Pius XII,
the Holocaust
and the Revisionists:
Essays

EDITED BY PATRICK J. GALLO

McFarland & Company, Inc., Publishers
Jefferson, North Carolina, and London

Frontispiece: Pius XII addresses the crowd after the July 19, 1943, bombing of Rome. Photograph from *Shepherd of Souls: A Pictorial Life of Pope Pius XII*, Margherita Marchione © Paulist Press, Inc. *www.paulistpress.com*

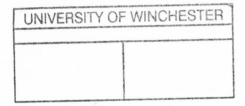

LIBRARY OF CONGRESS ONLINE CATALOG DATA

Pius XII, the Holocaust and the revisionists : essays / edited by
Patrick J. Gallo.
    p.   cm.
    Includes bibliographical references and index.

    ISBN 0-7864-2374-9 (softcover : 50# alkaline paper)

(DLC)2939   2005031094

British Library cataloguing data are available

On the cover: Pius XII delivers his 1941 Christmas radio address (photograph from Margherita Marchione's *Shepherd of Souls: A Pictorial Life of Pope Pius XII*, ©2002 Paulist Press, Inc., www.paulistpress.com)

Manufactured in the United States of America

McFarland & Company, Inc., Publishers
  Box 611, Jefferson, North Carolina 28640
   www.mcfarlandpub.com

To my wife, Grace,
our children, Laura, Andrew, Daniela,
our precious grandson Nicholas,
and Cecile and Martin, with love

Table of Contents

Introduction

In November 1938, Pius XI suffered a second heart attack. His health had deteriorated as he confronted the mounting crises that gripped the church and the entire world. On January 15, 1939, he met with all of the ambassadors to the Vatican and urged them to obtain visas to their respective countries, "for the victims of racial persecution in Germany and Italy." On February 16, 1939, the SS journal *Das Schwarze Korps* attacked the Pope as "the sworn enemy of National Socialism," and "Chief Rabbi of the Christians, boss of the firm of Judah-Rome."

In late February 1939, the 81-year-old Pope died. Before his death Pius XI had been preparing Eugenio Pacelli, his secretary of state, to be his successor. Pacelli's career was a steady ascent from his appointment first as nuncio to Bavaria, then as nuncio to the Weimar government, undersecretary of state, bishop, cardinal, and papal secretary of state in 1930. Cardinal Pacelli was a trained diplomat and an expert on German affairs. He subsequently registered 43 separate protests in violation of the 1933 Concordat. In April 1935, Pacelli made it abundantly clear in a speech at Lourdes that the church would never come to terms with the Nazis as long as they persisted in espousing a racial philosophy "contrary to Christian faith." He said to the quarter of a million in his audience:

> With the illusion of extolling new wisdom, they are really only lamentable plagiarists.... It matters little that they are inspired by a false conception of the world and life. Whether they are possessed by superstition of race and blood, their philosophy ... rests upon principles essentially opposed to those of Christian faith.[1]

Pacelli had drafted most of Pius XI's 1937 encyclical, *Mit brennender Sorge* (*With burning anxiety*), that clearly condemned the Nazi regime, its philosophy and its leader. One draft of the encyclical was written in Pacelli's handwriting. *Das Schwarze Korps* immediately responded, "The encyclical, the most incredible of Pius XI's 'pastoral letters'; every sentence in it was an insult to the New Germany." It also condemned Pacelli as an ally of the Jews and Communists in a series of subsequent articles. The Chief Security Office of the Reich, in its Situation Report of 1938, linked Pacelli with world Jewry, stating, "The slogans issued at the anti–German manifestations of world Jewry have once more clearly confirmed the political aims of the Vatican."

In a three-hour meeting with Cardinal Pacelli, A.W. Klieforth, the U.S. consul in Berlin, described his anti–Nazi views in a newly discovered report filed with the U.S. State Department in 1937. "He opposed unilaterally every compromise with National Socialism. He regarded Hitler an untrustworthy scoundrel, and a fundamentally wicked person. He did not believe Hitler capable of moderation, in spite of appearances, and he fully supported the German bishops in their anti–Nazi stand."[2] Klieforth further reported, "His views, while they are well known, surprised me by their extremeness." The cardinal secretary met with Joseph Kennedy, U.S. ambassador to Great Britain from 1938 to 1939. Kennedy's diplomatic papers, now unsealed, indicated that Pacelli said that his personal views could be conveyed to President Roosevelt. In their first meeting in 1938 Pacelli handed Kennedy a personal report that made it clear that any compromise with the Nazis "was out of the question," and he "made his personal disdain for them perfectly clear."[3] Pacelli added that "evidence of good faith" by the Nazi regime was "completely lacking."

The Reich attempted to pressure the German cardinals not to select Pacelli when the papal conclave convened in March 1939. The Nazi-controlled press began a propaganda campaign orchestrated by Goebbels, with *Das Reich* railing, "Pius XI was a half Jew, for his mother was a Dutch Jewess; but Cardinal Pacelli was a full Jew." Another newspaper made it clear that Pacelli "is not favorably accepted in Germany, since he has always been hostile to National Socialism."[4] The *Berliner Morgenpost* and *Der Stürmer*, a virulent anti–Semitic rag, followed with similar attacks. The latter publication was operated by Julius Streicher, a notorious anti–Semite and anti–Catholic.

After less than 24 hours of deliberations in conclave, the Sacred College of Cardinals elevated Pacelli to the papacy. On March 2, 1939, a small puff of white smoke rose from the vertical pipe over the roof of the Sistine Chapel, announcing to the throng standing in Saint Peter's Square that the church again had a supreme pontiff. On his 63rd birthday, the new Pope Pius XII appeared on the balcony on the central loggia of the façade of Saint Peter's and imparted his blessing, "Urbi et Orbi," to the city and to the world. The new pontiff was an experienced diplomat, and he was an expert on German affairs. His selection by the Sacred College of Cardinals in such a short deliberation indicated that they were acutely aware of the impending crisis and that they wanted a person with Pacelli's qualifications.

The day after his coronation Pius XII met Kennedy and again maintained that Nazism was antithetical to Christianity. Harold Tittmann, U.S. representative to the Vatican during the war, had this view of Pius XII: "With his diplomatic background, he was inclined to see both sides of a question, and this may have given others the impression that he was sometimes timid and reluctant to make decisions, especially in foreign affairs. In reality this was not the case. He was, in fact decisive."[5]

In its editorial of March 6, 1939, the *Palestine Post* cited the Pope's Lourdes speech as evidence of "his opposition to pernicious race theories." Four days later the *Jewish Chronicle* in London praised the election of Pacelli and also quoted his anti–Nazi speech in Lourdes. American newspapers, including the *New York Times*, lauded his selection. The *Jewish Chronicle* and a number of organizations, including the Synagogue Council of America, the Canadian Jewish Congress, and the Polish Rabbinical Council, all praised his selection as the new pontiff. The *Zionist Review* in London praised Pius XII's selection of Cardinal Maglione as the new secretary of state. It stated on March 16, 1939, that Maglione's appointment "confirms the view that the new Pope means to conduct an anti–Nazi and anti–Fascist policy."

Pius XII assumed the papacy with the world on the path to war and a crisis of unimaginable proportions. The Western democracies and the church were confronted with the challenges posed by the twin totalitarian forces of fascism and communism. Nazi Germany was poised to strike at Poland after having gained control of Austria and Czechoslovakia. The Nazis had begun the persecution of Jews, Christians, political opponents, and minorities and shipped them to concentration camps. The Nazi Holocaust, as the world would come to identify the monstrous atrocities after World War II, was in the not-too-distant future, posing new challenges and moral dilemmas for nations, churches, organizations, and individuals. "From the moment of his election in March 1939, Pius had a very clear concept of his most pressing task, which was the need to prevent the outbreak or spread of war from once again engulfing Europe in the kind of disastrous suffering and conflict that he had witnessed so closely only 25 years earlier."[6]

Few revisionists realize or take into account the tremendous burden of responsibility that Pius XII had to carry. The outbreak of the war and "the knowledge of the sufferings which such a war would entail, grieved the Pope immensely.... The extra burdens which the war imposed on the

Church, the moral and spiritual trials of clergy and laity alike, and the grievous attacks on the Catholic position in almost every European country also were of great concern."[7]

Following his 1941 Christmas message the *New York Times* editorialized, "The voice of Pius XII is a lonely voice in the silence and darkness enveloping Europe this Christmas ... the Pope had put himself squarely against Hitlerism."[8] Praise and gratitude for his efforts in the cause of peace and for his aid to the persecuted were lavished on the Pope during the war and the decade that followed. Historians, world leaders, the press—both secular and religious—governments, organizations, and those who had been rescued testified to the Pope's central role during these tumultuous years. The prevailing historical interpretation was that Pius XII was a positive and activist force. He attempted to bring an end to the war and gave aid and comfort to the persecuted.

During the war the Nazis and Communists launched a merciless propaganda attack on the Pope. This laid the foundation for the revisionism that emerged in the second decade after the end of World War II. In the mid–'60s a perceptible shift occurred for a number of reasons, not the least of which was the sensation caused by Rolf Hochhuth's play *The Deputy*, which opened in Berlin on February 20, 1963. In this pseudohistorical drama Pius XII is portrayed as silent about the treatment of Jews and connives in their deportation from Rome. This portrait conformed in many respects to the Nazi and Communist propaganda attacks during the war.

The term "revisionist historian" seems to be associated in some minds with those Holocaust deniers who co-opted the term in the 1970s. But beneath this veneer of revisionism was something sinister that was rejected by serious historians and writers who marshaled overwhelming objective documentation of the planned extermination of the Jews of Europe and the additional murder of millions of non–Jews.[9]

James McPherson has forcefully written, "History is a continuing dialogue between the present and the past. Interpretations of the past are subject to change in response to new evidence, new questions asked of the evidence, new perspectives gained by the passage of time. There is no single, eternal, and immutable 'truth' about past events and their meaning. The unending quest of historians for understanding the past—that is, 'revisionism'—is what makes history vital and meaningful."[10]

At present two types of books seem to sell, those that deal with World War II and with the Holocaust. Pope Pius XII seems to be a sure thing commercially for a commissioning editor especially and exclusively if the book takes a critical and one-sided stance on its subject. Unfortunately not all of these volumes have contributed to the historiography of the Nazi Holocaust or the role of Pius XII during these tragic events.

In recent years revisionist perspectives have taken such a sharp turn that alternative perspectives are shut out of the dialogue. This is reflected in the near-absence of books published by mainstream or academic publishers that present an alternative interpretation and analysis of Pius XII. Far too many reviewers view those that are published by small presses as defensive tracts and they are dismissed out of hand. Respected university houses have been complicit in this avoidance and have published volumes that do not meet the rigors of historical scholarship. Justus George Lawler has referred to the spate of anti-papal books as an "omnipresent papaphobia ... the startling phenomenon of slanted and bogus scholarship, where one might least expect it ... among the acknowledged professional exponents of candor, honesty, and rectitude."[11] These revisionist tracts tend to politicize and sensationalize their subject matter. They are received uncritically and are held up as the standard for acceptable publication even though the research and the objectivity is questionable at best. Daniel Jonah Goldhagen, who brought no original research to his latest tome but did bring slapdash scholarship and overblown moralizing, was published by a mainstream press. Those authors who present alternative analyses to the revisionists or who do not assume a posture of attack often find their manuscripts rejected or marginalized.

Pius XII revisionists tend to offer morality plays and not history, "a kind of Gresham's law where bad history drives out good history, making it difficult ... to determine where sensationalism, propaganda and martrylogy ends and history begins."[12] A selective group of revisionists begins with a determined premise and agenda and proceeds to quote each other and recycle the same conclusions. Goldhagen lauds the "considerable new scholarship" that has been published in recent years and proceeds to list a series of revisionists whom he uses to reinforce the existing orthodoxy. He lists James Carroll, David Kertzer, Susan Zuccotti, Michael Phayer, and Gary Wills. Though he did not list John Cornwell, Goldhagen does use much of his material, citing it in his notes.[13] Goldhagen makes sweeping provocative generalizations that are not supported by any new research.[14] In fact he largely uses secondary sources to support his preconceived theories. He omits context and evidence that might contradict his own preconceptions. José Sánchez observes: "Much of the investigation of Pius' behavior seems more like a legal procedure than a historical examination."[15]

Historians should search for and sift evidence, insist on sequence and chronology, provide context, and attempt to make as precise a reconstruction of the past as possible. Historians must immerse themselves in the times of their subject matter. Historical complexity is lacking in many revisionist accounts. Most revisionists fail to place events in context or else selectively quote the participants and dismiss out of hand eyewitness testimony that would provide a contrary account to theirs. Their approach to the subject matter is not rooted so much in history as in ideology that overtakes objective historical inquiry. David Kertzer, Daniel Goldhagen and their fellow revisionists take a prosecutorial stand, the pitfall of which leads them to omit key facts and at times to put forth very tortured arguments. Some revisionists do not adhere scrupulously to the discipline of the historian's detachment. Goldhagen for the prosecution is remorseless and makes a one-dimensional explanation of a complex subject. Anti-Semitism explains everything and everybody was anti–Semitic. This volume calls attention to the importance of understanding Pius XII's motivation and behavior in the context of the events as they happened rather than in the abstract.

Unfortunately the temptations of sensationalism, money, and notoriety drive ideology, and what emerges in some cases are polemics rather than legitimate historical inquiry. Some revisionists have moved from objective scholarship to advocacy and rants. Those writers who attempt to think outside of the box, or present a balanced perspective often have their manuscripts rejected or pushed to the margins. If they are successful in being published they are not by mainstream publishers or by most university presses. When they do see the light of day they face either intense criticism or are summarily dismissed.

It has been alleged that Pius XII remained silent with respect to the destruction of the Jews. The allegation connotes inaction and indifference. Pius XII allegedly said or did nothing in the face of one of the most horrific events in history. Some make sweeping assertions, such as "The one person other than Hitler who might have had the power to stop the Holocaust was the wartime pope, Pius XII."[16] Such a statement is proof that Gresham's law applies to writers and historians to whom virtual history is their guiding principle.

This volume calls attention to the importance of understanding Pius XII's motivations and behavior in the context of the events as they happened rather than in the abstract. We present a series of both original and previously published articles and essays that will critique several revisionist writers who make these allegations, including John Cornwell, David Kertzer, Michael Phayer, Susan Zuccotti, Daniel Jonah Goldhagen, Robert Katz, Gary Wills, and James Carroll.[17] Clearly Pius XII and the Holocaust is one of the most contentious subjects in the historiography of World

War II. The purpose of this volume is to provide alternative perspectives that are so clearly lacking and to engender true dialogue. It is hoped that it can contribute to the restoration of intellectual rigor and responsibility to the continuing discussion on this aspect of Pius XII and the Nazi Holocaust. Perhaps we can arrive at revisionism in the truest sense of the term.

CHAPTER 1

Beyond *The Deputy*: Origins of the New Revisionism

by Patrick J. Gallo

Richard Evans asks: "What is historical objectivity? How do we know when a historian is telling the truth? Do historians just select facts they need to support their own interpretations and leave the rest in the archives? Can we really say that anything historians present to us about the past is really true?"[1] These questions constantly preoccupy historians. John Gaddis has written:

> History like cartography, is necessarily a representation of reality. It's not reality itself; indeed if truth be told it's a pitiful approximation of a reality that, even with the greatest skill on the part of the historian.... And yet, with the passage of time, our representations become reality in the sense that they compete with, insinuate themselves into, and eventually replace altogether the firsthand memories people have of the events through which they've lived. Historical knowledge submerges participants' knowledge of what took place....[2]

Historical revisionism is a necessary approach to historical analysis provided it is based on new information, on facts, and on new methods not available to its predecessors. The historian adds, discards, or modifies only after careful scrutiny, carefully examining and weighing any predetermined biases. It's advisable to heed E. B. White's admonition that all writing slants the way the writer leans. Historical revisionism should attempt to enhance our understanding of history through the continual reinterpretation of not only existing data, but new data as well. It should be a process that opens up dialogue and not precludes it. A postmodern deconstruction approach leads people to believe that everything is at least relative and at worst the product of some evil conspiracy. History is seen as a matter of perception, language, and political agenda. There is no ultimate historical reality, and any truth can be recast.

When assessing the role of Pius XII and the Nazi Holocaust one must tread "a fine line between a critical approach based on today's values and knowledge." The greater the distance in space and time between author and subject, the more careful one must be in striking an objective and careful balance. Michael Marrus, a critic of Pius XII, analyzed the Nuremberg trials and wrote that too many writers have "prompted unwarranted moral judgments that apply our standards, our appreciations, our sensibilities, our knowledge, and our hindsight to the events of half a century ago." Far too many revisionists have failed to heed Marrus's admonition, including the author of that statement. A select group of revisionists has emerged asserting the same basic interpretation that has reached canonical status. They present a laundry list of charges in their indictment of Pius XII: "Thus a point by point refutation of the charges against the Pontiff is a Sisyphus task. One no sooner demolishes one count in the indictment than three others are added. And proving a negative is a philosophical impossibility."[3]

Why did the interpretation of Pius XII during the terrible years of the Nazi Holocaust that was once so positive take such a sharp and extreme turn? Is there hope that a balance will be achieved so that an accurate assessment, or rather an approximation of the truth, will emerge?

Pius XII reigned as supreme pontiff from his ascendancy in 1939 to his death in 1958. His pontificate was challenged by the horror of a global war, the Nazi Holocaust, the genocide of the Poles, the imprisonment and murder of the religious of his church, and the liquidation of other minorities and opponents of the regime. At the same time he was challenged by Stalin's totalitarian regime that persecuted and murdered millions. Hitler and Stalin made it clear that National Socialism and Communism were irreconcilable with Christianity and in particular with the Catholic Church. In turn Pius XI and Pius XII acknowledged that the Catholic Church was fundamentally incompatible with both of them. Pius XII considered both as not only challenges to the Catholic Church but to all of Christendom. He felt that the Nazis threatened the survival of Western civilization. According to John Conway:

> The seeming ineffectiveness of the Christian faith in such a world was a heavy tribulation to have to bear. The attitude of the Papacy towards these events was therefore the result of long and difficult deliberation.

The Pope's problem was how to maintain the authority of the Holy See, both as the spiritual guardian of faith and morals for members of the Church, and as a significant diplomatic organization, whose voice and policy would not be respected even by those governments and peoples who acknowledged no allegiance to the Church.[4]

How was Pius XII to deal with a regime of rabid racial fanatics bent on expansion, persecution of their political and "racial" enemies, and the destruction of Christianity? Conway writes:

The evidence is clear that Pius XII, perhaps more than most other popes, had given considerable thought to the political aspects of his role and conduct as supreme pontiff.... His ability to see the likely consequences of any particular course of action, particularly the disadvantages, undoubtedly deterred him from adopting any stance that could have incalculable, even disastrous, results not only for the cause of peace or for his own mission, but for the whole church.[5]

At the conclusion of World War II Pius XII witnessed the emergence and hardening of the Cold War, and was confronted by the Soviet Union's persecution of ethnic minorities and the church.

Unlike myth, history is not tidy, and the events that became known as the Holocaust are too complex to be dealt with simplistically. Raphael Lemkin, an international jurist, coined the term genocide at the close of World War II. Lemkin "struggled to find a way to define the novelty of Nazi atrocities against Jews." He took the Greek word genos, meaning a people in a nation, and combined it with the Latin suffix cide meaning murder. Lemkin, with the Armenian genocide as a referent, campaigned tirelessly to have the United Nations adopt the Genocide Convention and to recognize genocide as a crime against humanity.[6] "The word 'genocide' is a much contested and over used term." According to Eric Weitz, for genocide to occur, "there needs to be a demonstrable intent to destroy" in whole or in part "a particular population group."[7]

The terms genocide and holocaust gradually came into widespread currency after the war. In some circles the Hebrew word Shoah, meaning destruction, was preferred. During the war the term holocaust was used and understood to connote "victim" offered as sacrifice or the widespread destruction by fire. Shoah was "used to describe punishments visited by God on Jews."[8] Yehuda Bauer believes that genocide and holocaust are related but distinct. In his estimation holocaust is a "radicalization of genocide: a planned attempt to physically annihilate every single member of a targeted ethnic, national, or racial group." Dan Stone disputes Bauer's position: "It is my contention that these 'historical' grounds for defending the Holocaust's uniqueness are in fact ideologically driven attempts to maintain the Holocaust as a kind of 'sacred entity.'"[9] According to Norman Finkelstein, "The claim of Holocaust uniqueness is a claim of Jewish uniqueness," and serves a political purpose. Finkelstein casts a critical eye:

> Appropriating a Zionist tenet, the Holocaust framework cast Hitler's Final Solution as the climax of millennial Gentile hatred of Jews.... The irrational essence of Gentile anti–Semitism is inferred inductively from the irrational essence of the Holocaust.... Taken apart or together, these propositions do not withstand even superficial scrutiny. Politically, however, the argument is highly serviceable.[10]

Eric Weitz forcefully argues that the Nazi Holocaust must be compared with other genocides and "to insist on the incompatibility with other genocides, we place it outside of history."[11] Weitz says:

> Genocides have occurred since the earliest recorded history, from the Israelite destruction of numerous communities in Canaan, depicted in the book of Joshua, to the Roman annihilation of Carthage and its population. But beginning with the Armenian genocides they have become more extensive, more systematic, and more thorough.[12]

Those revisionists who tend to center on single individuals, in this case on Pius XII, do so from the specific prism of the Nazi Holocaust. In doing so they fail to provide context. Weitz writes:

> The specific policies even genocide, were not preordained; they would emerge in the context of political and social developments— including, critically, total war — in the 1930s and 1940s. But a society in some way purged and purified on the basis of race was the lodestar of Hitler's politics, and the state would be both sextant and sail, the instrument that would chart and implement the course.[13]

The current bibliography on the Nazi Holocaust lists some thousands of volumes. According to Mark Mazower, "The millions of victims of state violence in China and the Soviet Union rate only a small fraction of this attention, the killing fields of Cambodia and Rwanda still less ... the Holocaust has been turned into a moral touchstone, an unparalleled example of evil that we are exhorted to keep constantly in mind." Dan Stone counts some 50 genocides since the end of World War II.[14]

The Nazi Holocaust took place in the midst of a global war that killed upwards of 50 million to 60 million people. At the time, the reports of the atrocities were viewed in a larger context and were not linked specifically to the special fate of Jews. For government officials and the man on the street the atrocities took place in terms of what one knew and what one believed at the time. "Until mid–1938, Jews were rarely put into concentration camps as Jews. The Nuremberg laws seemed to guarantee at least life and limb."[15] Tragically, the window of opportunity to flee persecution was a narrow one. The victims in the concentration camps until late 1938 were Communists, Socialists, clergy, and other "undesirables."

The war was the most important influence in the enactment of the Final Solution "Everything happened so fast. Forget the talk of blueprints for destruction festering in Hitler's mind over decades: genocide was the product of military success after 1939 and the political dilemmas this brought in its wake."[16] Christopher Browning maintains that Hitler's war in the East was in essence a racial war.

What was the American perspective of the events in the '30s and '40s? Peter Novick observes that until the latter part of 1942 "Jews were, quite reasonably, seen [by Americans] as among but by no means as the singled-out victims of the Nazi regime."[17] From the outbreak of the war and America's subsequent entrance, the attention of the public and government officials in the United States was focused entirely on military events. During this period there was little known with any certainty, and "the fragmentary reports reaching the West were often contradictory...."[18] Afterward reports of atrocities against Jews began to accumulate but these, like the numbers, were often contradictory. "If American newspapers published relatively little about the ongoing Holocaust, it was because there was little hard news about it to present — only secondhand and thirdhand reports of problematic authenticity." Furthermore Novick states that just as the American mainstream press contained little about the Holocaust, "the same was true of much of the Jewish press."[19] Throughout the war years Americans were convinced that Hitler and the Nazis were evil. Few Americans were aware of the scope of the Nazis' program to annihilate the Jews. The lack of awareness was common even among highly placed officials.

When we confront the issue of knowledge in the "narrow sense is how knowledge is framed."[20] It involves "distinctions among varieties of awareness, consciousness, belief, attention."[21] The persecution of Jews was placed within the context of the persecution of other victims. This framework persisted for the duration of the war. Yehuda Bauer wrote:

> Information regarding the Holocaust became available in late 1942. Perhaps naturally, though, people refused to internalize it. To protect themselves against the impact of the information, Jews themselves refused to believe it, and many of them refused to internalize the information until after the war. Until information is internalized and becomes knowledge, action is not possible. It took time until information was believed.[22]

Susan Zuccotti, a revisionist historian, explains why Holocaust information was not credible. With reference to the Gerhard Riegner report of August 11, 1942, she states: "But again, this was information from opponents of the Third Reich, and thus dismissible as enemy propaganda.... We cannot assume that information with hindsight to be correct should have been recognized as such at the time."[23] However, Zuccotti does not apply that same standard to the Vatican and Pius XII, who she contends had full knowledge of the death camps. The Vatican did not have the intelligence network of the major powers. Yehuda Bauer makes a distinction between information and knowledge. He states that as late as 1944, "the information had not jelled into knowledge, and it was rejected by many government officials, the military, and the general public, Jews and non–Jews alike — as preposterous."[24]

At present it is intellectually acceptable to target certain individuals and groups responsible for not doing anything or enough with regard to the atrocities that we now identify as the Nazi Holocaust. This is connected to the broader historiography of victimhood that reflexively vilifies Western civilization, Christianity, or specific world leaders such as Roosevelt, Churchill, and Pope Pius XII. The sense of rage and guilt over the Nazi Holocaust simply cannot find an adequate expression or means of resolution. The death of Hitler, the destruction of the Nazi regime, and the punishment of various war criminals seemed anticlimactic and unsatisfying.

Despite the constant stream of books and articles on the subject, we are still a long way from understanding or coming to terms with the explosion of evil that took place in the '30s and '40s. In some circles Pius XII has been conspicuously singled out as a surrogate for the failure of governments, organizations, and other individuals to respond to the plight of the Jews and other minorities. Carl Amery views Pius XII as a symbol: "To accuse him is to accuse ourselves. Pius XII was not only God's 'deputy'; he is our 'representative'— the representative of our inhumanity!"[25] The Catholic Church has a defined structure and hierarchy. In addition it possesses a structure of defined beliefs that is often countercultural. Together these factors have led revisionists to attach "responsibility" for action or alleged inaction in current contexts and place it at the doorstep of a single individual — in this case Pius XII.

Revisionists ignore the fact that the Vatican is a tiny temporal state and did not have the military or intelligence resources that were available to the world powers. Zuccotti, Cornwell, and many revisionists equate the Vatican's information gathering capabilities with those of the major Western powers. At the outbreak of the war the Vatican's secretariat had a total staff of 31 including archivists. David Alvarez has carefully studied Vatican intelligence capabilities and concludes:

> There was no Vatican intelligence service.... It has become increasingly clear that during World War II, the Vatican was actually rather poorly informed about events. Both the British and French ambassadors to the Holy See reported to their foreign ministries their surprise at discovering how weak the Vatican was in this regard. The British envoy noted that for news of the war the Pope relied primarily upon the BBC.[26]

Pius XII also relied on D'Arcy Osborne, British minister to the Vatican, for information since the nuncios were not well informed. The major Western powers were constrained by public opinion, the lack of knowledge, inertia, and the pressures of the war. Cornwell singles out Dr. Josef Müller as the Vatican's main conduit of information during the war. Given the limitations of its source of intelligence, it was not unusual for the Vatican to be cautious in evaluating the information that it received. José Sánchez cautions the historian: "To move from the fact of persecution, to the knowledge that they were killing many, to the belief that they were going to kill all is a big leap. It was not commonly believed by the Allied leaders, who with their espionage services were probably in a better position to know German aims."[27]

To understand the origins of the revisionist position with regard to Pius XII we need to examine the Vatican's conflict with both Hitler's and Stalin's regimes from the '30s onward. The Vatican was in increasing conflict with Mussolini's and Hitler's totalitarian regimes. The Vatican was under constant assault from Mussolini and Hitler throughout the '30s and '40s.[28] The Nazis regarded the Catholic Church in particular as their nemesis and took a series of measures as part of their systematic war on Christianity. The Catholic Church represented a formidable opponent, which the Reich sought to eliminate. The reasons for the conflict with the Catholic Church and their efforts to destroy the church within the Reich territories will be explored more fully in the following selection. Both Pius XI and Pius XII had condemned the eugenic policy and euthanasia program of the Nazis. Pius XI in 1937 also condemned Hitler's regime and his racial policies and followed this with a condemnation of totalitarian Communism.[29] Nothing brought home the reality of the Nazis' systematic persecution of the church than the imprisonment and execution of thousands of Catholic priests, seminarians, and religious. Revisionists ignore this dimension of the Nazi-church confrontation since it opens up many issues that contradict their assertions.

With the outbreak of the war Pius XII officially adopted a policy of neutrality, refusing to allow the Holy See to "endorse the justice of their respective crusades."[30] The Pope refused to endorse the Nazis' invasion of the Soviet Union as an anti–Bolshevik crusade. The official stance of impartiality was pure fiction since the Pope's sympathies were clearly with the Western democracies from the very outset of the war.[31] Hitler's Reich realized this and grew angrier at each new piece of evidence of Pius's pro-allied sympathies that served only to further stoke their fury.

In turn Hitler, the Nazi radical elite, and Stalin were adamant that Christianity in general and the Catholic Church in particular had to be eliminated from the scene. The Vatican viewed the twin totalitarian ideologies as fundamentally antithetical to Catholic doctrine and their differences were irreconcilable. Hitler and Stalin blamed Pius XII and the Catholic Church for the suffering of millions of Jews and Catholics. These accusations were constantly repeated in their propaganda war against the Catholic Church.

In June 1942, the Catholic bishops in the Reich territories signed a pastoral letter that was read from every pulpit throughout the Third Reich. The bishops condemned Hitler's policies of official murder of the innocent and of those "judged unproductive citizens."[32] In her weekly column for the *New York Times*, Anne O'Hare McCormick wrote:

> When the history of this new reign of terror is written, it will appear that the strongest centers of opposition to the claims of the God-Sate were not the universities, trades unions, political parties, courts or organized business. In Germany and the occupied countries the institution that stands up most stoutly against the pretensions of the Nazi New Order is the Church.[33]

William Donovan, director of the Office of Strategic Services (OSS), reported to the president, "the anti–Nazi church elements have organized in cells ... of both the clergy and the laity, have saved thousands of Jews ... by clandestine action undertaken at great personal risk."[34] OSS agent DeWitt Poole also reported to Allen Dulles, OSS station chief in Zurich, on "the clergy's splendid behavior in defense of Jews," and felt sorry that this could not be publicized without endangering priests in Nazi-occupied territories. He recommended "that as much material as possible about this particular point be ready for the moment where it can serve to refute accusations on this point."[35]

The Nazi propaganda machine was relentless in its attacks on the Pope. In May 1943, the Nazi-controlled Paris radio blamed the Catholic Church for having unleashed the war.[36] *Aujourd'hui*, the Nazi-controlled Paris newspaper, charged "Pope Pius was responsible for the hostile attitude of the French clergy toward German authorities and that his last speech had a particularly disquieting effect."[37] The Vatican's response was reported in the *New York Times*: "recalling the Nazi charges that the Catholic Church in Germany had invited oppression by opposing Adolf Hitler's theories of 'racialism....'"[38] In a speech delivered on January 30, 1943, Hitler attempted to revive the myth that Nazi Germany was the last bulwark against the Bolshevik tide of conquest.[39] This brief sampling of the mutual conflict highlights the fact that the groundwork for the attack on Pius XII was laid in part by the Third Reich.

The Communist attacks on the church began in the '20s and increasingly centered on Pius XI and Pius XII. For example, William Z. Foster, the American Communist leader, in 1949 restated the basic communist tenet that religion and socialism were contradictory and irreconcilable. Religion was considered a tool of the capitalists to exploit the proletariat with its "imaginary eternal rewards and punishments," which made it an opiate for the masses.[40] In short the churches were simply the façade for the ruling class. In addition Communist leaders around the globe concluded, "The Catholic Church is and has been one of the strongest and most consistent counter-revolutionary forces in society." Papal announcements and appointments were viewed as part of the Vatican's sinister character.[41]

By 1930 the Communists were convinced that the Vatican was instigating a military intervention against the Soviet Union. American Communists declared, "The alliance of cross and cannon is open and brazen.[42] Stalin conducted a propaganda war that coincided with that of the Nazis, both of which aimed at undermining the church's authority and credibility. *Izvestia* charged that despite the Vatican's claims to neutrality, it had worked to support the Nazi regime in its destruction of other nations. It went on to attack the Pope for his alleged silence relative to the persecution of Jews and other minorities. This was disingenuous since Russia and the current regime had a long record of persecuting Jews. Responding to *Izvestia*'s accusations, the *New York Times* said that they were without validity and questioned how anyone could believe the Communist propaganda against the church.[43] *Izvestia* maintained that the church was pro–Fascist.[44] This led Herbert L. Matthews to assert categorically, "...the Pope's feelings are unquestionably anti–Nazi and anti–Fascist...."[45]

The initial charge that the church had been silent in the face of Nazi atrocities came from Communist Russia. As the war progressed, Stalin was in a position to control Poland and sought to control vast areas of Eastern Europe.[46] The Soviet regime concluded that it was absolutely necessary to break the loyalty to the Pope and to eliminate the power of the church in Eastern Europe. The obvious motive was to break the bond of trust between the people and church. This would open up the entire area to Soviet influence and control. On March 18, 1944, the New York State Legislature passed a resolution deploring *Izvestia's* charges against the Vatican and stated that they were made on behalf of the Soviet government. The resolution also pointed to Pius XI's and Pius XII's condemnation of Fascism and Nazism and "all other forms of totalitarian government both in public and private pronouncements dating back to 1932."[47]

On February 9, 1945, Moscow continued its assault on Pius XII. The bishops of the Russian Orthodox Church devised a statement aired on Moscow radio that accused the Pope of condoning fascism by attempting to excuse Germany for its crimes.[48] "The Russian Orthodox bishops were especially pleased that the Vatican postwar hostility to the Soviet Union was based not on ideological anti-communism and anti-materialism with which the Orthodox would have to agree, but on resistance to the expansion of Soviet influence in Eastern Europe, with which the Orthodox could not agree."[49] Herbert L. Matthews responded to the bishops in an article in the *New York Times* titled "Stalin's Hand Seen in Vatican Attack."

In February 1945, *The Protestant* published a petition signed by 1,600 U.S. Protestant ministers and religious leaders that repeated some of the common misrepresentations of the Pope's conduct during and after the war. The petition was addressed to Franklin Roosevelt, Winston Churchill, and Joseph Stalin, which was curious since it was the Pope who had opposed Hitler's regime and was now in opposition to another totalitarian government. The petition urged that the Vatican should have no influence in postwar discussions and it declared, "The papacy has thrown its weight into the present human struggle on the side of the enemies of democracy."[50]

Boris Stern, the former Soviet ambassador to Italy, added the Vatican was a "tremendous danger to world peace and post-war security." *The Bolshevik*, a Communist Party magazine, asserted that Pius XII was a friend of Germany and approved of Hitler's policies.[51]

Pius XII had recognized that Nazism was the immediate danger to the church and the Western world, while Communism was a danger in the not too distant future. The Pope opposed both and did not sacrifice his opposition to Nazism with an obsessive preoccupation with Communism, as a number of the revisionists have contended. Some revisionists fault Pius XII for his opposition to communism but fail to answer a fundamental question: In the light of history, was he wrong?

Latter-day revisionists may have forgotten that Stalin was a bloody tyrant who reduced his own people to virtual slavery. The kulaks resisted the forced collectivization campaign. Stalin decided on a "policy of the liquidation of the kulak as a class."[52] Most of the kulaks were liquidated between 1929–1930. "From all over the country convoys including children and old people were moved 'by stages' toward their places of exile. The trains were packed with people dying of cold and thirst."[53] By 1933 at least 300,000 families had been deported.

By the early '30s nearly 10 million persons were sent to forced labor camps. In an early purge, 98 of the Communist Party's Central Committee and 300,000 party members were shot. In one two-year period, one and a half million people had been killed. "The NKVD was, as the phrase went, the 'unsheathed sword of the Revolution.' As such its functions went beyond those pertaining to the political police even in other totalitarian systems, since even prior to 1936 its activities were not limited to uncovering and uprooting actual treason and dissent, but were meant to uncover and destroy every potential threat to the regime...."[54]

Purges extended to all facets of Soviet life, including the intelligentsia and the army. Stalin stayed late into the night personally signing death certificates. "Every arrest helped to build the magnificent Bonfire of Fear. Every arrest threw a little chip of its own onto to the mysterious nocturnal fire which needed to burn forever; only constant fear kept the country and the system stable."[55] The infamous Gulag of Kolyma in the northeast corner of Asiatic Russia, a godforsaken region of marshland and permafrost, had a 100 percent death rate that claimed three million.[56] Between 1937 and 1938 the NKVD had arrested seven million people. "By the end of 1938 mass repression obviously had to be slackened. The prisons and forced labor camps were overcrowded to the bursting point."[57] For each year from 1948 to 1953 the average number of those in various camps was in excess of two million.[58]

Russia has had a long history of anti–Semitism.[59] In 1939 and in the early part of 1940, "the Soviets were probably killing more people in eastern Poland than the Germans were in the west."[60] Stalin remained silent about "the genocidal slaughtering of the Jews by the Nazi conquerors of Poland." He remained silent even after the invasion of the Soviet Union.

He "paved the way for the extermination of 1.5 million unsuspecting Jews in White Russia and the Ukraine."[61] Stalin's sins of omission and commission during the war "cost the lives of at least one million Soviet Jews in addition to the 500,000 to 600,00 who died in prison or were slain as a result of the purges."[62] His anti–Semitism grew obsessive in the postwar years. In his last years "the anti–Zionist and anti–Jewish motif prominent as treason and dissent became identical in his mind with Soviet Jews."[63]

After World War II was concluded, Stalin extended his control and repression of the peoples of Eastern Europe. As the Red Army marched across Eastern Europe, the Soviet military administration began the construction of concentration camps. The most brutal were set up in Eastern Germany, and two of the camps were located at Sachsenhausen and Buchenwald, the sites of former Nazi camps.[64] Stalin killed many more people than Hitler and Mao combined. "But they are disputed icons of evil, since they have had, and still do have, their ideological apologists...."[65] The revisionists fail to factor into their accounts Stalin's murderous record on human rights during Pius XII's pontificate.

At the end of the war the Pope, in a different international setting, fought the expansion of Communism. He sought to protect the interests of the Catholic Church within the Soviet bloc that often brought him into conflict with the great powers. Though Pius XII disapproved of Catholic cocooperation with Communist regimes in Eastern Europe, he didn't intervene when an agreement had been reached with them. This was an implicit acceptance of those accords.

The Soviet regime brought bishops and priests before show trials reminiscent of those held by the Nazis. In 1949, Pius XII vigorously denounced the Hungarian Communist government for the imprisonment of Cardinal József Mindszenty to a life sentence.[66] Indeed the Pope's stature among the Catholics of Eastern Europe was enhanced because of his willingness to fight communism beyond the Iron Curtain where the Western powers were limited in what they could do there. It is no accident that decades later another pontiff, John Paul II, would play a leading role in the collapse of communism in Poland and in Eastern Europe.

Communist propagandists systematically charged Pius XII with a variety of crimes, and *Prace*, the Czech Communist magazine, said that he was a Nazi stooge. It went on to charge that Pius XII agreed to "a solution of all Eastern European peoples in favor of Germany" and also agreed that Goebbels was to succeed Hitler. Soviet historians claimed the Pope and Hitler had agreed, "The Vatican would send into Soviet territory, German army agents for implanting Catholicism, so that the occupants could organize espionage and sabotage."

M. M. Scheinmann, a Soviet writer, repeated the assertion that the Pope was obsessed with the need to conduct a crusade against the Soviet Union, which rendered him silent with regard to the persecution of the Jews.[67] According to Scheinmann, "In consequence acts of any anti–Soviet government, however criminal, were to be ignored or even approved."[68] The Soviets, of course, ignored their own history in the treatment of Soviet Jews, which continued well into the Cold War.

After the war Stalin began a systematic persecution of Jews. Alan Bullock has written, "Stalin succumbed to the same virus of anti–Semitism as Hitler, substituting the Jewish world-conspiracy of capitalism and Zionism, with its headquarters in Wall Street...."[69]

Leon Poliakov extended communist accusations and argued in *Commentary* that Pius's anticommunism caused him to keep silent on the Holocaust, saying:

> The humanitarian activities of the Vatican were necessarily circumscribed with prudence and caution. The immense responsibilities on the Pope's shoulders and the powerful weapons the Nazis could use against the Holy See undoubtedly combined to prevent him from making a formal public protest, though the persecuted hoped to hear one. It is sad to have to say that during the entire war, while the laboratories of death worked to capacity, the Pope kept his silence.[70]

The revisionists have adopted many of the allegations leveled at the Pope by the Nazis and, most particularly, from the Soviet Union. John Cornwell calls Pius XII *Hitler's Pope*. In an all-too-familiar refrain, he maintains that the Pope's fears of the Nazis "were overshadowed by the aggression and goals of Communism.[71] David Kertzer agrees that the Vatican and Pius XII embraced Fascist regimes as "a God-sent bulwark against the great socialist evil."[71] Harold Tittmann, who had personal and official dealings with the Pope, has written, "There were absolutely no signs that the Pope was pro–Fascist or pro–Nazi. In fact, the opposite seemed more the case."[72] Michael Phayer's thesis is that Pius XII refused to speak out against the Holocaust because he wanted a strong Germany as a bulwark against the spread of Soviet Communism. Phayer and his fellow revisionists cannot provide documentation to prove that this was papal strategy.

The charge that the Pope was silent during the Holocaust implies callous indifference and inaction. It has become unquestioning orthodoxy.[73] Phayer claims the Pope "did little for Jews in their hour of greatest need." While he concedes that Pius XII was able to save Jewish lives through his papal nuncios, he still asserts that his gravest failure "lay in his attempt to use a diplomatic remedy for a moral outrage."[74] From the vantage of hindsight, what would Phayer have wanted the Pope to do? Use the Swiss guards? Issue verbal moral thunderbolts on the Nazi criminals or use direct and indirect action to save lives? Phayer et al. ignore what he actually accomplished or don't evaluate the factors that constrained a particular course of action. Leon Poliakov was skeptical that even a firm public protest would have had any impact or would have saved any Jews. Clearly the revisionist school believes that "outspoken denunciations of Nazi crimes could have saved more Jewish lives, even if they have to admit that there was nothing the Holy See could do to force the Nazis to end their campaign for a 'Final Solution.'"

While John Cornwell still accepts the revisionist view that Pius XII was silent and by implication paralyzed to act, he has recanted to some extent: "I would now argue in the light of the debates and evidence following *Hitler's Pope,* that Pius had so little scope of action that it is impossible to judge the motives of his silence during the war, while Rome was under the heel of Mussolini and later occupied by the Germans." The revisionists might well heed John Conway's assessment: "The overall picture to be drawn from these volumes [*ADSS*] is therefore the significant reduction of papal influence during these years of war and terror. The evidence makes clear that, despite the pope's sincere efforts to mitigate the effects of the war and to bring relief to its victims, his initiatives were spurned and his advice ignored as the forces of violence and destruction escalated."[75]

The revisionists speculate but cannot demonstrate from the vantage point of the present that Jews could have been saved or the Nazi Holocaust averted. The Pope saved at least 850,000 Jews and probably many more due to a different course of rescue. The revisionist volumes abound with historical errors of fact compounded by unfortunate and unhistorical unproven hypotheses.

Was Pius XII in fact silent? What in fact was his approach in dealing with the many who were persecuted? What in fact did he do to save Jews and the persecuted? The revisionists fail to fully explore what Pius XII actually said, both in private and in public, and in particular how the Nazis reacted to his statements. Yehuda Bauer believes that a Nazi elite, possibly a couple of hundred, saw Jews as a major threat. The elite included Hitler, Josef Goebbels, Alfred Rosenberg, Julius Streicher, Wilhelm Frick, Otto Thierack, Hans Frank, Heinrich Himmler, Reinhard Heydrich, and Hermann Göring.[76] Would a public protest have deterred the radical racial fanatics from enacting or have stopped the slaughter of Jews? Would such protests have saved more Jews than the course of action taken by the Pope? What would have been the result of a public protest? Would more lives have been in danger because of this perceived provocation? What were the practical possibilities at the time? José Sánchez states: "Here, the historian has to step outside of reality and venture into the realm of virtual history. There are probabilities but no certainties. It is at this point that the historian, scholar or amateur, can devise any scenario he wishes without fear of contradiction, for who can criticize or defend against an event that never happened." What is asked, Justus George Lawler maintains, "Is not a deed which would achieve the cessation of the Jewish slaughter, but merely a statement, a proclamation, a word."[77]

The allegation of Pius's obsession with communism "implies a monomania, an exaggerated, panicky, narrow-minded reaction to the Bolshevik danger."[78] Michael Phayer's central thesis is that the Pope refused to speak out against the Nazi Holocaust because he wanted a strong Germany to serve as a bulwark against the threat of Soviet expansion. Phayer turns speculation into an assertion that he cannot document to prove that Pius or Vatican officials in fact pursued this strategy. Saul Friedlander, an early advocate of this same position, admitted: "Obviously, this is no more than a hypothesis which no text explicitly proves." What is forgotten or simply ignored is that the Soviet regime, just as the Nazis, represented a major threat to the survival of Western democracy and the survival of the church. When the Allies urged the Pope to make a public condemnation of Nazi atrocities, Pius XII maintained that he could not condemn one totalitarian regime and not the other. The Allies dropped their request when they learned that the Pope intended to condemn both regimes, fearing that this would alienate Stalin.

Pius XII sought an accommodation with the Soviet government. Throughout his tenure as nuncio to Germany and then as Vatican secretary of state he sought to conclude a concordat with Moscow. Revisionists try to have it both ways by criticizing the Pope apparently for not speaking out against Nazism, but for doing so against Communism. Some even criticize the Pope for his firm position against the Soviet Union but not his courage. In an effort to obtain the support of American Catholics for the lend-lease program to Russia, President Roosevelt hoped to get the Pope to intervene with American bishops. In his letter of September 3, 1941, Roosevelt wrote the Pope and stated, "Insofar as I am informed, churches in Russia are open ... there is the real possibility that Russia, as a result of this conflict, recognize freedom of religion." The Vatican and other State Department officials were amazed that such a letter could have stated such inaccurate information. Despite this, Pius XII joined President Roosevelt when the immediate goal was the defeat of Nazi Germany and "that the only way to overcome the former was an Allied victory, even if this meant assistance from Soviet Russia." Harold Tittmann has written the Pope "detested the Nazi ideology and everything it stood for." He concludes, "Thus Pius XII himself had joined the President in admitting that Hitlerism was an enemy of the Church more dangerous than Stalinism and that the only way to overcome the former was an Allied victory, even if this meant assistance from Soviet Russia." The Vatican made it clear that they could not openly condemn Nazi Germany without also condemning Stalinist Russia. Allied leaders expressed their displeasure with this view, fearing the disintegration of a fragile alliance.

The emergence of revisionist interpretations of Pius XII must also be seen in terms of how and why the Nazi Holocaust came to permeate the American mind. The Holocaust was rarely discussed for the first two decades following World War II. For a number of years after the war the fate of European Jewry was barely mentioned, in part because only a minority of the prisoners liberated in Dachau, Belsen, and Buchenwald were Jews. The Americans liberated Dachau and Buchenwald, the British Bergen-Belsen. In his famous 1945 broadcast from Buchenwald, Edward R. Murrow never used the word Jew when he referred to the liberated prisoners. In the public mind in both the United States and Great Britain these camps became emblematic of Nazi barbarism. The distinctiveness of the extermination camps in the East was ignored at the Nuremberg trials. Auschwitz was liberated by the Red Army, and along with Treblinka, Belzec, and Sobibor they played less of a role in the media of the United States and Great Britain. The camps in the East whose victims were all Jews were closed before Allied forces got there or were liberated by the Soviet Army "with few American reporters and photographers in attendance."[79] Eric Weitz writes:

> Today we understand the very particular role the genocide of Jews played in the Nazi system. But in 1945 and 1946 with the revelations and reports about the Bataan Death March, the outright murder of Allied prisoners of war, the Nazi bombings of London and the ravages of Poland and other Eastern European countries, it would have been hard to make the case that the extermination of Jews had a special characteristic ... the Allied refusal to highlight the victimization of Jews was part and parcel of the immediate aftermath of a war in which so many people had suffered.[80]

For some time after the war the terms genocide and holocaust had not taken hold or been applied to the attempted annihilation of European Jewry. To many the unfolding documentation of one of the most horrific events in human history was an embarrassment. With the emergence of the Cold War the Nuremberg trials quickly faded from memory and

Americans wanted to return to some degree of normality in the decade of the '50s. The civil rights revolution and the Vietnam War dominated the American consciousness throughout the '60s. By the '70s the subject came to the fore in America.

Present concerns shape and determine what of the past we remember and how we remember it. The past is filtered through the prism of the present. This is no less true of the historian in America. Americans who came to accept the admonition "never again!" witnessed with relative indifference the genocides in Cambodia, Kosovo, and Rwanda with the exception of occasional journalistic coverage and a few Hollywood depictions.

Though American Jews put the Nazi Holocaust on the American agenda, the fact is American culture and society became receptive to that initiative. "We are not just 'the people of the book,' but the people of Hollywood film, of the television miniseries, of the magazine article, and the newspaper column, of the comic book and the academic symposium."[81] In the late 20th century the growth of a "victim culture" provided many Americans the necessary anchor to identify with the Nazi Holocaust. In 1978 nearly 100 million Americans watched all or part of the *Holocaust*, a television miniseries. This was a significant event in the "entrance of the Holocaust into the American consciousness."[82]

The Nazi Holocaust also became politicized. The political right invoked the Nazi Holocaust in the cause of anti–Communism. To those on the right of the political spectrum the Nazi Holocaust was rooted in the very nature of totalitarianism, which they identified with Soviet communism. "For leftists, the claim that American elites abandoned European Jewry during the war has been used to demonstrate the moral bankruptcy of the establishment, including liberal icons like FDR.

"For liberals, the Holocaust became the locus of 'lessons' that teach the evils of immigration restriction and homophobia, of nuclear weapons and the Vietnam War."[83] Richard Breitman takes issue with David Wyman's thesis that American policy makers, American society and American Jewish leaders abandoned Europe's Jews. The Nazi Holocaust became a moral referent for those in the political center.

The political right and left presented monocausal interpretations of complicated subjects with the lines of good and evil sharply drawn. Something so complex as the Holocaust cannot be monocausal.

Five years after Pius XII's death, Rolf Hochhuth, an unknown playwright, helped to create a climate that cast these issues in a psychological rather than in historical perspective. *The Deputy (Der Stellvertreter)* was staged in Berlin in February 1963, a few months after the close of the first session of the Second Vatican Council. This historic assembly infused the Catholic Church with new perspectives and changes, especially in its relations with other Christians and Jews. At the same time Americans were confronted by the moral challenges of the civil rights movement and increasingly by the war in Vietnam. Before the debut of *The Deputy,* the trial of Adolf Eichmann brought out the horrors of the Holocaust. Eichmann's trial in particular resonated with Jews around the world, during which many relived the Holocaust. The televised trial for the first time forced the American public to confront the Holocaust as a distinct event. For younger American Jews it was their initial encounter with the Holocaust. Moreover, war was imminent in the Middle East, and Israel was battling for its survival. In addition the discovery of Anne Frank's diary in 1962 created the desire for explanations and for attaching responsibility. Outbreaks of violence by neo–Nazis in Germany were another contributing factor.

In the '60s the New Left, both a political and cultural movement, gained momentum in many college campuses. Its social agenda brought them into conflict with the Catholic Church and it used Pius XII as the means to attack the church's positions on abortion and other matters. It's in this mix of circumstances that revisionism would flourish, and that Pius XII would emerge as a substitute, or surrogate, of the conscience of us all. This psychological transformation distorted the historical perspective for years to come, and by placing blame on Pius XII it helped explain the inexplicable. In summary, the initial attacks from Nazi Germany and the Soviet Union, a series of political and social events, biased revisionism, and political theater all created a mythical interpretation in contradiction to the historical record. Revisionists have not been impervious to the ways in which the Nazi Holocaust has gripped the American mind. In the mid–'60s leftist academic circles continued to maintain that Pius XII hated Bolshevism more than he hated Hitler. The Pope would also be blamed for helping to create the anti–Soviet atmosphere that resulted in the Cold War. These charges were based on little evidence and were largely fictional creations.

Hochhuth, an anticlerical Protestant and a former member of the Nazi Youth, was a disciple of Erwin Piscator.[84] Piscator was the founder of a quasi–Marxist school of drama known as "political theater," which used the criterion of political correctness and not historical reality to put prominent individuals on stage for public condemnation. Hochhuth was part of the post–World War II trend in theatre called "Documentary Theatre" or "Theatre of Fact." Hochhuth's seven-hour play filtered the Communist critique of Pius XII through a psychological prism. The Pope, whom the playwright contends had pro–Nazi leanings, is held up to public pillorying for his alleged silence; however, Hochhuth also reverses field and admitted the Pope aided Jews to the best of his ability. The image of an immobilized Pope emerges from *The Deputy*, whose alleged silence would later come to take a wider connotation of indifference, apathy, inaction, and even anti–Semitism. According to Hochhuth the Pope's concern with Vatican investments made him indifferent to the annihilation of the Jews. Hochhuth particularly criticizes Pius XII for failing to save the Jews of Rome, who were loaded on trucks in front "of the very door of the Vatican." One of *The Deputy*'s clergy laments, "A vicar of Christ who sees these things before his eyes and still remains silent because of state policies, who delays even one day ... such a pope ... is a criminal." Decades later Susan Zuccotti would continue with this theme in her book, *Under His Very Windows*. This would even lead to the outrageous assertion by John Weiss that Pius XII, "Supported the Nazis ... even if it meant the murder of priests."[85]

Few revisionists note that in 1940 Pius XII sent out a secret instruction to the Catholic bishops of Europe entitled *Opere et Caritate* (*By Work and by Love*). The letter began with a quotation of Pius XI's encyclical *Mit Brennender Sorge*, which attacked Nazi doctrines and ordered that all people suffering from racial discrimination at the hands of the Nazis be given all help.[86] The letter was to be read in churches with the comment that racism was incompatible with the teaching of Catholicism. The Nazis were infuriated and took steps to suppress and confiscate copies of the encyclical. The *New York Times* reported, "Vatican Denounces Atrocities in Poland; Germans Are Called Worse Than Russians."[87] On January 26, 1940, the *Jewish Advocate* praised the Vatican Radio's," outspoken condemnation of German atrocities in Nazi occupied Poland." Josef Goebbels, Nazi propaganda chief, ordered the arrest of anyone listening to the Vatican's broadcasts, which he deemed, "more dangerous for us than those of the communists." The papal encyclical *Mystici Corporis Christi* (*Of the Mystical Body*) clearly exhorted not only Catholics but non–Catholics as well to come to the aid of the persecuted victims regardless of nationality or race and specifically referred to Jews.[88] Vatican Radio's broadcast to France in June 1943 stated, "whoever distinguishes between Jews and other men is unfaithful to God and is in conflict with God's command." The *New York Times* reported, "Pope Is Said To Plead For Jews Listed For Removal From France." Eleven days later it followed with, "Vichy Seizes Jews: Pope Pius Ignored."[89] In one of his many wartime communications to the Vatican, Chief Rabbi Isaac Herzog of Palestine wrote, "The people of Israel will never forget what his Holiness is doing for us."

The Deputy was subsequently translated into 20 languages and captured the public and academic imagination. What was ignored by most people was that the playwright admitted in the afterward, "...the action does not follow the historical course of events ... I allowed my imagination free play."[90] Hochhuth's play did little to illuminate or inform but it did ignite public controversy. Despite the fact that the play was fictional and highly polemical and was not based on historical evidence, it was widely acclaimed. It found favor with the media and the public at large interested in the sensational and scandalous. Robert Kempner, the former deputy-chief prosecutor at the Nuremberg trials, protested Hochhuth's portrait of Pius XII. Sir D'Arcy Osborne, Britain's ambassador to the Vatican during the war, stated, "Pius XII was the most warmly, kindly, generous, sympathetic (and, incidentally saintly) character that it has been my privilege to know in the course of a long life."[91] Pius XII, who had been hailed by Jews and Gentiles, survivors, government leaders, and heads of rescue organizations, was to undergo a major departure in the public and academic consciousness. The left's critique of Pius XII had been mediated through a third-rate literary piece and gave rise to a generation of revisionist scholars and journalists.

In recent years revisionism has become politicized with not so hidden agendas. Nowhere is the politicization of history by its practitioners more evident than in the writings of a number of revisionists. John Cornwell continued Rolf Hochhuth's depiction of Pius XII, as *Hitler's Pope*. Daniel Goldhagen recklessly asserts that there is a moral equivalent between the Roman Catholic Church and the Nazi Party. He also contends there is an unbroken line between Christian teachings and the Holocaust. "Having established his own idiosyncratic standards of righteousness, he can easily enough criticize all those who do not adhere to these archetypes...." This sweeping contention is supported by no new research. Instead Goldhagen makes use of highly selective quotations from other authors, most of whom adopt the same pejorative viewpoints about the Catholic Church's record. Rabbi David Dalin adds his scathing criticism, "On and on the factual errors go, the sloppy handling of dates, persons and places all culminating in the selective use [or ignoring of evidence to portray Eugenio Pacelli, later Pius XII] as the fount of the era's anti–Semitism."[92] Goldhagen uses the Nazi Holocaust as a moral cudgel, and some revisionists use it as an ideological or political weapon. Dalin vents his fury at "Goldhagen's misuse of the Holocaust to advance an anti–Catholic agenda."

Why did the Pope remain silent? According to the revisionists, not only was he obsessively concerned about communism, he was also fundamentally an anti–Semite.[93] Goldhagen continues with this rant as part of his moral salvo, "The elements of Pacelli's anti–Semitic collage were the kind Julius Streicher would soon offer the German public in every issue of his notorious Nazi newspaper, *Der Stürmer.*"[94] He equates Pius XII with Streicher, a fanatical anti–Semite who was "somewhat pathological." In the hands of such revisionists Pius XII becomes a Faustian figure who is driven by power, a betrayer of the Jews. Neither Goldhagen nor Cornwell are professional historians. Cornwell is a below-average journalist whose research is shoddy at best.

The contrast between objective scholarship and advocacy is illustrated by two examples cited by Cornwell and Goldhagen.[95] The first incident occurred in 1917 and the second in 1919. In September 1917, Pacelli who was nuncio to Bavaria, received a letter from Dr. Moshe Cossman Werner, Munich's rabbi. Rabbi Werner asked Pacelli for help in getting the Italian customs authorities to release some palm fronds to be used in the coming feast of the Tabernacles. Because of the wartime restrictions the palms had been held up in a railway station in Como, Italy. Pacelli passed on the request to his superior, Cardinal Pietro Gasparri. Pacelli said that he had informed Werner that since the Vatican did not have diplomatic relations with Italy it was unlikely that he should expect a favorable response from Italian authorities in time for the Jewish feast. Pacelli's letter also noted that the rabbi was asking for help in a matter that not only involved civil rights, but that also sought cooperation in the celebration of non–Catholic religious rites, which was forbidden by canon law at the time.[96]

Gasparri replied that the Vatican could not act because, in fact, the Vatican did not have diplomatic relations with Italy. When the matter was explained to Werner, "he thanked me [Pacelli] warmly for all that I had done on his behalf." Cornwell takes this incident in part and states that this was a "diplomatic sleight of hand," and that Pacelli's letter "has lain buried in the files of the Secretary of State until now."[97] Cornwell's endnote shows that he quoted the letter from a book that was published in 1956. He uses this incident as evidence that Pacelli was an anti–Semite and asserts, "Pacelli rejected a poignant plea of his Jewish brethren that might have brought spiritual consolation to the many thousands." In truth, given the circumstances at the time, Pacelli could not set himself above canon law even though this canonical prohibition has since been lifted. Diplomatic relations with Italy came seven years later with the Lateran Accords.[98]

To prove Pacelli's inherent anti–Semitism, both Cornwell and Goldhagen also use a letter written in 1919. Bolshevik revolutionaries had taken power in Bavaria, and Pacelli became their target. Pacelli was repeatedly threatened with bodily harm. The Bolshevik revolutionaries took over the

Royal Palace. "In a letter to Rome, sent over Pacelli's signature, the letter described the attack"[99] on the Munich nunciature by a band of Communist radical thugs led by "...a young man about 30 or 35, also Russian and a Jew. Pale, dirty, with vacant eyes, hoarse voice, vulgar, repulsive, with a face that is both intelligent and sly." Goldhagen leaps to the attack, "Implicit in Pacelli's letter is the notion of Judeo–Bolshevism, the virtually axiomatic conviction among Nazis, and modern anti–Semites in general, and within the Church itself that Jews were the principal bearers and even the authors of Bolshevism." According to Frederick Schweitzer, "This mode of thought is the feat of an archaeologist who fashions a dinosaur from one bone and a ton of plaster of Paris, an indication that Goldhagen's temperament is more that of an advocate than an historian."[100] Cornwell falsely claims that this is a ticking time bomb laid in the Vatican secret archive. There is nothing secret about the archive since any scholar can have access to it. Despite Cornwell's claim, he did not first discover the letter; it had been in print for several years and was well known to serious scholars. Goldhagen and Cornwell either deliberately or out of ignorance fail to state that his description was by an aide, not Pacelli, who did not witness the event. The letter was either drafted by his assistant and signed by Pacelli, or was written by him on the basis of a report or memo he had received. The letter in essence accurately described the facts of the event. The letter addresses the revolutionaries, not the Jewish people, and the author of the letter does not associate "Jewishness with Bolshevism," but a specific Bolshevik revolution and a specific group of Jewish revolutionaries at a specific moment in time.[101]

The revisionists citing this letter do not inform the reader about the surrounding climate throughout Europe. As a result they pluck this letter out of the events of the day. The Bolsheviks came to power during World War I and took Russia out of the war. The Allied powers intervened with military force, ostensibly to reestablish the second front. In reality it was intended, as Winston Churchill put it, to "nip Bolshevism in the bud." The Allied intervention failed, as did the efforts of the White Russians to reestablish Tsarist rule. The Bolsheviks followed with the formation of the Communist International (Comintern) to propagate their version of revolution to the rest of the world. "It would be difficult to exaggerate the fear and terror that these events spread amongst many parts of the population in Western and Central Europe."[102]

Despite a promising constitution, the Weimar Republic faced continued crises as various factions attacked the government and one another. In an atmosphere approaching civil war, armed Spartacists sought to depose the Ebert government. Berlin — eventually all of Germany — would probably have gone Communist but for the Free Corps that marched in and crushed the Red centers of resistance. The threat of violent revolution from both the left and the right gripped Munich in 1919. In the first six months of 1919 political violence was an everyday occurrence in Munich. For a brief period the Communists seized power and proclaimed a Bavarian Soviet Republic. Kurt Eisner ran the Bavarian Socialist Republic. "To many Bavarians Kurt Eisner, an elderly Jew, was the very model of a revolutionary...."[103] His situation hopeless, Eisner resigned in February and then he was assassinated. Martial law was declared and a socialist government was declared.

On April 13 the Communists seized power, deposed the anarchists and proclaimed a second council of republic closer to the Russian model. The Communist Party, though small, contained a number of tough young men mainly of Russian–Jewish origin. The leaders of the new council were Eugene Levine and Max Levien, who set about confiscating food and arms, censoring the press, organizing a Red army, and taking hostages of the population. Lenin gave Levine his support and inquired as to the number of hostages he had taken. Shortly thereafter the Congress of the Third International established the Communist International (Comintern). The Munich Communists committed a number of violent acts. Most foreign diplomats left Munich during these dangerous times but Pacelli remained. In another incident, machine-gun fire from a car sprayed Pacelli's residence. On another occasion a group of Bolshevik thugs broke into the residence and brandished revolvers at Pacelli. Pacelli boldly confronted the assailants and turned them away. A violent mob surrounded Pacelli's car with the intent of overturning the vehicle. Once again Pacelli confronted the mob and convinced them to stop.[104] The Free Corps drove the Communists from power. Eugene Levine and some of the communist leaders were tried and executed for high treason. "The revolutionaries' dream of a chain of Bolshevik republics, linking Bavaria, Austria and Hungary to the Soviet Union, effectively collapsed." It is in this mieleu that the 1919 letter must be viewed and evaluated. Goldhagen and his fellow revisionist continue to ignore a letter written by Cardinal Pacelli to Cardinal Pietro Gasparri. The letter, dated November 14, 1923, was written five days after Hitler's abortive putsch to seize control of the Munich government. In the letter Pacelli denounces the National Socialist movement and notes that the cardinal of Munich had already condemned the persecution of Bavaria's Jews.[105]

An adage states "A picture is worth a thousand words," however, with the caveat that the picture indeed is a true one. Revisionist authors and their publishers thrive on the sensational in order to sell their wares. A photograph that accompanied an article written by James Carroll for the *New Yorker* illustrates revisionist legerdemain. Pius XII is seen saluting German soldiers who it appears are wearing the combat helmet of World War II. In the context of the article the reader is left with the impression that the Pope was given an honor guard by the Third Reich. What the *New Yorker* and Carroll didn't tell their readers was that the photograph was taken of Cardinal Pacelli before he became pope. The Weimar government extended this courtesy to all diplomats, including Pacelli. That same photograph was used a year later in a *New York Times Magazine* article critical of Pius XII and was recycled again in another article written by Carroll for the *Atlantic Monthly*.

The same photograph had additional life when John Cornwell and his publisher, Viking Press, used it on the cover of the book. They enhanced its effect by blurring some of the figures. In short the soldiers in the photo wore Weimar not Nazi uniforms, but the impression coincided with the provocative title, *Hitler's Pope*. One additional sleight of hand took place when the door of the car in the photo was cropped so that the reader would not be able to identify the 1920s vintage of the vehicle.

A number of pressure groups and individuals police the public discussion of the Holocaust.[106] Upon the publication of Cornwell's book Abraham Foxman, national director of the Anti Defamation League, seized Cornwell's most outrageous charges and said in a television interview that "Pius XII was callous at best and an anti–Semite at worst."[107] Mr. Foxman, Viking Press, and the scandal-driven media ran with the sensational charges without further investigation into Cornwell. Goldhagen is also able to get by with his charge that Pius XII was an out-and-out anti–Semite. The line between objective scholarship and shoddy "research" was never called into question.

Cornwell claimed that he applied for access to Vatican archival material, "reassuring those who had charge of crucial documents that I was on the side of my subject (Pius XII).... For months on end I ransacked Pacelli's files which dated back to 1912 in a windowless dungeon beneath the Borgia Tower in Vatican." Though the title of his book may indicate he uncovered new documentation, Cornwell did not cite a single document about Pius XII's relationship to Hitler. Cornwell was not granted access to any archival documents after 1922. Hitler was not politically significant prior to that date. There was no ransacking of Vatican files because the files ran from 1922 backward, not forward, but Cornwell gave his readers a different impression. Also any scholar has access to the Vatican's archives to do scholarly research. You do not have to reveal beforehand your essential point of view in order to be granted access, nor must it agree with that of the Holy See. One does not work in a dungeon; the Vatican archive is an underground vault where files are stored and may be obtained only by working with an archivist. Lastly, Cornwell did not work months on end. He was given a pass for three weeks. Cornwell began research on May 12 and ended on June 2, 1997. Most days he was never there, and he spent an average of one to two hours when he did consult the archives. This does not deter Goldhagen and many of the other revisionists who continue to cite Cornwell as a reliable source.

Professors Norman Finkelstein and Ruth Bettina Birn provided a devastating critique of Goldhagen's earlier work, *Hitler's Willing Executioners*. The authors, in *A Nation on Trial: The Goldhagen Thesis and Historical Truth* argue that the historiography of the Holocaust has been politicized and further criticized his research and interpretations.[108] Abraham Foxman called on Finkelstein's publisher to drop the book and Leon Wieseltier, literary editor of the *New Republic,* personally intervened with his publisher to squelch its publication.[109]

It seems that revisionists are unfamiliar with the Vatican documents that have been published to date. For example Michael Marrus, a Holocaust historian, has implied that either something sinister or damaging to Pius XII may be found in a record of what the German cardinals said in the two meetings they had with Pius XII in 1939.[110] The fact is the record of that meeting is available to anyone familiar with the Vatican documents.[111]

Vatican documents (*ADSS*) also show that from 1941 onward the Vatican leaders were prepared to instruct their officials to offer help to the persecuted including protests against those atrocities to governments where such papal pressure might be effective. The documents relating to Slovakia, Romania, Hungary, and France are a clear indication these interventions went beyond the defense of merely Catholic interests or the laity.[112] Frederick Schweitzer says that an indication of Goldhagen's failure to research properly is his "passing reference to the Vatican's 11-volume work published in response to Hochhuth's gauntlet.... He makes no use and shows no knowledge of the volumes beyond dismissing them as highly selective in order to shore up Pius XII's reputation with the Jews."[113]

The revisionists fail to consult recently declassified OSS documents that show Pius XII's collaboration with anti–Hitler conspirators in Germany that extended from 1929 to 1945. Richard Breitman, who has been authorized to study the new series of documents, has said, "In general, the Germans considered the Pope as an enemy...," they planned "to take him from Rome to the north ... but the proposal was rejected because the majority [Nazis] knew that Pius XII would never leave Rome, and that the Vatican was on the side of the Allies ... Berlin distrusted the Pope and the Vatican, because it knew they hid Jews."[114] What impressed Breitman was the depth of Nazi hostility for the Pope and the Catholic Church. Other documents found in the foreign ministry archives of various governments also reveal that the Vatican provided the Allies with information regarding Axis troop movements. Few revisionists are aware that as early as 1939 Pius XII had created a special department for the Jews in the German section of the Vatican Information Office. Some 36,777 documents were processed in favor of the Jews. This doesn't take into consideration the thousands of false identity papers that were distributed to the countless numbers who were being persecuted. In addition the Vatican Information Bureau also aimed at the restoration of families separated by the conflict and responded to thousands of queries about refugees and missing military and civilians, and sought to ensure their spiritual and material assistance. New available documentation, *Inter Arma Caritas*, reveals that 20 million messages were transmitted despite the obstacles thrown up by the Nazis and the Soviet Communists. The Vatican Information Office had just two employees in 1939 and grew to 600 by 1943. By 1941 about 2,000 requests for help were sent daily to the Vatican Information Office. The requests for assistance grew so numerous that Vatican Radio was employed to request information, to forward information, or to answer inquires regarding refugees and missing persons. It also broadcast news and messages gathered by nunciatures and papal delegations. By 1944, Vatican Radio was broadcasting 63 weekly programs and transmitted 27,000 messages a month.

Among the laundry list of indictments leveled against Pius XII is that he never mentioned the Jews in his wartime statements or in any of his public statements. Once again revisionist critics fail to read what is already on record. Jews are specifically discussed in the context of their persecution in two encyclicals, *Summi Pontificatus* and *Mystic Corporis Christi*. Yehuda Bauer has written, "Antisemitism was not just one of the aspects of Nazi ideology. Rather, it was one of the two central pillars, the other being the demand for world domination by the Germanic peoples. Nazi racialism was, in a very real sense, a by-product of its anti–Semitism.... Only the Germanic peoples were fully human.... Antisemitism stood at the center, not only of ideology, but the decisive actions of the Nazi regime."[115]

Hitler assembled his ideas about Jews in *Mein Kampf*, "The racial question gives the key not only to world history, but to all human culture." According to Hitler the rise and fall of civilization depends on the "racial preservation of the nation ... so the resurrection of Germany depends on the clearest knowledge of the racial problem and hence of the Jewish problem."[116] The sole purpose of the state was to maintain the purity of the Aryan master race. The only problem according to Hitler was the Jews, whose "vileness," was part of their blood, that their "race" was inferior in all respects and had defiled Germany. Hitler maintained that Judaism is not a religion "they are a race" of bloodsucking parasites which contaminated the Aryan race. "He instilled in his followers redemptive anti–Semitism according to which the Jew, defined by race, is all-powerful and all-malignant. This was the idealistic element in the poisonous fantasy: the threat of one's perdition, the promise of one's salvation."[117]

Hitler's ideological obsession was quickly enacted into policy. "The desire to expand to the east and control Europe was motivated by a phantasmagoric racial-biological ideology in which the enemy was controlled by Jews; therefore, the Jews were, from the Nazi point of view, the main enemy."[118] To understand this malignant worldview is to understand the mindset of the Nazi racial fanatics confronted by the Western democracies and the papacy. Nazi ideologue, Alfred Rosenberg in his diatribe, *Myth of the Twentieth Century*, formulated a scientific theory of racism. "The Jews ... not a people ... a parasitic "antirace," which must be extirpated...."[119] Konrad Lorenz posited the natural law of the Aryan master race. "In Hitler's twisted cosmological vision, the eternal enemy of the Aryans, the race that possessed the power to create, was the Jew, the embodiment of evil, the agent of the racial pollution that had undermined and destroyed one civilization after another."[120]

The questions remains: If Pius XII attacked Nazi racialism or employed the term race, what did most people in Europe think of at the time? What in fact did the Nazi radicals think? The Pope had already gone on record in 1935 and 1937 condemning the Nazi's pagan cult of race.[121] Most often the Nazis and the outside world associated the usage of the term with Jews. Certainly this was the case in Nazi Germany, whose ideology was based on a superior master Aryan race and considered Jews a race apart. David Kertzer, a revisionist historian uses the term "racist anti–Semitism" himself.[122] Documents abound with Nazi references to Jews and race; the terms were inextricably bound together. SS General Heinrich Himmler wrote Joachim von Ribbentrop on January 29,1943, expressing his displeasure with regard to Italian resistance to the Final Solution. He wanted Italian Jews, "and other foreign nationals of Jewish race to be removed from the Italian occupied area of France."[123] Nazi racial policies were never directed only against Jews; "the immense elasticity of race thinking is evident in an array of other comments and programs ... the Nazis demonstrated the easy slippage between biological and cultural definitions of race."[124]

The assertion that Pius XII was silent or never used the word Jew in his public statements has become dogma.[125] Apparently the revisionists or their research assistants have never read his encyclicals carefully enough or choose not to. In his first encyclical, *Summi Pontificatus (Of the Supreme Pontificate)*, known in English as "Darkness over the Earth" he quoted St. Paul, saying, " The spirit, the teaching and the work of the Church can never be other than that which the Apostle of the Gentiles preached: "there is neither Gentile nor Jew," using the word "Jew" specifically in the context of rejecting racial ideology. Pius XII urged resistance to the attacks on Judaism and instructed Catholics that they "should confront such wickedness by saying: Non licet; it is not allowed!" On October 28, 1939, the *New York Times* praised the encyclical: " Pope Condemns Dictators, Treaty Violators, Racism."[126] The Jewish Telegraphic Agency on October 27 reported that, "the unqualified condemnation which Pope Pius XII heaped on totalitarian, racist and materialistic theories of government in his encyclical ... caused a profound stir.... Although it had been expected that the Pope would attack ideologies hostile to the Catholic Church, few observers had expected so outspoken a document...." The Allies subsequently dropped 80,000 copies of the encyclical on Germany with the hope of arousing anti–Nazi sentiment.[127] The Gestapo sought out anyone reading or distributing the encyclical. Alfred Rosenberg condemned the Pope as antiracist.

Eight days after the Allies issued a human rights declaration that in general terms condemned the treatment of Jews, Pius XII delivered his Christmas message of 1942. The Pope denounced the Nazis, and in particular the persecution of "hundreds of thousands who, without any fault of their own, sometimes only by reason of their nationality or race, are marked down for death or gradual extinction." The pope employed the Latin word "stripes," but "which had been used throughout Europe for centuries as an explicit reference to Jews."[128] While condemning totalitarian governments he acknowledges the responsibility of the church and urged Catholics to provide shelter to those in need. On Christmas Day, the *New York Times* in its editorial praised the Pope for his moral leadership: "This Christmas more than ever he is a lonely voice crying out of the silence of a continent ... when he assails violent occupation of territory, the exile and persecution of human beings for no reason other than race or political opinion."[129]

Roberto Farinacci, editor of Italy's official Fascist newspaper, sprung to the attack and wrote, "The Church's obstruction of the practical solution to the Jewish Problem constitutes a crime against the New Europe." The revisionists conveniently ignore the reactions to Pius XII's public pronouncements either by individual Nazis or the Nazi press. "But in fact the 1942 message was not as cryptic and incomprehensible as latter-day critics would suggest." On January 22, 1943, SS General Reinhard Heydrich, Himmler's deputy, denounced the Pope for repudiating National Socialism. "His speech is one long attack on everything we stand for. 'God,' he says, 'regards all peoples and races worthy of the same consideration.' Here he is clearly speaking on behalf of the Jews. He is virtually accusing the German peoples of injustice towards the Jews and makes himself the mouthpiece of the Jewish war criminals."[130] Revisionists would be better served if they consulted the Nazi press's reaction to papal and Vatican prouncements including: the *Berliner Morgenpost, Das Reich, Der Sturmer, Frankfurter Zeitung, Volkisher Beobachter, Der Andriff, Der Judenkenner,* and *Der Weltkampf,* since they predictably followed suit and used Heydrich's own words. The Reich's secret services wrote that Pius XII "defended the criminal Jews of war."[131] Cornwell and Goldhagen and most of the revisionists completely ignore Nazi reaction to papal pronouncements in order to prove their case.[132] In December of 1942 Goebbels denounced the Pope for having taken the side of Jews in the Christmas message.[133] The Nazis and the entire world understood that the Pope was referring to the Jews. It is important to note that Heydrich, just two days before his condemnation of Pius XII, had presided over the Wannsee conference that planned the "Final Solution." Asserting Pius XII was "silent about Nazi mass murder is a serious error of historical fact," because his 1942 Christmas message "put the Pope squarely against the Holocaust," Martin Gilbert says of the Pope's critics.[134]

Most revisionists selectively use *Mystici Corporis Christi* and omit the fact that Pius XII unequivocally states that Jews and Gentiles are one and that he denounced racial hatred as incompatible with Catholic doctrine. He also denounced the Nazis' euthanasia programs.[135] Did the Nazis understand to whom the Pope was referring? In May 1943 the Nazi-controlled *Aujourd'hui* accused the Catholic Church of inviting oppression in the Reich by opposing Hitler's racist theories. Harold H. Tittmann's recently published memoir provides further insight into Pius XII's conduct during the war. Tittmann recounts his discussions with Dr. Josef Müller, the anti–Nazi middleman between the Pope and the German resistance. Tittmann records, "Dr. Müller said that during the war his anti–Nazi organization in Germany had always been very insistent that the Pope should refrain from making any public statement singling out the Nazis and specifically condemning them and had recommended that the Pope's remarks should be confined to generalities only." He further said the policy of the resistance was to allow the German hierarchy to carry out "the struggle inside Germany...."[136]

Some revisionists such as Michael Marrus have even blamed Pius XII for not condemning Kristallnacht in 1938, even though he was elevated to the papacy a year later. When Lord Rothchild organized a protest meeting in London in response to Kristallnacht, Cardinal Pacelli sent a statement of Pius XI expressing his solidarity with the persecuted Jews. That statement was read publicly at the protest meeting. Professor Marrus is unaware that the sixth volume of the *ADSS* contains the supporting documentation of the Vatican's protest.[137]

Robert Wistrich has used the so-called Bérard report as proof that the Vatican/Pius XII did not oppose anti–Jewish restrictions. Leon Bérard, Vichy's Vatican ambassador to the Holy See, sent a report dated September 2, 1941, in which he stated that the Vatican "had no quarrel with us" over the anti–Jewish statutes. Implied of course is papal Vatican anti–Semitism. What Wistrich, Zuccotti, and like-minded revisionists do not mention is that there is ample documentary evidence to show that Bérard's report was not only unauthorized, but was firmly contradicted by the Holy See. Cardinal Maglione, papal secretary of state, clearly stated that Bérard had made exaggerations about Vatican policy.[138] In short the report was written by and at the request of a representative of the Vichy government.[139] In her book *Under His Very Windows*, Zuccotti alleges that the Vatican knew in 1941 of the concentration camps and less than a year later the start of the extermination process. Justus George Lawler notes:

> ... in *The Holocaust, the French, and the Jews*, virtually no one — social workers, members of Jewish or Christian agencies, officials of the free French government, church leaders whether Catholic or Protestant — seemed to know of or believe in the existence of the death camps. Zuccotti here is all magnanimity, generously forbearing, and detailed [pp. 145–54] in her condonation of this nescience and incredulity.[140]

The revisionists reject out of hand all contemporary and eyewitness testimonies that may challenge their assumptions. The historian's tools include the analysis of written documents of the period, of diaries, of letters, and of testimonies of those contemporaneous to the events. The task of the historian is to subject eyewitnesses and participants to the crucial tests of accuracy and authenticity, not to select some that prove a case and ignore others that do not. Personal testimonies are extremely useful when cross-checked with, and borne out by many other testimonies, and are at least as reliable as a written document of the time. The historian must be careful not to rely too heavily and uncritically on German documents of the time since "the documents of the perpetrators were often designed to mislead rather than to inform, to hide rather than to reveal."[141] The secular press both Gentile and Jew, world leaders, diplomats, eyewitnesses, thousands who had been rescued by the Vatican, and various participants who attest to Pius XII's motives and actions are summarily dismissed.

Susan Zuccotti says that those who were rescued and attributed it to papal intervention have "shown the gratitude to be misplaced. Men and women of the Church in Italy certainly deserved to be recognized and thanked, but the pope had very little to do with their activities. Those sheltered could not have known it was the work of the Pope. Jewish leaders who praised Pius XII knew better and were doing so for other reasons. Why were so many observers mistaken? The error was often rooted in benevolent ignorance."[142] Zuccotti's sweeping dismissal of eyewitness testimony favorable to another point of view amounts to arrogance and academic elitism. One might add: Were the journalists at the time ignorant of papal interventions when they filed their reports? What about the diplomats who dealt directly with Pius XII or those who were saved by the Vatican? Even highly placed diplomats who were housed in the Vatican, or those directly aided were, according to Zuccotti, benevolently ignorant. Harold Tittmann writes from firsthand knowledge, "And it was only rarely that records were kept by the Vatican officials of conversations the Pope had with his intimate collaborators or even with important visitors from the outside, such as ministers, ambassadors, or private individuals offering information or suggestions. Sometimes, if the Cardinal Secretary of State or one of the undersecretaries happened to be present, reference would be made in their published documents to what the Holy Father had said, but only briefly." Tittmann's recently published memoir also has revealed that Pius XII maintained "special accounts" in New York banks administered by Archbishop Spellman. In addition the Pope had a "personal and secret account" that was unknown to Spellman. Pius XII revealed the existence of these accounts in a strictly confidential meeting with Tittmann on June 19, 1941. These accounts were "used exclusively for charitable purposes" during the war. This supports the 1966 testimony of Father Robert Leiber, who stated, "The Pope sided very unequivocally with the Jews at the time. He spent his entire private fortune on their behalf." The British historian Sir Martin Gilbert has dismissed the claims of the revisionists that rescue activity was independent of Pius XII. "I am on the side of those who argue for the connection between the Pope and the Catholic rescuers. You cannot say that the Pope is the supreme head of the Catholic Church and did nothing, and then, in the next breath, speak of all these wonderful acts of Catholic charity and rescue — especially by senior men of the Church who pledged fidelity to the pontiff— and claim that the Pope had nothing to do with their rescue efforts." On July 21, 1943, Archbishop Andrea Cassulo, apostolic nuncio in Romania, wrote Cardinal Luigi Maglione in which he refers to numerous protests on behalf of Jews. A. Safran, the rabbi of Romania, expressed his gratitude to Cassulo for papal assistance. On April 4, 1941, he wrote, "In these hard times, our thoughts go more than ever to what the Supreme Pontiff has done in favor of Jews in general and to Your Excellency in favor of Romania and Transylvania. These deeds will never be forgotten. In addition Rabbi Safran recounted the intervention of Cassulo noting that "he succeeded in having no more deportations."[143]

Elio Toaff, who would become chief rabbi of Rome after the war, wrote in tribute to Pius XII that Italian Jews, "more than anyone else ... had the opportunity to appreciate the great kindness, filled with compassion and magnanimity, that the Pope displayed during the terrible years of persecution and terror." Rabbi Toaff was in Italy at the time and witnessed many of the events that tragically came to Italy and its Jews. Golda Meir, upon the Pope's death, said, "During the ten years of Nazi terror the Pope raised his voice to condemn the persecutors and to commiserate with their victims." According to Zuccotti's standard, Albert Einstein was benevolently ignorant when he wrote in 1940, "Only the Church stood squarely against the path of Hitler's campaign for suppressing the truth.... I feel a great admiration because the Church alone has had the moral courage and persistence to stand for intellectual truth and moral freedom." Apparently Leo Kubwitsky, secretary general of the World Jewish Congress was also benevolently ignorant when in 1945 he gave Pius XII over $1 million (at the present value) for "charity works" and expressed "his gratitude to the august Pontiff for his work in support of persecuted Jews." The Pope in return decided, "the sum should go exclusively to needy persons of Jewish origin."[144] When Pius XII died on October 9, 1958, the tributes were so numerous that it took three issues of the *New York Times* to report them all. Tributes came from the world's major rabbis, world leaders, those rescued, and the secular and religious press.

Indeed we are a culture of book and film. Revisionism has more recently been projected to the wider culture in fiction. Daniel Silva's *The Confessor* accepts the silence of Pius XII during the Holocaust as a given. His main plot is based on a fictional meeting between a high Vatican official and a Nazi Foreign Office official during which the former collaborates in the Nazi plans for the extermination of the Jews. A far-right cabal of traditionalist Catholics plans to stop by all means necessary the new liberal pope from admitting the church's guilt for aiding and abetting the Final Solution. Gabriel Allon, a secret Israeli agent, is Silva's hero. Allon saves the pope from assassination but also exposes the wartime sins of the church. So here we have a Jew saving a pope, a reversal of the wartime Pius XII who apparently failed to save the Jews.

Fiction took to the screen with Constantin Costa-Gavras's film *Amen*, based on *The Deputy*. Costa-Gavras, a left-wing filmmaker, thought the time was right to put Hochhuth's version of Pius XII onto film. All of the charges are laid out once again in this caricature that sacrifices history on the altar of the cinematographic pamphlet. Thus, revisionism is thrust into the popular culture as a sine qua non and has become orthodoxy. Revisionists fail to examine events in context and in terms of the culture of that day and not our own. "What we have is the worst kind of revisionism, which treats history like a loose-leaf notebook. Historians remove the pages that disagree with their opinions" and speculate, substituting those that support their thesis.[145]

Revisionist dogma has arrived at a point in which the Church under Pius XII was as responsible for the Holocaust as the Nazis who carried it out. They maintain the Pope was silent and thus complicit in the Nazi Holocaust. All too often they give the impression that opposition to the Nazi regime was easy, without risk, and a matter of will or goodwill. Pius XII has became the antihero of a black legend The historical reality of the pontificate of Pius XII has nearly been lost in the increasingly strident agenda-driven revisionism of recent years. In the hands of some revisionists Pius XII is used to promote an agenda, whether it's to settle old scores, to place blame elsewhere, to demand reparations (Goldhagen), to attack current positions of the church and the centrality of the papacy, or to use the Holocaust to take sides in intramural Catholic disagreements. Goldhagen's latest rant is a bitter attack on Christianity in general, and on the Catholic Church and Pius XII in particular. According to John Conway, "His is a sneering disparagement of other analysts for moral equivocation, a dismissal of most contemporary scholarship, and a hunger for the black-and-white, the simplest of historical explanations."[146] Georg Denzler says of Goldhagen, "This is an artificial construction of half-truths in the service of an ideology. And it is so full of extraordinary factual mistakes that it amounts to a pattern of falsehoods and distortions."[147]

> The question separating Pius XII's accusers and defenders in the future will continue to be whether he should have done more to publicize his moral condemnation of Nazi atrocities; or whether his exercise of ethical responsibility enabled him to save more lives. Pius XII chose what he considered the realistic course and left the door open to negotiation. Nonetheless, he was not silent, as we have shown. On the contrary, he steadfastly proclaimed Catholic teaching.[148]

Revisionist historians have presented a number of proposals after the event that would have theoretically saved some or most Jews during the Holocaust. William Rubenstein warns everyone, "one must at all times be aware of what was actually proposed at the time in the West and what has since been proposed, often many decades later by historians who are able coolly to reflect on the events of the Holocaust, possessing knowledge well known today but unknown at the time. Proposals for rescue made many decades later — that is, suggestions not actually made by anyone during the war itself — are ipso facto highly suspect if not historiographically illegitimate."[149] Those who were present in the '30s had Hitler ahead of them. Hitler's persecution of political and racial enemies began almost immediately after he assumed power and increased in intensity and scope throughout the '30s.[150] Saul Friedlander contends, "In all major respects the regime depended on Hitler. Especially with regard to the Jews...."[151] Though we in the early 21st century have Hitler and the Nazi Holocaust behind us we should not lose sight of the fact no Hitler, no Holocaust. Hitler's Final Solution required Hitler. "He carried a very specific brand of racial anti–Semitism to its most extreme and radical limits."[152]

There is something unsavory in the animus underlying some of the revisionist works. Whatever we make of Hitler and the Nazi Holocaust, we must never forget Emil Fackenheim's famous dictum about granting no posthumous victories to Hitler. We hardly honor the martyred millions by singling out a single individual and bearing false witness against that person. According to William Rubenstein, "...it cannot be emphasized too strongly that the responsibility for the Holocaust lies solely and wholly with Adolf Hitler, the SS and their accomplices, and with no one else. In searching for a rational explanation of modern history's greatest crime, it is important that we not assign guilt to those who were innocent."[153]

CHAPTER 2

The Road to Dachau

by Patrick J. Gallo

The revisionists fault Cardinal Pacelli for having negotiated the 1933 concordat with Germany. They claim that it legitimized the regime and destroyed the Catholic Center Party — and the direct political involvement of the church, which they theorize, could have held Hitler in check. They make the same mistake as the German politicians and industrialists at the time who thought Hitler could be controlled.[1] According to Goldhagen, "it included the church's liquidation of the Catholic Center Party ... effectively legitimating Hitler's seizure of power and his destruction of democracy, which Pacelli and Pius XI welcomed."[2] Cornwell alleges that Pacelli was motivated by the imposition of papal absolutism on the church within Germany. Some revisionists claim the concordat was the result of a deal that delivered the parliamentary votes of the Center Party to Hitler, thereby giving him dictatorial power.[3] Though Michael Phayer argues that this is inaccurate, he does agree "the agreement inhibited the German bishops from speaking about matters not directly related to the Catholic church.[4] Revisionists often rely on the recollections of the former chancellor, Henrich Brüning, whose own intrigues proved disastrous.[5]

The revisionist interpretation displays an astonishing ignorance of the literature regarding Hitler's rise to power. They zero in on one aspect without placing the concordat within the framework of German politics in the decades of the '20s and '30s. Revisionists are prone to historical amnesia. I suggest as a starter that they re-read Alan Bullock's *Hitler: A Study in Tyranny* and William Shirer's *The Rise and Fall of the Third Reich*, then proceed to Richard Evans's *The Coming of the Third Reich*, and everything in between on German politics in the '20s and '30s.

After 1919 the three parties responsible for the adoption of the Weimar Constitution — the Social Democrats, Catholic Center, and the Democrats—

were unable ever again to obtain a majority. They were able to form a ministry with a majority in the Reichstag only if they took in the other parties. In short they extended their reach to agree to disagree on major issues. Violent political clashes occurred throughout 1919 and the following year.

Henrich Brüning, the floor leader of the Center Party's deputies in the Reichstag, became chancellor at the end of March 1930 and tried to rule by emergency powers until the Reichstag was dissolved in July 1930. "...Brüning himself was at best a fair weather friend of Weimar democracy."[6] During the summer of 1930 the economic crisis in Germany deepened, and his economic policy of retrenchment was making the situation even worse. Brüning used the president's emergency powers to put his fiscal program into effect by decree. He also placed restrictions on democratic rights and civil liberties, "...thus began the dismantling of democratic and civil freedoms that was pursued with such vigor under the Nazis."[7] The chancellor was greeted by a storm of criticism for what he had done.

In the presidential election of March 1932 Hindenburg defeated Hitler. "A few days after the election Brüning was persuaded to enact a decree outlawing the SA and SS. The effect of this act was to ruin the politically naïve Chancellor, for it was not only ineffective but brought a concerted storm of protest from the right."[8] It provided an opening wedge for General Kurt von Schleicher, who sought to establish a government of the right that would include the Nazis but would not give them control. "Austere in appearance, secretive, inscrutable, given to taking decisions without sufficient consultation, denied the gift of rhetoric, Brüning was not the man to win mass support from an electorate increasing appalled at the economic chaos and political violence that were plunging the country into a crisis whose dimensions beggared even those of 1923."[9]

As a result of the mounting economic crisis Brüning's government fell, since he was unable to hold a coalition together. "The inability of the German parties to combine in support of the Republic had bedeviled German politics ever since 1930, when Brüning had found it no longer possible to secure a stable majority in the Reichstag elections. The Communists announced that they would prefer to see the Nazis in power rather than lift a finger to save the Republic."[10] From that time in May 1932, "all that stood between the republic and Hitler were the whims of a senescent President, Schleicher's faculty for conniving, and the blinded simple mindedness of Franz von Papen."[11]

In August 1932, the Nazis approached the Center Party, which could along with them bring a majority into the Reichstag. Goebbels recorded,

"We have got in touch with the Center Party, if merely by way of bring-ing pressure to bear on our adversaries...."[12] One immediate result of these negotiations was the Center Party's support of Hermann Göring as pres-ident of the Reichstag. Göring maneuvered a session in which the Nazis voted with the Communists in a no-confidence motion that resulted in the Reichstag's dissolution and a new election. After the 1932 Reichstag elections the Nazi Party was by far the largest party in Germany, with the Social Democratic, Communist, and Center parties behind in that order. It should be noted that the Center Party, "spanned a socially varied con-stituency, and its Reichstag delegation included a number of Protestants."[13]

The Catholic Center Party never took an independent line and was always ready to make an accommodation with any government in order to protect its own interests. These maneuvers were not orchestrated by the Vatican or by Pacelli, but by Monsignor Ludwig Kaas, the leader of the party, and Heinrich Brüning. Like many of the other parties in 1932–1933, they did not recognize the danger of a Nazi dictatorship. In fact they con-tinually negotiated with the Nazis, hoping to use them for their own ends.[14]

Hitler became chancellor in January 1933. "Far from being inevitable, Hitler's success owed much to luck and even more to the bad judgment of his political opponents ... the divisions and ineffectiveness of those who opposed him, and the willingness of the German Right to accept him as a partner in government."[15] The Nazis had no intention of maintaining a democracy. Hitler made no secret of what he meant by the politics of legal-ity. He said, "The Constitution only marks out the arena of battle, not the goal. We enter the legal agencies and in that way will make our party the deter-mining factor. However, once we possess the constitutional power, we will mold the state into the shape we hold to be suitable."[16] Hitler moved quickly to consolidate his power in 1933 with the elimination of all who stood in his way to complete domination of Germany. He had no intention of being restrained by the constitution, the Jews, the Communists, the Social Demo-crats, or the Christian churches— and most especially the Catholic Church.[17]

The pretext for smashing the Communist Party and the establish-ment of arbitrary power was the Reichstag fire of February 27, 1933.[18] The day after the fire, Hitler promulgated a decree signed by the president "for the protection of the People and the State." Described as a defensive meas-ure against the violence of the Communists, it suspended the guarantees of individual liberty under the Weimar Constitution. Article 2 permitted the government to take over full powers in any federal state. Article 5 increased the penalties for crimes of high treason and sabotage to one of death. The death penalty was also imposed in the case of conspiracy to assassinate members of the government.[19]

In February 1933 Göring banned all Catholic newspapers in Cologne, a presage of a total ban to come on the Catholic press throughout Germany. On Hitler's command the SA destroyed the meetings of Christian trade unions and the Catholic Center Party. Hitler made an appeal for the church to negotiate with the Third Reich. At the same time he threatened the destruction of the church unless an agreement was reached immediately.

On March 21, 1933, Hitler presented the Reichstag with the Law for Alleviating the Distress of the People and the Reich (Enabling Act) that contained five clauses. The first and fifth clauses gave the government the power to enact laws without the cooperation of the Reichstag. The second and fourth clauses stated that this power should include the right to deviate from the constitution and to conclude treaties with foreign states. The third provided that laws enacted by the government should be drafted by the chancellor, and should become effective on the day after publication.[20]

The Center Party's vote was crucial to its ultimate passage. With the Center Party's consent the government would have the necessary majority for its passage. Hitler assured Dr. Ludwig Kass that he would write a letter "concerning revocation of those parts of the Reichstag fire decree which prejudiced the civil and political liberties of citizens; the letter would also stipulate that the decree was to be applied only in specific circumstances."[21] Hitler also promised a concordat in the near future. The Center Party faction was typically indecisive, given traditionally to opportunism. Its members finally agreed to support it, concluding that they were in no position to prevent its passage. "After all, in conjunction with the promised letter, would not the Enabling Act bind Hitler to legality more effectively than he was bound at present?"[22]

The Center Party's leadership announced that they would vote for the bill, "a fitting close to the shabby policy of compromise with the Nazis which the Center had followed since the summer of 1932."[23] The promised letter never arrived. Brüning and Kaas concluded that unless they voted in favor the nation would be plunged into bloody anarchy. The Center Party leadership's critical vote gave Hitler unchecked power that he used to snuff out all political opposition.[24] Ludwig Kaas resigned in May 1933 and Brüning succeeded him as leader of the party. "All of the Party's deputies and officials tendered their resignations and gave Brüning full power to reappointment them or find replacements.... So the Center Party now, de facto replaced the idea of an elected Reichstag by an appointed one."[25] Brüning moved even closer to the Nazi regime. The concordat then was finalized in July, well after the passage of the Enabling Act. The Enabling Act sealed the process of abdication by the political parties, a process that had started in 1930 when the Great Coalition was shattered."[26] It is this set of facts that revisionists don't even factor into their analysis of the concordat.

In March 1933, the concentration camp at Dachau was established at a site where a munitions factory once stood. Theodore Eicke was the first commandant of the camp. Dachau was intended for political prisoners. The first group to be interned included Social Democrats, Communists, and homosexuals, who were guarded by the SS. Later political dissidents and other "undesirables" from occupied countries were interned there. Hitler was particularly concerned with the "Jewish" problem and threats from the extreme left. The Catholic Church, however, was a special threat. Throughout the '30s Alfred Rosenberg, a Nazi ideologue, singled out the Catholic Church for his venom. According to Rosenberg the clergy, the Catholic hierarchy, and the Vatican poisoned German blood. Christianity was portrayed as the distorted product of Semitic tribes.[27] Dachau was not "an improvised solution to an unexpected problem of overcrowding in the gaols, but a long-planned measure the Nazis had envisaged virtually from the very beginning."[28]

From 1919 to 1933 Pacelli was able to negotiate separate concordats with Baden, Prussia, and Bavaria but failed to reach an agreement with the Weimar government due to the objection of the Socialist bloc in the parliament. From the Vatican's point of view a concordat with the new government would secure the legal status of the church in Germany, particularly in matters such as education and marital law. It was believed that it would be able to gain new rights for the church.

Pius XI instructed his secretary of state to conclude a concordat with the new regime. Contrary to the revisionist charge, Pacelli did not initiate the negotiations but acted on the instructions of the Pope.[29] He was under no illusions about the person with whom he was dealing. As early as 1925 he reported to his superiors that Hitler was a violent man who "will walk over corpses" to achieve his objective. The cardinal, "was extremely frank and made no effort to conceal his disgust at the proceedings of Herr Hitler's government.... Cardinal Pacelli equally deplored the actions of the German Government at home, their persecution of the Jews, their proceedings against political opponents, and the reign of terror."[30]

Franz Van Papen, the new vice chancellor, traveled to Rome to express the government's desire to conclude a concordat with the Holy See. German Catholic leaders, independent of the regime, followed suit and underscored the necessity of insuring the rights of the church. Negotiations intensified from May to July of 1933. In the interim Hitler concluded the Four Power Pact, a peace agreement with France, Great Britain, and Italy.

In reality this agreement recognized the new regime and gave it legitimacy. At the same time Hitler concluded a concordat with the Protestant churches. In June he proceeded with the arrests of thousands of supporters of the Catholic Center Party.

The concordat was concluded on July 20, 1933, and was ratified by Pope Pius XI on September 10. On paper the regime had made significant concessions. "To the Nazis, however, the Concordat was no more than a truce in the fight against the Catholic Church."[31] Both Pius XI and Cardinal Pacelli understood that without an agreement they faced the elimination of the church from Germany. Neither supported or sympathized with the Nazis. Pacelli was faced with the dilemma of having no agreement at all or an agreement though flawed which held out the basis to mount a legal challenge. He chose the lesser of two evils. Cardinal Pacelli, in a conversation with Ivone Kirkpatrick, the British minister to the Vatican said, "The spiritual welfare of 20 million Catholic souls in Germany was at stake, and that was the first and, indeed, only consideration," in agreeing to the concordat. He went on to say that the Holy See, "had to choose between an agreement on [Nazi] lines and the virtual elimination of the Catholic Church in the Reich." Ivone Kirkpatrick cabled London explaining what Pacelli told him: "a pistol had been pointed at his head and he had no alternative.... Not only that, but he was given no more than a week to make up his mind (and) it was a case of then or never...."[32] Both the Pope and Cardinal Pacelli calculated that their first duty was to secure the civil guarantees for the autonomy of ecclesiastical institutions and their activities.

Many Germans and European leaders thought Hitler to be a bulwark against Communism. The key to British foreign policy was the attempt to divert Hitler's energies and pressures eastward. If a war occurred, Britain hoped that it would be she who would stand on the sidelines, conserving her energies while Germany and the Soviet Union became exhausted in a long conflict. Both Pius XI and Cardinal Pacelli were opposed to Nazism and Communism and viewed them as, "the outgrowth of those destructive and revolutionary forces that arose out of the First World War that had such a devastating effect on the moral and spiritual basis for leadership throughout the world."[33]

The Vatican did not, as Goldhagen outrageously claims, welcome Hitler to power or desire the destruction of democracy in Germany. This is another version of Cornwell's thesis, with Goldhagen making the Catholic Church the moral equivalent of the Nazi Party. The concordat was not an approval of the Nazi regime, but an attempt to provide a framework to control it. It was intended to secure the legal rights of German

Catholics. Hitler was certain that there would be opposition from the anticlerical wing of his own party. Ever the opportunist, Hitler reached an accommodation albeit for the short term. On July 26 and 27, 1933, *L'Osservatore Romano* published Cardinal Pacelli's two-part article in which he firmly denied the concordat in any way constituted an approval of National Socialism. He made it clear that it was an agreement "both with a totalitarian state and against a totalitarian ideology."[34]

In their indictment of Pius XII the revisionists conveniently omit what Hitler really meant by the politics of legality, and ignore the failure of German political leaders and the economic and political crisis that gripped Germany in the '30s. Moreover, they seem to ignore that it was the Western powers that legitimized Hitler's regime. The Soviet Union's Treaty of Berlin in May 1933 made it the first power to grant recognition to the Reich. This was to be a treaty of friendship and neutrality. In addition the four-power treaty between Italy, Germany, Britain, and France meant a tacit acceptance of Nazi Germany into their ranks. Finally, the Vatican was to conclude separate agreements (concordats) with 30 other governments.

Contrary to the revisionists' contention, the concordat did not cause the downfall of the Catholic Center Party, since it had already been weakened if not eliminated by March 1933 when Hitler eliminated all opposition parties.[35] In order to ameliorate the persecution of its membership, the Center Party began its own dissolution weeks before the concordat was signed. Moreover, as demonstrated earlier the party had made shabby deals with the Nazis in an effort to attain or maintain its national standing. The claim that Pacelli sacrificed the Center Party in order to obtain the concordat is patently false and rests on the unsupported evidence of Heinrich Brüning's memoirs that is refuted by other contemporary evidence. Brüning and the key players in German politics underestimated Hitler's ruthlessness and guile in their desire to use the Nazi Party for their own political ends. The concordat, as the revisionists maintain, did not silence the German clergy from speaking out. "...The Concordat set forth traditional Church teaching about politics and the clergy."[36] It restated the church's teaching limiting the clergy's direct participation in party politics.

The first formal protest filed with the Reich under the terms of the concordat concerned the government-sponsored boycott of Jewish businesses. By October 1933 Cardinal Pacelli registered a protest with the German Foreign Ministry concerning, "...difficulties and persecutions, carried to virtually every degree, which the Catholic Church in Germany is now enduring in open violation of the Concordat."[37] The Nazi radicals resented any legal constraints on their totalitarian goals and rejected Hans Kerrl's view that Christianity and National Socialism could be combined.

Five days after the ratification of the concordat the German government announced the passage of the Law for the Prevention of Genetically Diseased Offspring. The law provided for the sterilization of individuals that would "insure the perfection of the Aryan race." This was followed by the Law for the Prevention of Hereditarily Diseased Progeny that made sterilization compulsory. Approximately 320,000 to 350,000 individuals would be sterilized. "Social hygiene was to be swept away; racial hygiene was to be introduced in its stead."[38] Both laws were in direct conflict with Pius XI's encyclical Casti Connubii (On Chastity and Marriage), issued on December 30, 1930, that stated in unequivocal terms the church's position on sterilization. The encyclical had condemned all countries including, the United States, that had introduced sterilization statutes.[39]

The Nazis clashed with the Holy See because it protested the German statutes. Eugenic sterilization contravened canon law and the Nazi eugenics and euthanasia programs struck at the core of Catholic teaching on the sanctity of human life. Konrad Lorenz, Nazi theorist, maintained that for the Aryan race to survive and thrive the weak and feeble members of society had to be eliminated. According to Lorenz, in nature the weak did not survive, and it contravened natural law for the strong to care for the weak. Thus, this thinning of the population strengthened the Aryan master race. "Euthanasia was for Hitler a program to rid the German people of anyone considered mentally or physically deficient — any perceived weakness in the collective gene pool."[40]

Contrary to Goldhagen's assertions, the church in fact had opposed the Nazis eugenics and euthanasia programs. As Henry Friedlander notes, "The Catholic Church was on record in opposition to negative eugenics and particularly sterilization, and both the Vatican and the German bishops denounced the sterilization law."[41] Two additional papal decrees were issued in March 1931.[42] Both Goldhagen and David Kertzer ignore the 1930 encyclical and the church's history of opposing the eugenics movement.[43] Nazi euthanasia was not merely a preface to the Final Solution but an integral part of the Holocaust.[44] "Most Holocaust historiography treats the Nazi Euthanasia program as a step along the path of the Final Solution ... rather than as an actual chapter in that event."[45]

Das Schwarze Korps called for the enactment of a euthanasia program in 1937. Hitler thought it best to institute a program in wartime. The euthanasia program would eliminate the weakest members of society, known as "life unworthy of life." The early victims of this cruelty were disabled children who were given overdoses of sedatives. Hitler refused at first to issue a euthanasia law, believing that the people would not accept the killing of fellow Germans. With the outbreak of the war as a cover,

Hitler "wrote a brief authorization on his personal stationery" that, "granted" the mentally and hereditarily sick people the "grace" of death.[46] The evolution of Nazi anti–Jewish policy was intertwined with eugenicist measures targeted against "non–Aryan Germans, at Poles, and at Gypsies.... The genocide of these three groups grew out of the same biomedical vision, although the timetables, modalities, and the dimensions of murder of each group differed significantly."[47] Goldhagen's concern is solely on the murder of Jews and eschews an interpretation of the genocide in a more universal framework.

In October 1939 Hitler's secret decree, the General Foundation for Institutional Care, extended the euthanasia program to adults. This program was code-named T-4 after the address of the euthanasia-program headquarters and the staff administering the program located at Tiergartenstrasse 4 in Berlin.[48] The General Foundation of Insane Asylum and Nursing Homes employed staff in the killing centers. The Reich's arm distributed questionnaires to institutions to identify patients eligible for euthanasia. The killing of adults was by lethal injection or they were placed in carbon monoxide gas chambers and died of asphyxiation. "Mass gassings with carbon monoxide, that began in January 1940 at locations across Germany, proved most efficient. Victims were told to undress and to enter a room resembling a shower complete with surfaces, benches and a drain. Crematoria were erected nearby to dispose of the bodies." More than 70,000 Germans classed as feebleminded were gassed under T-4. Church officials clearly opposed the Nazis' euthanasia program.[49] On December 2, 1940, Pius XII forcefully condemned the killing of "life unworthy of life."[50]

The T-4 program was abandoned in August 1941 after it received protests from Catholic and Protestant sources.[51] Daniel Goldhagen and his fellow revisionists fail to mention this at all and don't report that the program developed a more extreme operation after the Vatican's protest. After 1941 euthanasia continued on the individual initiative of institutions and doctors. "They used drugs to starve patients to death, the 'natural method,' particularly for children, with the assurance of the medical bureaucracy that they would be removing burdens on the state and its war effort, 'useless eaters,' who were taking up beds needed for war-wounded soldiers."[52] The total number throughout the war was over 100,000. In Goldhagen's indictment of Pius XII one wonders if the author or his research assistants read Pius XII's 1943 encyclical carefully or if they read it through an unbiased lens.[53] *Mystici Corporis Christi* specifically in paragraphs 32, 43, 93 and especially 94 condemn the Nazis' killing of "life unworthy of life."[54]

By December 1933, the Nazis began tightening their control of the church with the passage of the Editors Law, which virtually shut down the Catholic press. The following year Interior Minister Wilhelm Frick followed with a prohibition against open discussion of church questions in the press, books, and pamphlets. Dr. Josef Müller brought information regarding the crackdown to the Vatican. Müller, an officer in the Military Counterintelligence (Abwehr), journeyed often to Rome with documentation of the regime's anti–Catholic campaign. In November 1934, Interior Minister Wilhelm Frick prohibited the open discussion of church issues in the press, books, and pamphlets.

Between 1935 and 1936 the Catholic clergy were imprisoned in a series of "Currency and Immorality" show trials. Hundreds of priests, monks, and nuns were accused of "perverted and immoral lifestyles," and imprisoned. This was accompanied by roving SA and Hitler Youth gangs who assaulted the clergy in the streets and disrupted church services. Cardinal Faulhaber, Cardinal Innitzer, and Bishop Sproll were also objects of these violent assaults. The campaign of violence was accompanied by a broad-based propaganda assault, both of which were intended to destroy Catholicism by eliminating all organizations supported by the church. The Reich government also moved to gain control of church finances.[55]

Both Göring and Frick in July 1935 called for the suppression of Christian church influence in public life. On July 21, 1935, Victor Klemperer recorded in his diary, "The struggle against Catholics, 'enemies of the state,' both reactionary and Communist is increasing." Klemperer's published diaries, *I Shall Bear Witness*, provide a day-by-day account of the interior of Nazi Germany and a compelling chronicle of the evolving persecution of Germany's Jews, Catholics, and Protestants. In September 1935 the anti–Jewish Nuremberg Laws were put into place.

In 1936 Hitler established the Ministry of Church Affairs, under the direction of Hans Kerrl, which sought to bring all of the churches under Nazi control. Church leaders resisted, clinging to whatever autonomy remained, and "blocked the dynamic momentum of Nazi ideology."[56] By 1939 most Catholic schools had been abolished. Catholic youth organizations were also replaced with those of the Nazi Party. As the Nazis trampled on the civil rights of Germans, the only place where they could hear a protesting voice was in church. But this too was hazardous, since informants or Gestapo agents carefully monitored the sermons of priests.

Zuccotti writes, "One result of Nazi violations of the German Concordat was yet another papal encyclical, *Mit brennender Sorge*, issued on March 14, 1937."[57] The first draft of the encyclical was written entirely by Pacelli and the second was written in his own handwriting. *Mit brennender*

Sorge (*With Burning Anxiety*) unequivocally denounced the Nazi regime. In tough language it went on to disapprove of the Nazi theory of "Blood and Soil," and the claim that faith in Nazi Germany was equivalent to faith in God. It went on to characterize the Nazi persecution of the church as "base, illegal, and inhuman." It referred to the spiritual oppression by the Nazis and the "war of annihilation against the Catholic Faith," as the Calvary of the church." The encyclical then singled out Hitler and attacked the "cult of idols," and the Führer's, "aspirations of divinity placing himself on the same level as Christ." One of the most significant portions of the encyclical was the clear statement "No, it is not possible for Christians to participate in anti-Semitism," that for Christians it is "inadmissible."

Diocesan officials in Berlin decided to have the Salvatorian provincialate print the encyclical instead of the Germania press. They felt that this would avoid detection by the Gestapo and also decided to use a stencil process to hide the site of the work. The Gestapo searched the Germania press for the encyclical. Konrad von Preysing, bishop of Berlin, sent the encyclical via a courier service throughout his diocese. Many pastors stored their copies in the church tabernacle to prevent detection and confiscation. Instructions were circulated to the pastors that the encyclical was to be read on Palm Sunday, March 21, 1937. SD chief Reinhard Heydrich ordered his police to be alert to the public reading and to arrest anyone who was distributing copies. The public reading caught the Nazis by surprise and "struck like a bomb." The Nazis correctly interpreted the encyclical as a direct attack on the state. Hans Kerrl, Reich minister of church affairs, said it "contained serious attacks against the welfare and interest of the German state," and attempted "to undermine the authority of the German Reich government and to harm the welfare of the German state internationally."[58]

Susan Zuccotti concedes that the encyclical was "undeniably outspoken," but then proceeds to criticize its alleged limitations. She claims the encyclical in part dealt only with church interests. Then she claims that it never mentioned National Socialism by name, and while it mentioned race, it did not mention Jews. In her brief discussion of the encyclical, Zuccotti does not discuss the "violations of the Concordat," or the persecution of the churches in Germany, whose aim was their total elimination. No mention is made of the religious who were sent to the concentration camps.[59] David Kertzer does admit that the encyclical "excoriated" the Nazi regime but he finds it wanting since it did not mention the persecution of Jews or anti–Semitism, but "it did produce an angry response from the Nazi government."[60] Kertzer does not fully explain or pursue the nature and extent of the "angry response."

The revisionists do not explain why the encyclical had to be smuggled past the Gestapo into Germany. Copies were printed in various locations and the underground Catholic network distributed them to the parishes throughout the country. The Gestapo and SS attempted to find the presses and were successful in locating 12 of them. The encyclical was circulated worldwide, and London's *Daily Telegraph* on March 22, 1937, reported, "The encyclical stated the Nazis had made it plain that they were waging a 'war of extermination' against the Church, and after countless rebuffs the Pope had decided to make a final stand." If the encyclical, as Zuccotti maintains, did not mention National Socialism then why did they take such pains to suppress its distribution? How did the Nazis react to the encyclical's contents?

The Nazi Press joined in the condemnation of the pope. The *VoelklisherBeobachate*r attacked, "the Jew God and His deputy in Rome," and *Das Schwarze Korps* called, "the encyclical, the most incredible of Pius XI's pastoral letters; every sentence in it was an insult to the new Germany." Hitler and Goebbels ordered that Catholic priests were to be brought to trial on charges of immorality and "slanders against the State." Hitler intensified the persecution of the church, but the encyclical did not moderate or halt his repressive policies.[61] Priests and other clergy were sent to concentration camps. In January 1938 Victor Klemperer sounded the alarm in his diary, "anti–Semitism has again been very much in the foreground (it rotates: now the Jews, now the Catholics, now the Protestant ministers)." The next month he noted, "Priests imprisoned, priests expelled from the pulpit...."[62]

Revisionists barely mention the internment of clergy in general and Catholics in particular. Why not? Is this not worth exploring since it might balance and disprove the view that both Pius XI and Pius XII were Nazi sympathizers? Might it also shed light on the depth of resistance to the Nazis? Pius XII did not make a vigorous public condemnation of the imprisonment of the religious in concentration camps.

Clearly Pius XI and Pius XII were not indifferent to the plight of their church and the persecution of its members. How could they possibly have sympathized in any way with a regime that imprisoned and killed their members? Goldhagen and Kertzer, who see the compatibility between Christianity, anti–Semitism, and the Holocaust, might, if they cared to, alter their sweeping indictments. Pius XII's approach to the plight of imprisoned Catholic clergy was the same as that to the persecuted Jews.[63] He was constrained by the realities of what he could accomplish by going public. It would provoke even greater retribution on the persecuted.

The Nazis' persecution of the churches was a combination of "political nihilism and ideological fanaticism." They set out to destroy the existing social order and were fanatically determined to create a pure Aryan super race. According to John Conway, "the Nazis antagonism toward the Churches arose from their intolerance of any compromise with a system of belief that spanned the centuries and embraced all men under a doctrine of equality before God.... The Nazi radicals were motivated not only by a desire for total control, but an ideological fanaticism that believed it possible to create an ersatz religion of blood and soil." Their mission was to create a secular substitute for Christianity.[64]

Hitler expressed his hatred of the Catholic Church in private dinner conversations. On one occasion he remarked to his dinner guests, "I hate the Jews because they have given that man, Jesus, to the world," and, "Bolshevism is Christianity's illegitimate child. Both are inventions of the Jew." To Hitler, Christianity was "the heaviest blow that ever struck humanity," it was "an invention of the Jew," and "the evil that's gnawing our vitals is our priests.... The time will come when I'll settle accounts with them." Hitler and the Nazi radicals were obsessed with the Christian churches. The Catholic Church was especially hated and feared. The recent release of declassified OSS intercepts of Nazi communications reveals the depth of that hatred and fear.

We have had for some time the records of both the private and public statements of Hitler, Bormann, Goebbels, Heydrich, Himmler, and members of the Nazi elite. Martin Bormann's "Circular on the Relationship of National Socialism and Christianity" makes it clear that the two are "irreconcilable," and links Christianity with Jewry. Josef Goebbels's diary entries are replete with similar references to Christianity, "He [Hitler] views Christianity as a symptom of decay. Rightly so. It is a branch of the Jewish race ... in the end they will be destroyed."

Victor Klemperer's diary entry with respect to Alfred Rosenberg's *Myth of the Twentieth Century* states that his, "main thrust ... repeated over and over, is against the Roman Church, against the Pope and Jesuits."[65] The German Catholic bishops met in 1939 for their annual conference in Fulda. Their pastoral letter was characterized by the *New York Times* "as one of the sharpest attacks ever made by Catholics against Nazis."[66] The regime retaliated by closing down the printing facilities used to print the letter.

With Hitler's approval, SS General Reinhard Heydrich issued a directive ordering the suppression of certain "secret" and religious societies. He also ordered the internment in concentration camps of all individuals connected with those organizations. The Gestapo proceeded to compile a list of sects that were prohibited by the regime. At the very top of the list was the Catholic Church. An officer of the SD described Heydrich's hatred of the church: "It was almost pathological in its intensity and sometimes caused this otherwise cold and calculating schemer to lose all sense of proportion and logic." Heydrich considered "political Catholicism" the most dangerous threat to the Nazi regime, and he insisted that the destruction of the church should take precedence over actions against Communists, Jews, and Freemasons. He was prepared to authorize the most extreme measures to ensure the destruction of this dangerous enemy.[67]

According to the best estimate some 2,771 clergymen were imprisoned in Dachau. Catholic priests, seminarians, and lay brothers accounted for 2,579 of the inmates. The Slavs, to Hitler, were subhuman and also had to be destroyed. Fifty percent of the Poles who died during 1939–1945 were non–Jews. Twenty-two percent of the Polish population perished during World War II and 18 percent of its clergy. Twenty-five percent of the 10,017 diocesan clergy in Poland in 1939 were lost. To cite one example, 80 percent of the Catholic clergy in the Warthegau region of Poland were deported to concentration camps. Sixty-five percent of the Roman Catholic clergy sent to Dachau were Polish priests. The higher clergy were not exempted from deportation. A disproportionate number of those sent to Dachau were the 1,780 Polish clergy, 866 of whom died in Dachau.[68] Three thousand additional Polish priests were sent to other concentration camps.

In addition, a total of 780 priests died at Mauthausen, 300 at Sachsenhausen and 5,000 in Buchenwald. With the Nazi conquest of Western Europe, hundreds of priests were shot or shipped to concentration camps, many dying en route. Also many nuns were either imprisoned or shot. Approximately 400 nuns were imprisoned in the Bojanowo concentration camp.[69]

Parish priests were sent to Dachau for quoting or reading Pius XI's 1937 encyclical or for providing false identity papers. Father Bernhard Lichtenberg, provost of St. Hedwig's Cathedral in Berlin, became known for his public evening prayers for the Jews, the fallen soldiers on both sides, and all the persecuted. He said prayers for the Jews on the evening of Kristallnacht. He called on all Catholics to protect Jews and asked to be deported with the Jews to the ghetto of Lodz. Lichtenberg was arrested by the Gestapo and imprisoned for two years. He died of heart failure while being transported to Dachau. The clergy were shipped to Dachau or to other concentration camps as part of the regime's war on the churches. The examples are too numerous to cite but are fully documented. Most priests who were arrested, exiled, or sent to concentration camps were targeted just because they were Catholic clergy.[70]

Dachau was a cruel parody of the Nazi totalitarian state, and all possible measures were taken to dehumanize the inmates, who lived in perpetual fear and anxiety. On their arrival, all prisoners were stripped naked and their hair was shaved. They were outfitted in ill-fitting prison uniforms — stripped jackets, pants, cap, and wooden clogs. To further dehumanize the prisoners they no longer had names, but were known by a number. One such inmate was Karl Leisner, a German seminarian, who became no. 22356. In 1934 Leisner had been called up for compulsory work service. While there he organized Sunday Mass for the other conscripts. The Gestapo considered this to be dangerous and they raided his home, seizing all papers and correspondence. Following a failed attempt to assassinate Hitler in 1939, Leisner commented that it was a pity that Hitler had escaped. The Gestapo arrested him, but Leisner did not back away from his statement. He was sent to Dachau the following year.[71]

In 1940, all priests who were imprisoned in other concentration camps were sent to Dachau. All Catholic clergy in Dachau were placed in three main barracks built for 360 people. Every morning came roll call, and then work within or outside the camp began. In bitter winter, some were given the task of removing the snow off the roofs without shovels. In October 1941, a group of elderly Polish priests arrived in Dachau. It was extremely cold but they were not given coats or hats and were forced to work outdoors. Only eight of the 530 survived.[72]

The diet of the inmates was calculated to produce constant hunger. In the morning there was a mug of black coffee and a slice of bread. In the afternoon a small cup of watery soup was given, and at night the fare was margarine and a piece of black bread. It didn't take long for an inmate to be reduced to a skeleton. After a day of hard labor and malnourishment, the inmates trudged back to the filthy, vermin-infested barracks. There was the constant fear of illness and of having to go to the contagious wards of the infirmary. Even the SS guards refused to enter. Priests volunteered to minister to the sick.[73]

A few priests committed suicide by throwing themselves onto the electrified fence surrounding the camp. Some despaired and just gave up, but most did not. They either prayed in private or held clandestine group prayer meetings. A secret makeshift chapel was placed in the corner of one of the barracks.[74]

Priests were not immune to beatings, starvation, or medical experimentation. From the very moment they entered camp, SS guards beat the prisoners in order to break their spirits. Father Andreas Rieser, who seemed unbroken, was singled out by one guard and beaten repeatedly. The guard then forced the priest to fashion a crown from a piece of barbed wire, a sick representation of Christ's crown of thorns. Beatings were frequent and took place without rhyme or reason. Karl Leisner tried to keep up the morale of his fellow inmates and helped others to survive. One evening two SS guards came into his barracks for an inspection, picked him out of the group and beat him unconscious. In one portion of the camp stood a crematorium that was used to dispose of those who died in the camp. When guards saw Father Johann Schroffner giving Father Schulez, a Polish priest, a blessing they were beaten and put into separate cells without food. Days later Father Schulez was given poisoned food and died. A camp "doctor" gave Father Schroffner a lethal injection. In November of 1942 Himmler came to Dachau and personally selected 120 young Polish priests for immediate medical experimentation. An additional 120 were selected for later experiments. Further citation of individual cases are too numerous to mention.[75]

Meanwhile in June 1942, the bishops in the Reich territories signed a pastoral letter that condemned Hitler's policies of official murder of the innocent and those judged "unproductive citizens." At great personal risk the bishops went on to acknowledge that the Nazis sought to completely destroy Christianity.[76] The letter was read from every Catholic pulpit throughout the Third Reich.

Pius XII was deeply distressed by the persecution of his clergy and expressed his anguish in the encyclical *Mystici Corporis Christi*.[77] Imprisoned camp detainees, especially Catholic priests and Protestant ministers, paid dearly whenever Catholic officials protested. Bishop Jean Bernard noted the reaction of his fellow inmates in Dachau with respect to any papal protest: "The detained priests trembled every time news reached of some protest by a religious authority, but particularly the Vatican."

Bernard went on to say that beatings and maltreatment intensified after any protest.

Many priests died shortly after they were liberated from Dachau and the other concentration camps—a direct result of the maltreatment and the illnesses that developed while they were imprisoned. Karl Leisner was one of those who perished afterward, but not before he was secretly ordained a priest while in captivity.[78]

CHAPTER 3

Pius XI, Pius XII
and the Führer:
Peter Godman Against
Two Men of God[1]

by Matteo Luigi Napolitano

Whenever a fresh book on Nazi-Vatican relations appears, discussions always arise concerning two Popes: Pius XI and Pius XII. But when a publisher announces that a book on these themes will make all others obsolete, then a reviewer has to proceed with extreme caution.

Peter Godman's *Hitler and the Vatican* is a test case in this regard, since its publisher, the Free Press, well before its publication announced it as a pinnacle of scholarly research into the church's record during the Third Reich. "Finally," the press release reads, "the full story of the Catholic Church and its connection to the Nazis can be told." The release continues: "*Hitler and the Vatican* is the most extraordinary look inside the secretive Vatican ever written." Is this a factual statement? Why would a publisher make such a claim?

Apparently the reason for flagging Godman's book as a scholarly masterpiece is that it draws heavily on the newly released archives pertaining to the pontificate of Pope Pius XI. But is this enough to justify such advertising hoopla? Consider only this one fact: Pius XI reigned from February 1922 to February 1939, and thus the new Vatican records stop short of World War II (1939–45), when Pius XII reigned and when the conflict between the Vatican and the Nazis was at its height.

Hence, the documents at the heart of this book hardly cover the entire relationship between "Hitler and the Vatican."

This is not to say that the prewar years are unimportant.... These documents shed invaluable light on these two churchmen, and if a historian is dealing with his topic effectively, there should be no need for a book's publisher to falsely advertise the book, especially when certain overstatements can be quickly shown to be fabricated.

Take for example, the Free Press' claim that "the Vatican" has praised Godman's scholarship without citing any Vatican experts, and especially in light of the fact that the Vatican's chief authority on the Third Reich Church, historian Father Peter Gumpel, SJ, is on record with a highly critical appraisal of Godman's new book.

There is no question that Godman's book makes use of the new archival material released by the Holy See since February 2003. But are Godman's interpretations of these primary documents accurate and judicious? Or are they often hasty and tendentious?

The author does not specify exactly how long he searched in the Vatican files, but there are indications that he rushed his work. Vatican records show that he carried out his research and writing in near-record time. He visited the secret archives between mid–February and mid–July 2003, and reports finishing the book on August 15. He did not renew his access card when the Vatican Archives reopened on September 15. It is a remarkable accomplishment to complete in six months a book on the Vatican and Nazi Germany that carefully analyzes a broad network of unresolved questions that have been debated for at least 40 years.

As for the equally difficult task of examining the archives of the Holy Office (Sant'Uffizio), Godman's research there would be tangential to the operations of the secretary of state. The Holy Office did not have a major role in conducting Vatican foreign policy. Its focus was on theology and doctrine, not on practical politics. Though a good deal of Godman's overall argument rests on connecting the Holy Office files to the Holy See's diplomatic dealings with the Third Reich, that connection turns out to be academic fantasy, the product of Godman's fertile imagination, not the view of Vatican leaders at that time.

This is an essential point, since Godman tries to prove that drafts of condemnations of Nazism prepared by the Holy Office were far more incisive and critical than any similar denunciations issued by Pius XI or his secretary of state, Cardinal Pacelli, as if there were a deep rupture between the Vatican and the Holy Office. That office served at the pleasure of the Pope and his secretary of state. Godman tends too often to present this relationship as a competitive one. He chooses not to mention that many of the Vatican's condemnations of Hitler, racism, anti–Semitism and extreme nationalism, carried to the world over Vatican Radio and in the pages of *L'Osservatore Romano* and *La Civiltà Cattolica* throughout the 1920s, 1930s and 1940s, were every bit as strong and critical as the unpublished drafts he found in the Holy Office.

Godman presents it as a tragedy that the Holy Office drafts on Nazism were not delivered by either Pius XI or Pacelli. But the contents of these drafts were delivered in the precise manner Pius or Pacelli decided they would be most effective.

One thing is certain. At the time of Pius XI's death (February 10, 1939), the moment Godman ends his book, the Vatican was everywhere recognized as an unswerving enemy of Hitler, especially among Jews themselves. One of the many closely following the events at the time, David Kleinlerer, commented on the Vatican's attitude toward the Nazis:

> The official attitude of the Church of Rome towards racial theory and the persecution of religious minorities has been in the last year been repeatedly expressed by the official organ of the Vatican, the Osservatore Romano, which has repeatedly exposed the absurdity of the Nazi racial theory and voiced powerful protests against the treatment according to German Jews and 'non–Aryans'" [David Kleinlerer, the *Jewish Post*, February 16, 1939].

Kleinlerer acknowledges the Vatican was carrying out precisely that clear moral leadership that *Hitler and the Vatican* spends some 250 pages trying to prove did not exist.

Godman maintains that "excommunication" was "one of the severest sentences" that could have been used against Hitler and his regime, because it would have signified "exclusion from the community of the faithful, to which Adolf Hitler nominally belonged" (p. 4, also p. 155).

This is disingenuous. While Hitler often flirted with the idea of being considered a Catholic, the Vatican never bought into this ploy. As the new archives reveal, the Holy See knew that whenever Hitler or any of his followers referred to Christianity, it was only in a hostile sense, in accord with their racist and pagan standards.

So how does Godman suggest that Hitler in any way belonged to the German Catholic Community? Only by obscuring the real situation by introducing the word "nominally."

Hitler had no present, continuing substantial connection with Catholicism.... Had he been even a "nominal" Catholic, he never would have embraced the repellent doctrines of Nazism to begin. According to the canon law of the time, Hitler and his henchmen automatically excommunicated themselves the moment they become apostates and/or engaged in murderous actions against Jews and Christians.

In his study of the new documents, Godman admits that "no sympathy" towards Hitler can "be read in Pacelli's dispatches." Yet when it comes to discussing the 1933 concordat with Hitler, he says that by signing that agreement Pacelli cast a decade-long "shadow on the policy of the Vatican" (p. 6).

The concordat was a way to save the Catholic Church's legal independence in Germany. As Nobecourt puts it, "the Holy See did not sign an agreement with a regime but with a nation." Pacelli was keenly aware that Hitler could damage the church by violating the terms of the agreement, which is exactly what happened. But Hitler would have done that and worse if the concordat had never been agreed to.

In the early pages of the book, Godman introduces what he says is evidence that reveals several of the Vatican "motives" for seeking an agreement with Hitler. His "evidence" is a handwritten memo by the former secretary of state Cardinal Pietro Gasparri.

After having quoted this document, Godman observes: "As secretaries of state to Pius XI and Pacelli, Gasparri lived in the Fascist Italy which, in 1929, had signed and ratified a concordat with the Holy See. That represented the model for them both."

Godman does not explain how the two concordats differed and most important what Gasparri's attitude toward Pius XI and Pacelli really was. If a parallel is to be established between the Italian and the German concordats, it would rest mainly on the similarities of the negotiation process. There is no mention of the situation when Gasparri wrote the lines quoted above on June 20, 1933. By June 1933, Gasparri had long been excluded from the Vatican state affairs; he had been removed from his commanding position in the Vatican on February 11, 1930, on the very first anniversary of the Lateran Pacts, and Pacelli's becoming secretary of state.

At this point in his life, Gasparri was a very disappointed man. The decision to remove him had been made by Pope Pius XI himself in order to counter the growing and dangerous proximity between Gasparri and the Fascists (as Italian intelligence records clearly show). Gasparri did not welcome the idea of yielding his office to Pacelli, whom he accused of treachery for having accepted a post that he considered his own until his death.

Godman's translation of Gasparri's memo is a bit misleading. He has Gasparri saying that "Hitler's party corresponds to nationalist feeling in Germany," whereas what Gasparri actually says is that "Hitler's party corresponds to the national feeling in Germany." "Nationalist" makes it more difficult to understand what was going on in international diplomacy at that time. That word makes it seem that Gasparri was saying the Catholic voters had identified with National Socialism, whereas what he actually said is that they turned to Hitler because he seemed to express the ideals of the nation, not because of the National Socialism he preached.

Godman follows this strategy most extensively in discussing *Mit Brennender Sorge*, the 1937 encyclical against Nazism, where he faults the Pope for not naming names. But if we grant that the Pope spoke clearly even without naming specific individuals in the 1934 instance, why would he be wrong to follow the same practice in 1937? By what logic can Godman accuse the Vatican of not having spoken clearly in *Mit Brennender Sorge*? Neither the Nazis nor the rest of the world had any doubt about what the encyclical said. Hitler reacted with fury. In Paris, London, Washington, and New York the encyclical was seen as a total rejection of Nazism. But Godman would have the encyclical say something other than what it says. He would have us believe that the world did not understand the encyclical. He is not interpreting a document; he is reinterpreting the world's response.

Nothing of much value can be found in Godman's comments on the pronouncements of the German bishops. For instance, he complains about von Galen's sermons of 1933 against euthanasia not mentioning the Holocaust. But the Holocaust was only planned by the Nazis at the Wannsee Conference in January of 1942. Here we find in Godman's book a strange anachronism, shifting the Holocaust back almost 10 years earlier.

Godman's analysis of the German political elections of March 5, 1933, is a further example of incomplete reporting. For instance, he quotes a dispatch sent by the Vatican nuncio in Germany, Orsenigo, to Pacelli on March 7, in which the nuncio explained that, among 31 million voters, one third were Catholic, and seven million of those had chosen Hitler. But this information needs further details, details that are in the same message from Orsenigo that Godman is discussing.

Godman talks about Orsengio's quest for "compromise and conciliation" with the Nazi regime: "The German bishops' condemnation of the Nazi movement — wrote Orsenigo on March 22, 1933 — had concerned only its religious, not its political ideas."

But this assertion doesn't take into account other facts offered by Orsenigo in his message to Pacelli. There he writes: "Unfortunately we cannot deny that the Catholic people apart from a few exceptions turned to the new regime with enthusiasm, forgetting the guidelines established by the episcopate at Fulda under the leadership of the Eminent Cardinal Bertram. To tell the truth (what seems to have appealed to them was), the political behavior of the Nazi movement, and definitely not its ideological-religious content. As a result, people became caught up in the first and detached themselves from the second."

This quotation informs us that the German episcopate had condemned not only the religious ideas of Nazism but also its ideological aspects.

What was Pacelli's approach to Nazism and anti–Semitism? Godman quotes a dispatch sent by the secretary of state to Orsenigo on April 4, 1933.

In this document Pacelli, in coordination with the concerned Jewish community outside of Germany, instructed Orsenigo to intervene in favor of a small group of Jews persecuted by the Nazis. The nuncio responded that intervention on his part would be impossible due to his official position, because any such action would be considered by Germany as an undue interference in its own domestic affairs and as "a protest against the government's law."

"That such an interpretation might be desirable and justified, on moral ground, never appears to have entered the nuncio's head," writes Godman.

But Orsenigo, it must be noted, had to take into account the more fundamental diplomatic rules. Had he actually criticized Germany's domestic policy, by general rule of international law the nuncio would be soon declared persona non grata (person not welcome). That would have meant the end of the Orsenigo's diplomatic mission to Germany and the impossibility for the Vatican to appoint another nuncio there. Godman omits to say that Orsenigo himself suggested as an alternative that a bishops' declaration be made in order to raise somehow the problem of the anti–Jewish persecution. That declaration was issued on April 8, 1933.

Hitler and the Vatican is based on a rich fund of unpublished Vatican documents, but how the book deals with these documents leaves a great deal to be desired. The book reminds us that writing on the church, the Nazis and the Holocaust has proved to be a dangerous minefield for many capable writers in the last 40 years, especially those who are tempted to claim startling new disclosures based on cursory and flawed examinations of evidence.

CHAPTER 4

Pius XI's Hidden Encyclical:
An Appraisal[1]

by George Sim Johnson

For decades there have been rumors of an unpublished encyclical attacking anti–Semitism, drafted for Pius XI shortly before his death in 1939 and apparently shelved by his successor Pius XII. The failure to release this encyclical has often been adduced as evidence for Pius XII's alleged compliant attitude toward anti–Semitism. Now that the draft of the encyclical has been published it is clear why its publication would have been a step backward in the church's relations with the Jewish community. (Georges Passelecq and Benard Suchecky, *The Hidden Encyclical of Pius XI*).

The publishers of the *Hidden Encyclical of Pius XI*, which presents the full text of the aborted document, are eager to promote this anti–Vatican spin. In fact, they recruited Gary Wills, the intellectual elite's favorite anti–Catholic, to write the introduction. But even Wills cannot avoid the conclusion that it is a very good thing that this encyclical on anti–Semitism never saw the light of the day.

In a long introduction, they present what is known of the history of the draft entitled *Humani Generis Unitas* (*The Unity of the Human Race*). And the facts they dug up make it clear why, regrettably, it was necessary that the church wait a few more decades before addressing its relationship with Judaism in a serious public document.

In the summer of 1938, Pope Pius XI heard that American Jesuit John LaFarge was visiting Rome. Pius XI had been impressed by a book LaFarge had written on racial justice. He summoned LaFarge to his summer residence and asked him to draft a papal encyclical denouncing racism and anti–Semitism, a topic Pius considered to be "most burning at the present time."

LaFarge was joined by two other Jesuits who had experience drafting papal documents. The three men went to work in Paris during the ominous summer of 1938. A lengthy manuscript was delivered to the Vatican in the autumn. We do not know if Pius read it. The document was shelved and Pius died a few months later. That is the end of story, so far as the hidden encyclical is concerned....

We do not know precisely why Pius XII chose not to pursue the drafting of *Humani Generis Unitas*, but it's not hard to guess. Pius could have had no use for a document which, as Wills admits, exhibits the serious limitations of what passed for Catholic "liberalism" in the 1930s.

The draft of *Humani Generis Unitas* starts off well enough, making cogent arguments against racism on the basis of the "unity" of the human race. The authors are eloquent about the dignity of the human person and how this dignity is subverted by, among other things, modern racialist philosophies.

When the document gets to the specific subject of the Church's relationship with Judaism, however, the authors drop all talk about human dignity and come perilously close to treating the Jews as religious and social pariahs. Imagine the reaction today if John Paul II were to say that the Jews' rejection of Christ is "the authentic basis of the social separation of the Jews from the rest of humanity." Or if he were to warn Catholics of "the spiritual dangers to which contact with Jews can expose souls."

The authors of the draft rightly condemn racial anti–Semitism, but then condone religious anti–Semitism. They buy into the outdated idea that there is a historical curse on the Jews, one that makes them outcasts from humanity. It is an idea that was roundly rejected by the Second Vatican Council in Nostra Aetate — and by John Paul II, who recently condemned "erroneous and unjust interpretations of the New Testament relative to the Jewish people and their presumed guilt...."

One lesson of the document is that even "enlightened" Catholic opinion in the 1930s had a long way to go in its understanding of the church's relationship with Judaism.

The "hidden encyclical' drafted for Pius XI bristles with these theological errors. And so its belated publication really marks a fortuitous nonevent....

CHAPTER 5

We Have Contended
with Diabolical Forces

by Patrick J. Gallo

From the latter part of September 1939 to 1945 the Vatican was in contact with the anti–Hitler conspirators in Germany. All of the revisionists cited thus far are either unaware of the available documentation or purposely refuse to consult it since it does not fit into their preconceived notions.[1] Wouldn't a discussion of this at least provide some balance and context? Indeed it might help to mute what has become a simplistic approach to a complex subject.

As soon as he was elected to the papacy, Pius XII sought to prevent the outbreak of another war and its extension to the whole of Europe. To this end he had to assume an outward stance of strict neutrality in order to gain the confidence of the contending parties. A skilled diplomat, he understood the complexities of international politics. "He was well aware of the diminished efficacy of moral appeals against such dark forces, and the steady erosion of the papacy's powers of persuasion."[2]

Pius XII made a fervent plea for world peace two days after his election to the papacy.[3] In the spring of 1939, events moved inexorably toward war. All of Czechoslovakia was absorbed into the Reich despite the Munich agreement in which Britain and France pledged to guarantee the new frontiers. In May 1939, Italy and Germany signed the Pact of Steel, a treaty that had been drafted by the Reich. The terms of the Pact of Steel obligated Italy to enter a war along with Germany.[4]

In an effort to avert a war Pius XII instructed the Vatican's nuncios to urge Germany, Italy, France, Great Britain, and Poland to negotiate their differences. The Pope had hoped to exert pressure on Mussolini in order to prevent his intervention in the current conflict.

From 1938 to 1939 Baron von Weizsäcker, Germany's second-highest Foreign Ministry official, and the Italian ambassador to Germany, Bernardo Attolico, were secretly working together against Hitler's aggressive policies. "...They were consciously trying to undermine relations between Nazi Germany and Italy, central to Hitler's strategy," and "to prevent joint foreign adventures." Attolico admitted though, "here in Berlin we must deal with dangerous fools who have no idea of the world.... In Italy things are not much better."[5]

In September Hitler had brought the Polish dispute to a climax. Mussolini could not restrain his ally, and his fate was clearly in the hands of Adolf Hitler. The conclusion of the Nazi-Soviet Non-Aggression Pact on August 24 was met with consternation and disbelief throughout the world. The pact gave Hitler the green light to start the attack on Poland, and war became inevitable.[6]

When German troops massed along the Polish border, Pius XII, in a last-ditch effort to avert war, sent a radio message from Castel Gandolfo to Hitler. "Nothing is lost in peace; everything can be lost with war.... Along with us, the whole of humanity hopes for justice, bread and freedom, instead of iron that kills and destroys."[7] President Franklin Roosevelt followed this initiative with his own appeal for peace. With the outbreak of war the Pope continued to urge that all parties go to the conference table to contain the spread of the war. In October 1939, Hitler made an offer of peace on his terms that was subsequently rejected by the British and French governments. Hitler had already decided to attack the West, and once victorious, to conquer the Soviet Union.

Convinced that Hitler was leading Germany on a path to destruction, the Oster-Canaris-Beck resistance group planned a coup. The resistance in part was centered in the Abwehr, Germany's military intelligence. Colonel Hans Oster was chief of staff and head of its Central Division, and Hans Dohnanyi served as director of political affairs in the same division. Hans Oster rejected Nazism: "he loathed it with a hard white heat that admitted no reservations, qualifications, or extenuating circumstances."[8]

Admiral Wilhelm Canaris, chief of the Abwehr, was a mysterious figure and a master of intrigue. He had a reputation for deviousness, but in reality he had a high moral sense of duty. "At bottom his revulsion against the Nazi pestilence was ethical and aesthetic. He detested its crudity, its contempt for established law and principle, and especially its inhumanity.... A person who could never have brought himself to do physical harm to anyone, he regarded the ruthless and often sadistic cruelties of the SS as the hallmarks of evil incarnate.... To snatch victims from the Gestapo and the SD was thus for Canaris ... a moral imperative."[9] General

Ludwig Beck was appointed chief of staff of the German army, and in 1939 warned Hitler against attacking Czechoslovakia.[10]

The objective of the Oster-Canaris-Beck plan was to persuade the leaders of the Reich's army to put aside their reservations and overthrow Hitler. They planned to obtain the British government's assurance to put aside an offensive, which they believed would have the effect of unifying the German army behind the regime. In return they would be in a position to move ahead with the coup, and reach a negotiated end to the war.[11]

The resistance's overtures to Britain began in 1938; however, British officials were still were under the illusion that they could do business with Hitler. In 1939, the British needed to be convinced that the resistance group was in fact genuine, and that they had the ability to mobilize an effective coup. In short could the resistance deliver on its proposals?

The resistance had to overcome the military's sense of duty in wartime. A move to overthrow the government was high treason. In addition there was substantial popular support for Hitler. Moreover, the resistance had to prevent a Western offensive and at the same time hope that Hitler did not proceed with an attack in the West. Once a coup was successful they needed "guarantees that the Allies would not exploit a revolutionary situation."[12] Whom could they select as a credible intermediary? They needed a person who could operate in secret, and who had the prestige to convince the Allies of their sincerity.

Hans Oster devised a plan to enlist Pius XII's help. The Pope was a known opponent of the regime. Oster's "sources of information amply assured him about the Pope's anti–Nazi attitude."[13] The Pope knew General Beck and Admiral Canaris and Dr. Hans von Dohnanyi from his days in Berlin. Dohnanyi was Dietrich Bonhoffer's brother-in-law. Bonhoffer was a distinguished Protestant pastor. Pius XII's diplomatic experience was beyond reproach, and he was an expert on German affairs. When he assumed the papacy he immediately "reserved the treatment of German questions to himself."[14]

The resistance needed a trusted envoy to take its proposals to the Vatican. Dr. Josef Müller, a leading figure in the Catholic resistance in Germany, was ultimately selected. Müller had been a staunch anti–Nazi and had acted to defend the church from Nazi persecution. Müller had many contacts in the Vatican, including his friend Father Robert Leiber, SJ, and Monsignor Ludwig Kaas, the former head of the German Center Party. Leiber was a personal aide to Pius XII and was his confidant. He had direct access to the Pope; Kaas served as administrator of St. Peter's Basilica.

The Pope knew Müller and had enlisted him for a mission in 1938. He was sent to visit all the bishops of Austria. Müller was to advise them on how to properly conduct themselves and on the dangers posed by the Third Reich.

Oster recruited Müller as an officer in the Abwehr and attached him to the Munich office. Müller's official assignment was to report on polit-ical developments in Italy and at the Vatican, thus allowing him freedom of movement from Germany to Rome. With this as excellent cover, Müller went to Rome in late September 1939. Müller first met with Kaas, who urged him to meet with Leiber. The Abwehr, conscious of the need for secrecy, used code names for the principal participants. Leiber became Gregor.

Following Father Leiber's initial meeting with Müller, the priest agreed to communicate the resistance's proposal to the Pope: "Would the Holy Father," he asked, "act as intermediary between it and the British Government to seek agreement on the suspension of military moves dur-ing a German uprising and on the nature of a future peace?"[15] Since the Pope knew Beck, Canaris, and Müller, he could assure the British of the authenticity of the resistance.

In mid–October Pius XII immediately agreed to act as intermediary, and Müller was duly informed. Father Leiber was both shocked and sur-prised by how quickly the pontiff responded. The Pope agreed to serve as intermediary with the conspirators' plan only if Hitler was removed first, and if the Allies agreed not to involve themselves in Germany's internal affairs. The pontiff was convinced that the resistance had to be heard in Britain.[16] Leiber privately thought that the Pope might have gone too far out on a limb. He realized, as did Pius XII, that the risks to the Pope and church were immeasurable if the Nazis found out about his involvement. Surely the Nazis and Mussolini would have taken measures to even the score. Pius XII was a realist who understood the use and limits of power. "He had little time for plans, no matter how well intentioned, which were lacking in assurance of execution."[17] This makes his involvement with Operation X all the more remarkable. "By collaborating in conversations, which had as their purpose the subversion of a foreign government and by passing that government's military secrets to its opponents, Pius seri-ously compromised the traditional neutrality of the Vatican and jeopard-ized his personal position as well as that of the papacy."[18] Leiber informed Müller in mid–October that the Pope had consented to act as intermedi-ary.

In subsequent meetings Leiber informed Müller that the British agreed to the exchanges. Müller made numerous trips to Rome and car-ried with him the X-Report, which was the correspondence between the German conspirators and British intelligence.[19]

On October 27, Pius XII made a powerful condemnation of totalitarianism and racism in his first encyclical, *Summi Pontificatus*, issued from Castel Gandolfo, the papal summer residence. He denounced the violation of treaties and the havoc wrought on the Polish people. He proceeded to assert his intention to fight against dictatorial encroachments and his determination to step forward boldly into "the immense vortex of errors and anti–Christian movements" and to fight the enemies of the church.[20] The Pope was aware of Hitler's recent speech delivered at the SS Ordensburg (youth leader training center) in which he screamed that he would crush the Catholic Church under his heel as he would a toad. Gestapo Chief Heinrich Müeller said, "The encyclical is directed exclusively against Germany, both in ideology and in regard to the German-Polish dispute."[21] Cornwell dismisses the encyclical out of hand, stating it was "full of rhetoric and equivocations."[22] The same may be said of the other revisionists, who also fail to place the encyclical in the context of the events of 1939 and specifically in the context of Operation X.[23]

During the weeks of intrigue neither Cardinal Maglione, his secretary of state, nor his two undersecretaries, Tardini and Montini, were aware of Pius's activities. The Pope also arranged things so that Müller and Sir Francis D'Arcy Osborne, Britain's ambassador to the Holy See, never met, and could truthfully state this as fact. The Pope did not at any point during these exchanges inform the French ambassador to the Vatican. The Pope would orally transmit his replies to Müller through Leiber. Pius XII met directly with Osborne and passed on information to him. Osborne "would then send the message to the Foreign Office. London's response would reach Berlin through the reverse channel."[24] Pius XII also directed that the Müller-Lieber meetings should be moved from the priests' apartment at the Pontifical University of Gregoriana to the Jesuit parish house of San Bellarmino outside of Rome.[25] The Pope also selected Monsignor Ludwig Kaas to meet with Müller every time he came to Rome. On the evening of November 6, 1939, Leiber met with Müller and told him that Pius XII was prepared to assist Germany achieve a fair peace "once conditions justify it." Leiber also said the Pope was ready to approach Roosevelt to assist in the negotiations provided the United States did not herself enter the war.

> The first outline of the celebrated "X" memorandum or report, which Müller, with the help of Leiber drafted while in Rome wasso-called because Müller's code reference for it was 'X.' Apparently, the copies prepared for London and Berlin were written on Vatican notepaper. The memorandum was supposed to outline the kind of conditions to which the Western Allies would be most likely to agree once Hitler was removed.[26]

The Pope had given his approval to the draft and when Müller brought it back to Germany "attached to it was Father Leiber's personal card with the message written on it that the bearer enjoyed 'the full confidence of his Holiness.'"

On November 23, 1939, Hitler summoned the leadership of all three military services—the commanders and general staff officers—to the Chancellery. In his address to the assemblage he told them of the necessity of the coming offensive. The speech bristled with threats directed against the "doubters," "deserters," and those who would foment revolution. "The struggle," he warned, "would be waged without quarter against anyone who failed to embrace the will to victory." Many of those present who had doubted Hitler came away greatly impressed. "Oster commented incisively that accusations of cowardice had once again made cowards of the brave."[27] This incident proved to be a mortal blow to the success of Operation X.

The Pope's contact with the resistance was to have an unintended result. Müller provided warnings on SD preparations for new assaults on the church. In addition Müller provided regular reports with respect to the atrocities the Nazis committed in Poland. Canaris ordered agents of the Abwehr to gather this information and then gave it to Müller to brief the Vatican. The Pope received a steady stream of reports that indicted Catholic priests and religious were either being shot or sent to concentration camps. Atrocities against the civilian population were a common occurrence. Shortly after the war began, "The Jesuit-operated Vatican Radio started to broadcast first-hand accounts of atrocities perpetrated by the Nazis in Poland as reported to the Holy See.... However, the Polish bishops hastened to notify the Vatican that after each broadcast ... the various local populations suffered 'terrible reprisals.'" With this thought in mind, Father Ledochowski, the superior general of the Jesuits and himself a Pole, gave the order to stop the broadcasts. The Communists also committed atrocities against "the overwhelming Catholic Polish people...." The Pope proceeded to write a secret communication in which he called upon all bishops to do everything within their power to save all victims from Nazi persecution.[28] By the end of the war over six million Poles, or 22 percent of the nation's total population, were killed. Nearly three million were Polish Jews and another three million were Polish Catholics.

On March 12 Myron Taylor, President Roosevelt's personal representative to the Vatican, sent a report to Washington on the Pius XII-von Ribbentrop meeting. Pius XII was not all that keen about meeting with the Reich's foreign minister, and treated him with cold courtesy. Joachim von Ribbentrop informed the Pope that Germany expected to win the war soon. When the Pope turned to Poland, Ribbentrop tried to cut him off and change subjects. The Pope would have none of it and proceeded to read a report detailing Nazi atrocities committed against Catholics and Jews. Then Ribbentrop met with Cardinal Maglione, who continually raised questions with reference to Nazi persecutions. Ribbentrop angrily protested and in effect said the cardinal secretary did not know what he was talking about. Maglione told him that the Vatican had been sending detailed reports about the persecutions to the Foreign Ministry for months and had never received a reply. Taylor reported to FDR that the Pope "took the Nazis to task for the persecution of the Church." The papal confrontation received extensive coverage in the *New York Times,* whose headlines and lead front-page articles read: "Pope Is Emphatic About Just Peace; His Stress on Indispensable Basis for End of Hostilities Held Warning for Reich: Pontiff in Ribbentrop Talk Spoke on Behalf of the Persecuted in Germany and Poland: Jewish Rights Defended."[29]

Vatican Radio and *L'Osservatore Romano* publicized the intelligence it received from Cardinal Augustine Hlond, archbishop of Gniezno-Posnan, regarding the persecution of the Polish clergy.[30] Revisionist Michael Phayer omits crucial details about the Vatican's efforts in Poland in an effort to prove papal indifference to the plight of those who were suffering. Phayer says the Vatican suspended its reports on radio, but fails to point out that this was just temporary. The Vatican was concerned that the British were altering and rebroadcasting its reports as propaganda. By January 1941 Vatican Radio resumed its broadcasts describing the events and conditions in Poland. Phayer is forced to admit that the Pope did use his nuncio in Germany to plead the Vatican's case.[31]

At first the British attached their own conditions to the conspirators' initiative. By the end of January 1940, the British had responded favorably to the proposals transmitted in the Vatican exchanges, but remained skeptical about the intentions of the conspirators. Meanwhile in February the Pope passed on information with respect to German military plans to the American ambassador.[32] Sumner Wells, United States secretary of state, traveled to Rome and met with Cardinal Maglione, who indicated that he knew of a plan to oust Hitler from power. Maglione, unaware of the Pope's direct involvement in Operation X, was sounding out Wells to see if he knew of such an effort. For his part Wells gave no indication that he was aware of such a plan.[33]

Hitler postponed the offensive until the spring, posing a dilemma for the resistance. Once the offensive began, all hope of deposing Hitler would be gone. There was a narrowing window of opportunity for the success of Operation X. Should the conspirators alert the Low Countries in specific

terms when an invasion was to take place? How should they do so? The
Vatican exchanges had offered the British much with minimal cost; however, for the resistance it was "equally imperative that it not encourage
complacency which would set up the Allies for Hitler's surprise attack."[34]

In May 1940, Müller traveled to Rome and informed Leiber that the
discussions with the British had little chance of success since Hitler's
offensive was imminent. The German generals could not be persuaded to
act and support a coup when faced with the prospect of an expansion of
the war. The anti–Nazi conspirators, "in a desperate effort to demonstrate
their good faith and forestall operations against France, the Low Countries and Scandinavia ... leaked word of Hitler's intentions to the Pope in
the expectation that the Holy Father would warn the intended victims."
Müller subsequently provided Leiber with the specific date of the German
offensive. Pius XII decided to act immediately, and secretly warned Brussels and The Hague of the impending attack. The Pope realized the invasion of the Low Countries and Scandinavia would expand and intensify
the war. Pius XII entrusted Cardinal Maglione with the mission of informing the Belgian and Dutch ambassadors that an invasion was imminent.
He selected Undersecretary Giovanni Battista Montini (later Paul VI), who
met with the British and French ambassadors to the Holy See on May 7,
and told them that an attack on the Low Countries would begin by the
end of the week. "The course he [Pius XII] adopted can be explained only
by the union of his sense of moral obligation with what he regarded as the
interest both of the Church and mankind."[35]

The Pope registered a protest against the Nazi invasion of a neutral
country. He personally wrote three separate messages that he made public condemning the Nazi aggressors. Following the invasion of the Low-
lands, the Vatican feared that Pius XII could be in grave danger if his role
with the conspirators became known. There was considerable concern later
that if Britain was successfully invaded the Germans might acquire documentary evidence of his involvement with Operation X. What the Vatican
did not know at the time was that the German embassy to the Vatican
failed to pick up any hint of the Vatican exchanges. Operation X, which
held out such promise in September 1939 was now at an end, but not the
Vatican's involvement with the resistance. Müller's continued trips to
Rome were not intended to gather intelligence about the Vatican.[36]

Hitler was convinced that the Vatican had a worldwide network of
agents that was supplying important information to Rome, the center of
anti–Nazi activity. Vatican Radio continued, but it was monitored carefully by Germany's House Special Service and by the German embassy in
Rome. The Vatican's postal facilities were cut off and all telephones were

tapped. Göring's interception service deciphered all telegrams sent to church officials in Germany. Reinhard Heydrich, Reich security director, formed a special unit with a large staff to spy on the Vatican. Heydrich declared, "our ultimate goal is the extirpation of Christianity."[37] The Nazis were subsequently successful in eavesdropping on the Vatican's signal communications and deciphering its diplomatic codes. The Italians and Germans found it relatively easy to read a major portion of papal traffic, or to tap the telephones of the Vatican's nuncios.[38]

The Vatican knew its systems were being monitored and had to be ever vigilant. Under the censorship arrangements imposed on the Holy See by Italy, all diplomats within Vatican City could communicate with their respective governments "by means of the papal diplomatic pouch but only on subjects directly related to their representational missions. Since the security of the Vatican's diplomatic pouch could not be assured, Allied diplomats had to be careful in their reports."[39] Diplomats were under constant surveillance by the Fascist secret police, which was able "to monitor the activities and contacts of Allied diplomats inside papal territory."[40]

The Vatican was successful in hiding a secret transmitter in the Saint Callistus catacombs. Father Michael Müller, no relation to Josef Müller, was the director of catacombs. Father Müller, a Salesian priest, came to Rome in 1939 and received his doctorate at the Gregorian University. Father Müller was the direct liaison between Pius XII and the German Catholic Church. He brought messages from the Vatican and transmitted them to Germany, and personally brought responses back to the Pope. There was total secrecy and no records of any kind were kept. Müller would shed his priestly garb, don shabby clothes, and make his way from the Vatican to Saint Callistus. The messages to be transmitted were written on tiny scraps of paper hidden in his shoes or socks. His meetings with the Pope sometimes lasted as long as three hours. On a number of occasions Pius XII wept, moved by tragic news that Müller had brought. During the German occupation of Rome the Germans raided the catacombs, presumably searching for weapons hidden by the Italian partisans. It's not clear if they suspected that it contained a Vatican transmitter. The Italian seminarians on duty at the catacombs were kept in the blazing sun while a search party went through the catacombs. The Saint Callistus catacombs have a number of levels with so many twists and turns that one could easily get lost. The Italian cleric who led the search party through the maze directed the search so that the transmitter would not be found.[41] Frank Gilardi, then a seminarian, was a guide at the catacombs. He was present during the raid and substantiates Müller's use of the transmitter.[42]

In the final analysis the Vatican did not have an intelligence service to speak of. The Secretariat of State and most nunciatures were under-staffed and were not adept in their methods of gathering intelligence. Alvarez notes that in 1939 the Secretariat of State had employed only 31 individuals, including archivists and typists. The foreign ministry of Norway had 119 and the Netherlands had 80.[43]

The SS in the latter part of 1944 presented Hitler with a report of what it knew about Josef Müller's ties to the Vatican. The OSS in 1945 confirmed Müller's links to the resistance in Germany and the Vatican.[44] The Pope's contact with the German resistance did not end in 1940. There is ample documentation in the OSS archives to prove his continued contact and involvement with the resistance throughout the war.

Pius XII was fully aware of and in contact with those elements involved with four attempts to kill Hitler prior to the 1944 Army bomb plot. The SS concluded that the Vatican was directly involved in the assassination plots. Evidence indicates that Pius XII knew by name those who were involved in the various plans to stage a coup, and the conditions they attached to a settlement with the Allies. Throughout the war Monsignor Kaas met with agents of the resistance and kept the Pope informed about all assassination plots. All of the plots involved the establishment of a democratic government in which the Catholic Center Party would play a central role, and the withdrawal of German military forces to prewar boundaries.[45]

The resistance was dealt a crippling blow after the fourth attempt to kill Hitler failed. Hitler ordered Himmler to amalgamate the Abwehr and the SD. This meant the virtual destruction of the anti–Nazi conspiracies. Hans Oster had already been removed from his position on suspicion that he was involved in some way.

Lieutenant Colonel Claus Shenck von Stauffenberg was convinced that he alone could assassinate Hitler.[46] Stauffenberg was appointed chief of staff to the commander of the General Army Office in Berlin. This made it possible for Stauffenberg to rebuild the weakened ranks of the anti–Hitler conspiracy. General Ludwig Beck joined Stauffenberg's circle of conspirators.

Dr. Josef Müller was arrested in 1943 and tried in the spring of 1944. Lieutenant Colonel von Stauffenberg, the key player in the July plot to kill Hitler, was present in the courtroom.[47] Stauffenberg sent a representative to Müller's cell just a few weeks before the failed bomb plot. Müller was told to be ready to present his credentials in Rome.

Pius XII's involvement in all of the plots underscores the fact that he was positioning the Vatican to be the first government to recognize a new German democratic government. It also proves that he was not obsessively concerned with communism to the exclusion of Nazism. He officially maintained neutrality, which was the historic position of the Vatican; behind the scenes he was clearly pro–Allied.[48]

Pius XII's involvement with the German resistance also sheds light on revisionist criticism of his opposition to unconditional surrender. Susan Zuccotti imputes papal naiveté and sinister motives. She maintains that Vatican officials should have realized the hopelessness of negotiations, since the Allies were insisting on unconditional surrender. "But the Pope regarded the policy a calamity that would draw the Russians deeper into Europe."[49] What she doesn't mention is that Winston Churchill and the U.S. State Department were concerned about this very same possibility. In addition Zucccotti cites an article written by Father Robert Leiber as her only source, which has no direct bearing on the larger picture. Zuccotti, with no further documentation, asserts that the Pope's affinity for the German people entered into his consideration, which might be taken a step further in the mind of the reader to conclude that he was pro–Nazi. Zuccotti, again with no evidence to support her own naïveté, continues, "But, he believed, the Germans would call on him only if he demonstrated neutrality and good will. He could not, then, denounce the Holocaust or any other Nazi atrocities."[50] Which Germans, the anti–Nazi conspirators? Is Zuccotti really serious in maintaining that this provided the pope the perfect excuse not to denounce the Nazi Holocaust? Zuccotti shows an appalling ignorance of Allied diplomacy at the time, the complicated international context, and the fact there was a war going on. She is unaware of the documentation, old and new, which clearly shows the persistent papal involvement with the anti–Nazi conspirators. The fact of the matter is the Vatican attempted to negotiate in secret with them in order to obtain a new regime, and a compromise peace with a newly installed democratic government.

The Pope opposed the unconditional surrender policy of the Allies for a variety of reasons. Since a negotiated settlement was out of the question, unconditional surrender would rally the German people in defense of their homeland. An ancillary result would be to strengthen the regime's hold on the country. Most importantly it would undercut the resistance in that it would discourage new and key members from coming on board. It produced additional fear and hesitation in the ranks of the resistance. Would the Allies reach an agreement with a new set of players or would they insist on unconditional surrender? They did modify unconditional surrender when it was applied to Italy in July 1943.

A bloodbath followed the abortive bomb plot of 1944 that discouraged any further assassination attempts by anti–Nazi political or military elements.[51] Finally, a completely destroyed Germany would create a power vacuum in the heart of Europe. The economic and political reconstruction of postwar Europe would be put in jeopardy. Zuccotti may have conveniently forgotten that this was exactly the situation that confronted the United States at the conclusion of the war. The Soviet Union did come to dominate Eastern Europe and East Germany. Europe was on the brink of disaster in 1947 until the Marshall Plan rescued the continent from this catastrophe. In 1947, the United States realized the political and economic consequences that the unconditional surrender doctrine had on Europe and reoriented its foreign policy. Pius XII's opposition to and awareness of the pitfalls of the unconditional surrender doctrine are shared by many historians of the World War II era.

The Pope continually attempted to bring an end to the horror of the war. Weapons of mass destruction were employed, leaving a continent in human and physical ruin. Pius XII agonized, despaired, and grew despondent over his impotence to stop the slaughter. The adoption of unconditional surrender in 1943 provided an insurmountable obstacle to his quest to achieve a termination of the killing. Unfortunately, Zuccotti and Robert Katz cannot see this as the underlying motive of the Pope. Revisionists brush aside the real evidence of the Pope's frustration and speculate that successful results could have been achieved by hurling verbal thunderbolts from Rome.[52] Even had the Vatican had a first-rate intelligence network, Pius XII could not have overcome those factors that constrained his diplomatic efforts to end the war.

Finally, Pope Pius XII was consistent in his assertion about the responsibility of a Christian to resist unjust aggression. "A people threatened with an unjust aggression, or already its victim, may not remain passively indifferent, it would think and act as befits a Christian.... Their defense is even an obligation for the nation as a whole, who have a duty not to abandon a nation that is attacked."[53] He stated this in many forms both during and immediately following the end of World War II.

Dr. Josef Müller survived his imprisonment, escaping execution. In their first private audience after the war the Pope said he had prayed for Müller every day of his imprisonment. He embraced Müller and said, "We have contended with diabolical forces."[54]

CHAPTER 6

The Pope and the Shoah[1]

by Justus George Lawler

A shadow hovers over virtually all discussions of Pius, particularly since his treatment in *Der Stellvertreter* by Rolf Hochhuth. (Possibly not since *Uncle Tom's Cabin* has a third-rate literary effort had such a widespread and controversial impact.) But that shadow is not his condemnation of the pope — largely on his part a propaganda effort, easily dismissed — but his defining the terms of all subsequent discussion, so that what is asked of Pius is not a deed, an action, which would achieve the cessation of the Jewish slaughter, but merely a statement, a proclamation, a word. As a consequence, the immense literature which grew up around the figure of the pope persistently employs Hochhuth's (Protestant) language, as thought Pius's preached word would have some kind of automatic, intrinsic, even sacramental efficacy. Hence, too, all those dreary tracts focusing on "speaking out," "public condemnation," "never saying a word," "les silences," "das Schweigen," etc.

In any event, neither understanding nor judgment — save of condemnation — seems contemplated by the critics of Pius. While one should pity the pope in his plight, one need not praise him. But neither can one bury him under the steaming compost-heap of invective — "Hitler's pawn," "ideal pope for Hitler's unspeakable plan" — that John Cornwell piles up around Pius's memory, that Carroll naively adds his husks of spoilage to, and that Wills burrows into with ill-concealed relish. Of Pius's statement that he had "condemned on various occasions in the past the persecution that a fanatical anti–Semitism inflicted on the Hebrew people," Wills again plays fast and loose (the word is "squinting") with historical fact: "That is a deliberate falsehood. He never mentioned the Holocaust." Of course, that word was not in currency during Pius's time — but let it pass.

In proof of "deliberate falsehood" Wills refers to "the Pope's Christmas message of December 4, 1942 (meaning December 23), the one speech that is cited to prove that he did speak out against the Holocaust." (A strange circumlocution here: "the one speech that is cited"— as though the straw-man of indeterminate "citers" exhausted the matter, and the words of the pontiff himself were not worthy of examination by historian Wills. Never mentioned are these people who have cited only one speech; the reason being that Cornwell doesn't provide Wills with the names. Though there is some indication that Cornwell, on whom Wills is totally dependent, did glance at parts of the entire message with his now celebrated assiduity and freedom from bias: "no discrimination, no insight," "lengthy and dry ser-monizing," "denial and trivialization," etc. Wills himself appears to be aware of the two sentences only. Ignored by both writers, as well as most other commentators (John Morley excepted) is the context of this "one speech": the passages preceding the sentences which are "cited to prove that he did not speak out against the Holocaust," and the passages that follow immediately; all of which of course must be read as a unified state-ment. The first passage relates to the complicity of Christians in the moral disintegration before and during the war; the second to the plight of the Jews; and the third to the destruction of civilian centers— a recurrent theme in all the major addresses of this pope, as demonstrated in the discussion of Phayer's *The Catholic Church and the Holocaust* in chapter two.

It is obscene to call this a "paltry statement" as Cornwell does— on a page Wills must have misused when rifling through Cornwell's swollen satchel for facts, opinions, and quotations. Whether the statement repre-sents a "deliberate falsehood," is contradicted by the testimony of British and American representatives to the Vatican both of whom affirmed Pius's sincerity in believing he had spoken out clearly enough, and in a manner "plain to everyone." As to Wills' and other carpers' much quoted response as to "why he did not name the Nazis ... [because] he would have to name the Communists too," what is truncated or intentionally omitted here is Pius's belief that in the words of the American representative to the Vati-can: "this ('naming of the Communists too') might not be wholly pleas-ing to the Allies." Several critics of the statement also detect a clue to the alleged insignificance of this passage in Pius's rhetorical scheme — and therefore also in his mind — because it occurs near the end of a lengthy address. One doesn't know what has happened to the notion of perora-tion, the summation and climatic finale to a speech....

Wills justifies his "deliberate falsehood" and "false claim" accusations in the name of that virtue he has trumpeted as his own paramount attrib-ute: "But the issue of honesty arises when arguments are made defending Pius with false readings of history." This statement with which one must agree, certainly if they are "readings" such as Wills assembled with regard to Rahner, Benoit, Glock and Stark, "the hidden encyclical," and Nostra Aetate. Wills then recites, in an exercise of his own patent dishonesty, that "it is out of these two sentences ... that he (Pius) would later construct a claim to have attacked anti–Semitism, specifically, on various occasions." But Pius claimed no such thing, and to assert other is indeed a "deliberate falsehood..."

As to the all-important broader issue of the Holocaust, as early as his Christmas address of 1940, Pius declared: "It is a comfort to Us that through the moral and spiritual assistance of Our representatives and through Our financial resources, we have been able to give support to a great number of refugees, homeless, and emigrants, including non–Aryans." In the paragraph preceding this quotation — and proleptic of John Paul's introduction to the document "We Remember" — Pius had also declared: "The laws and morality of international warfare have been so callously ignored that future generations will look back on the present war as one of the darkest periods in history. Our thoughts anticipate with anxiety the moment when the complete chronicle of those who have been killed, maimed, injured, captured, those who have lost their homes and their relatives will be known in all its details. What we know already, however, is enough to rend our heart." Now this is certainly not the statement of someone who, according to current and past critics, was intent on clouding the historical record out of fear of future obloquy. Nor could it have referred to any other warring nation than Germany, which had invaded in the months before the address Poland, Belgium, Holland, Luxemburg, France, Denmark, and Norway.

It should also be emphasized this message was delivered at a time when the first rumors of what is now called the Holocaust were just beginning to be independently confirmed. It is also when the aerial attacks violating the "morality of international warfare — which the pope had first condemned two weeks after the outbreak of hostilities, and several times thereafter — were launched by the Axis powers against such cities as Warsaw in 1939, Rotterdam, Coventry, and London in 1940–41. Again, it seems obvious, without 'mentioning names' whom the pope is accusing. In the context of living through one of the darkest periods in history," Pius spoke of embracing not just Christians but Jews as well: "...those who are children of the Church of Christ, and those who because of their faith in the Divine Saviour, or at least in Our Father Who is in Heaven — all who are very dear to us."

In June, 1941, speaking of "sin as exalted, excused, and the master of human life," he gave this illustration: "...individuals and families are deported, transported, separated, torn from their homes, wandering in misery without support." Six months after the Christmas address of 1942, in an Allocution to the College of Cardinals which was published in *L'Osservatore Romano* (June 3, 1943) and in *La Civiltà Cattolica*, Pius mentioned specifically his concern for "...those who are tormented because of their nationality or race by major miseries and by more acute and grievous suffering, and who are sometimes even fated, without guilt, to extermination." If these are not condemnations of "the persecution," inspired by anti–Semitism, then we need to revise our dictionaries. But we have to revise our thinking as well: why do students of the era persist in following almost blindly in the footsteps of Hochhuth, and displaying his obsession with "silence" and with the need for public statements, declarations, even excommunications—the latter demanded by a number of captious critics—rather than with deeds and actions?

Nevertheless Wills persists: "Pius never explained his silence on the Holocaust." Yet he did proffer publicly and privately the reason for his circumspection: "Every word directed by US to the competent authorities and every public reference have to be seriously pondered and measured by US in the interest of those who suffer, in order not to make — even unintentionally — their situation more grave and insupportable." Two months before the Allocution, the Vatican Secretariat of State, after noting that "in order to avert (evitare) the massive deportation of Jews," it had involved its representatives in Italy, Slovakia, and Croatia. However, it added, "an open sign of this would not seem advisable lest Germany, knowing of this declaration of the Holy See, should intensify its anti Jewish measures."

Wills and his cicerone, Cornwell, believe the 1942 Christmas address to have been evasive and trivializing. Wills condemns it as "an address that refused to name Jews or Nazis or Germans specifically." Less than six months earlier in a broadcast to the British people, Churchill had said, "Since the Mongol invasion ... there has never been the methodical butchering on such a scale..." but never mentioned Jews.... Pius was clearly much-more specific (than Churchill), and much more clearly understood...."

But in fact the 1942 message was not as cryptic and incomprehensible as latter-day critics would suggest. Officials in the Reich main Security Bureau (RSHA) of the assassinated Reinhard Heydrich — architect of the Wannsee extermination program of January 1942, and heir presumptive to Himmler—clearly understood to whom this address was directed and to what it referred: "...the pope has repudiated the Nazi new Order ... clerical falsification of the Nazi world view.... The Pope does not refer to the National Socialists by name ... but (pace Cornwell and Wills) he is clearly speaking on behalf of the Jews..., he makes himself the mouthpiece of the Jewish war criminals." Owen Chadwick in Britain and the Vatican attributes these responses to the German Foreign Office. This is certainly a less anecdotally driven datum than that of the opportunist, Count Ciano, to which Cornwell gives credence.

Moreover, Bishop von Preysing of Berlin in March of 1943, three months later, also clearly understood what and to whom the Pope's address referred. In one of the letters in Actes et Documents..., he wrote to Pius, a long-time personal friend, about the deportation of "thousands and thousands of Jews whose probable fate is that which your Holiness has indicated in the Christmas message...." Pius's "full response" is rarely reproduced since it would not reinforce the post–Hochhuth image in *Der Stellvertreter* embraced more by Catholic than Jewish critics — and in fact, the acknowledged motivation of Cornwell's *Hitler's Pope*. After noting that he had referred to the fate of the Jews in that message, Pius observed that his statement "was brief, but it has been well understood."

He went on to say that his love and concern were extended to all who were in anguish, but that he could do nothing effective for them except to pray. However, that "full response" to which I referred above as being rarely cited, is Pius's declaration to von Preysing: "But We are decided, as circumstances advise or permit, to speak out once again in their favor" — and about which Phayer observes dryly: "Whatever the circumstances the pope had in mind evidently never came to pass," whereas a more pertinent observation would have to do with the proven fatuity of mere "speaking out," when action was called for. Nevertheless, one assumes the "circumstances" were those surrounding his allocution to the College of Cardinals six months after the Christmas message.

Moreover, through all the messages delivered after the outbreak of hostilities was the refrain condemning weapons of mass destruction ... along with the repeated denunciation of wanton violators of the principle of noncombatant immunity.... If the Pope's well publicized statement were so utterly ignored by military leaders ... what would have been the response to similar statements, raised in condemnation of their Nazi counterparts.... At the very least those statements would have been ignored.

CHAPTER 7

The Pope Pius XII Controversy: A Review Article[1]

by Kenneth D. Whitehead

One of the most remarkable of phenomena in recent years had been the revival of the controversy over the role of Pope Pius XII during the Second World War, and specifically, over that pontiff's stance with regard to Hitler's effort to exterminate the Jews. First played out over 30 years ago, beginning during the 1950s, the controversy centered on the question of whether Pius XII was culpably "silent" and passive in the face of one of the most monstrous crimes in human history — when his voice as a moral leader and his action as head of the worldwide Catholic Church might possibly have prevented, or at least have seriously hindered — so it is argued — the Nazis in their ghastly plans to implement what they so chillingly called the Final Solution (Endlösung) to a long and widely perceived "Jewish Problem" in Europe.

The controversy over Pius XII has not only been rekindled. It has extended to include other modern popes and, indeed, the Catholic Church herself as "anti–Semitic." An unusual number of books and articles have continued to fuel this controversy.

The controversy which arose around the wartime role of Pius XII, though, did not arise until nearly two decades later, almost five years after the pope's death. It was in 1963 that a crude but powerful stage play about the pontiff, *The Deputy*, became a surprise hit in both Europe and America.

The action of the play is principally carried forward by a young Jesuit priest in the Vatican service who learns of the Nazi extermination camps in the East. He is able to bring this information to the attention of the pope himself, but the latter proves unwilling to "speak out" against the gigantic moral evil he has been confronted with. Pius XII is presented as a man "who cannot risk endangering the Holy See.... (Besides) only Hitler has the power to save Europe from the Russians." Or again: "The chief will not expose himself to danger for the Jews."

Hochhuth's thesis about all this was simple: "A deputy of Christ who sees these things and nonetheless lets reasons of state seal his lips ... (is) criminal."[2] What the pope should have done was equally clear to the playwright; in the play, the pope is advised to "warn Hitler that you will compel five hundred million Catholics to make Christian protest if he goes on with these mass killings."[3] How the pope might possibly "compel" anyone to act merely by speaking out is not specified, but it is intriguing to think that Hochhuth, a non–Catholic, even imagined that the pope might possess such power. Is it possible that some subsequent resentment against Pius XII is similarly based on an erroneous belief that a Roman pontiff somehow does have the power to tell Catholics what to think and to compel them to act, but that Pius XII stubbornly refused to do so in order to help the Jews?

Yet for all of its inaccuracies and even crudities, *The Deputy* was a huge success. It was translated into more than 20 languages and, virtually by itself, launched the original Pius XII controversy

Few probably ever stopped to consider whether there might have been any special circumstances related to wartime conditions or to the Vatican's international position and special history which might have militated against the pope's speaking out.

The fact that this viewpoint predominates today tends to give the critics of Pius XII somewhat of an advantage, since they are generally able to gain immediate broad acceptance of their assertion about what the pope and the Church should have done during World War II. The defenders of Pius XII, on the other hand, generally have to scramble even to get a public hearing, much less persuade public opinion in their favor; more than that, they are too often apt to be dismissed as mere knee-jerk Catholic apologists.

Almost immediately following the controversy stirred up by *The Deputy*, an extensive controversial literature, both scholarly and popular, about Pope Pius XII and his wartime role grew up. This literature included questions not only about why he was silent about the Holocaust against the Jews, but about whether, in fact, he was all that silent; about what his policies and actions were with regard to the Jews and other war victims— in other words; what specifically, did he do, if anything, for Jews and other war victims? Other pertinent questions included what his attitudes and aims were towards the Nazis, the Communists, and the Western democracies. Did he, as is still often implied and sometimes even plainly stated, "collaborate" with the Nazis because of his fear of Communism and Soviet expansionism? Finally, what credit or responsibility belonged to the pope for actions taken, or not taken, by Catholics throughout Europe in favor of the Jews?

All of these questions (and a few more) are pretty extensively if not exhaustively covered in the ... books under review here. Five of these authors take a more or less frank anti–Pius (or anti–Church) view (Cornwell, Kertzer, Phayer, Wills, and Zuccotti).

This major escalation of the controversy began in earnest when *Vanity Fair* magazine in its issue of October 1999 published a preview and excerpt from the then forthcoming book of John Cornwell's, *Hitler's Pope: The Secret History of Pius XII....* The excerpt from the book published in *Vanity Fair* was typical — and sensational....

While the *Vanity Fair* lead-in to Cornwell's book did not come from the pages of the book itself, the author nevertheless readily accepted this kind of sensational publicity for what he had written....

Moreover, some of the implications and effects of this broader public controversy themselves go beyond just the words and acts of Pius XII during the war with regard to the Jews. In the course of an excellent review-article in the *Weekly Standard* concerning some of the very same books being reviewed here, for example, Rabbi David G. Dalin noted the striking fact that some of the bitterest attacks on Pius XII have been made by disaffected Catholics. These include, especially, the books by ex-seminarians John Cornwell and Gary Wills — as well as another book, not reviewed here, ex-priest James Carroll's *Constantine's Sword* ... Rabbi Dalin noted:

> Almost none of the books about Pius XII and the Holocaust is actually about Pius XII and the Holocaust. The real topic proves to be an intra–Catholic argument about the direction of the Church today, with the Holocaust simply the biggest club available for liberal Catholics to use against traditionalists.[4]

This is not true of all the books critical of Pius XII, of course; but it is a prominent and, significant for some, perhaps surprising, element in the present revived Pius XII controversy. Rabbi Dalin believes it "disparages the testimony of Holocaust survivors and thins out, by spreading inappropriate figures, the condemnation that belongs to Hitler and the

Nazis." He objects to what he calls an "attempt to usurp the Holocaust and use it for partisan purposes."

However, it is not the case that dissident Catholics are the only ones prepared to use the Pius XII controversy for partisan purposes. In yet another lengthy review article in the *New Republic* of some of the same books under review here (along with some others), Daniel Jonah Goldhagen, author of the very widely noticed 1996 book *Hitler's Willing Executioners*,[5] launched a generalized attack not only on Pius XII, but on the Catholic Church as a whole as a thoroughly anti–Semitic institution "at its core."[6] In his earlier book, Goldhagen found it possible to fix collective guilt upon the German people generally for the crimes of Hitler and the Nazis; in his *New Republic* article, he makes the same charge as far as Catholics and the Catholic Church are concerned charging Christianity and, specifically, the Catholic Church with "the main responsibility" for the anti–Semitism which issued in the Holocaust....

As encountered in his article, his historical references are so generalized and careless and imprecise — and even inaccurate — while his tone is overwrought and exaggerated, that one actually hesitates to say how bad his article really is; one hesitates for fear of seeming to share in his intemperance!

All of the books we are reviewing here ... deal with pretty much the same set of facts, most of them long on the record in the voluminous Pius XII literature....

Since the anti–Pius authors believe that the pontiff should have spoken out and acted more vigorously to help the Jews, they naturally tend to concentrate on those instances when he failed to do so, in their view, and to downplay or explain away those instances that might call their thesis into questions. As Rabbi Dalin, not unfairly describes this approach: "It requires ... that favorable evidence be read in the worst light and treated to the strictest test, while unfavorable evidence is read in the best light...."[7]

My overall impression is that all of the authors, in one degree or another, are focused so narrowly on the pope and the Jews that they sometimes fail to see and appreciate the larger picture concerning what was going on, namely that there was a war going on! It was a total war too, and one that was being conducted on a worldwide scale; and for those who found themselves inside the territories controlled by the Axis — and this included the Vatican for most of the war — wartime conditions necessarily limited their ability to function in so many different ways that it cannot be assumed that they were entirely free agents in any respect.

As for the pope and the Vatican Secretariat of State, responsible for managing the affairs of a worldwide church under these difficult conditions—

and with a small staff of only about 30 people in all, including clerical help — it has to be realized that they at all times and constantly had other and pressing concerns besides just following and reacting to what was happening to the Jews.[8]

Speaking as a former practicing diplomat myself, I sometimes found the apparent expectations of some of these authors concerning the church actors in this drama could or should have been doing in the actual situations described to be simply unreal.

Another assumption of most of these authors, especially those in the anti–Pius camp, is that Pius XII was necessarily free in the conditions of war and occupation that obtained to speak out or to make public protests in the way that they think he should have, looking at things from their post–Holocaust perspective. Both before and during the war, the 107-odd acre Vatican City was entirely surrounded by a hostile Fascist regime in Italy, which, not incidentally, also controlled the Vatican's water, electricity, food supply, mail delivery, garbage removal, and indeed, its very physical accessibility by anybody. John Cornwell admits that Mussolini could have taken over the Vatican at any time — if sufficiently provoked (or prodded by Hitler).[9] The Italian Foreign Minister, Count Galeazzo Ciano, recorded in his diary of March 1940 that Mussolini seriously considered "liquidating" the Vatican; for the pope it was not an imaginary threat but an active possibility for most of the war.[10]

From September 1943 to June 1944 Rome was under harsh German military occupation, and it was during this period that Hitler seriously considered occupying the Vatican and abducting the pope, as a number of sources attest and as some our authors do not fail to record....[11]

Another assumption quite unproven that seems to be taken for granted on the anti–Pius side is the notion that if the pope had only spoken out, his words would necessarily have been heeded, if not by the Axis governments and their satellites, at least by the Catholic peoples of Europe, who presumably could or would then have opposed what their governments were doing. This assumption seems both unrealistic and unlikely, quite apart from the penalties that citizens in the Axis countries and their satellites would have incurred for opposing their governments.

By the time the war came, there was a firmly established pattern of Axis rejection of Vatican protests; on any given occasion, the pope had to expect that, in all likelihood, his words would not be heeded. As the war progressed, this unhappy reality was made quite explicit by the Germans. For example, by June, 1942 — after numerous appeals had already been made specifically on behalf of Jews — the Vatican Ambassador to Germany, Cesare Orsenigo, reported to G.B. Montini, the future Pope Paul VI, who had just lodged one more appeal on behalf of a Jewish couple, as follows: "I regret that, in addition, I must add that these interventions are not only useless, but they are even badly received; as a result, the authorities show themselves unfavorable to other ... cases." Perhaps the surprising thing, again, is that the Vatican continued to lodge protests anyway under such conditions.

Yet Michael Phayer thinks that "because Church authorities left Catholics in moral ambiguity by not speaking out, the great majority remained bystanders."[12] Susan Zuccotti describes Fascist-style Croats engaged in persecuting the Jews as "devout Catholics," presumably ready to take orders from the pope if only he had been willing to issue the orders.[13] Such views grossly exaggerate both the degree of the Catholic commitment of anybody actually prepared to persecute the Jews in this fashion and the influence any pope or bishops could possibly have had on them, or in a Nazi-ruled Europe generally.

For in that time and place it must also be remembered that there were in force very severe penalties for opposing the actions of these totalitarian governments. There were thus a few other reasons besides the pope's failure to speak out that may have persuaded people to be "bystanders." As early as 1936, for example, priests in Germany were being arrested simply for expressing sympathy for Jews and others in concentration camps. Even before the war, again, "ordinary Germans who were caught with hectographed copies of Bishop von Galen's sermons against the Nazi euthanasia program — a celebrated instance where a Churchman did strongly speak out — or who discussed it with colleagues, were arrested and sent to concentration camps."[14] Speaking generally, those who criticized Nazi action against the Jews "faced imprisonment." ...Merely listening to Vatican radio was a criminal offense in wartime Germany.

After the war began, "hostile civilians who ... refused to obey a German order were denied any right, and, indeed, could be killed with impunity by German soldiers without resort to legal process...."[15]

In the midst of this generalized slaughter, since the pope disposed of no material means, and since the governments on all sides intent upon the pursuit of the war were more or less deaf to the entreaties he did from time to time make, the Vatican at least tried to do what it could do to ameliorate the situation. In this effort, diplomacy was the Vatican's primary chosen means, not only in dealing with belligerent governments but also in attempting to help victims of the war, including Jews. Pius XII has been strongly criticized for preferring to use the means of diplomacy rather than plainly denouncing gross evil. Michael Phayer sees what he calls the pope's "attempt to use a diplomatic remedy for a moral outrage" as Pope Pius's "greatest failure."[16] Yet the pope was not following a policy that was original to himself; it was the traditional policy of the Vatican....

In short, the idea that Pope Pius XII should — or could! — have simply "spoken out" against the evils of Nazism runs up against some rather inconvenient realities — which some of the present-day writers on the Holocaust seem to have paid too little attention to.

There were other reasons why Pius XII chose to follow the course that he did. He was pressured for his "silence" by both Axis and Allies, for example, from the earliest days of the war. More than once he stated ... that he was not speaking out in order not to make the situation worse for the victims.

In answer to a formal diplomatic protest lodged by the Italian ambassador to the Vatican, the pope said:

> The Italians are certainly well aware of the terrible things taking place in Poland. We might have an obligation to utter fiery words against such things; yet all that is holding us back from doing so is the knowledge that should we speak, we would simply worsen the predicament of these unfortunate people.[17]

Here the pope was not talking about possibly making things worse just for Jewish victims. At this point in time (May 1940), it was Catholic Poles who were indiscriminately slaughtered in great numbers. As one historian later wrote: "...on average, three thousand Poles died each day during the occupation (of Poland), half of them Christian Poles, half of them Jews...."[18]

The pope and his associates repeated on various occasions this same justification for not speaking out. In February 1941, for example, the Pope commented that silence was "unhappily imposed on him."[19] This was no mere excuse. At the Nuremberg Trials of Nazi war criminals after the war, Field Marshal Albert Kesselring testified that Pius XII no doubt did not protest "because he told himself quite rightly: 'If I protest, Hitler will be driven to madness; not only will that not help the Jews, but we must expect that they will be killed all the more.'"[20]

It is surely something of a truism to say that historical figures could have "done more" or acted differently, but it is also beside the point. The proper task of history, it would seem, is to understand what someone did and why. When Pius XII is instead charged with "silence," it is very hard to deal with the questions — it is like an unprovable negative.

Actually, Pius XII and the Vatican were heavily involved in relief work throughout the war, quite apart from what the pope said, or did not say; on the "silence" question. Margherita Marchione, among other authors, points out that other agencies involved in relief work were similarly "silent." She notes that the World Council of Churches, for example, left any possible denunciations of crimes to its member churches—just as the Holy See regularly left it to the Catholic bishops to say whatever seemed necessary or helpful....

In February 1943, at a meeting called to examine the problem of helping Jews threatened by the Nazis—a meeting which included the papal nuncio as well as a pastor from the World Council of Churches—the Red Cross articulated its reasons for deciding not to issue any protest statement; protests, in the view of the Red Cross, would jeopardize the relief work the agency was carrying out in favor of war victims.... [21]

In this connection, people have often asked why Pius XII did not excommunicate Hitler.... Certainly any such excommunication would have constituted a provocation, if that was what the pope, like the Red Cross, was trying to avoid....

More than that, though excommunication might have been effective back in the ages of faith, when a head of state had to contend with strong feelings about excommunication on the part of his subjects, in today's secularized world it was not likely to have much effect.

More than that, Hitler had long since "excommunicated" himself. Nor does it seem that those who proved capable of engaging in the Nazi killings could have been much influenced by being told that they had been excommunicated. Excommunication would have amounted to an ineffective gesture (like speaking out). More important for the pope would be what could effectively be done under the circumstances.

So what did the Vatican do for war victims, including Jews? Pope Pius XII set up both a Pontifical Relief Commission and a Vatican Information Service; the former was designed to provide aid in the form of whatever funds, goods, medicine, or shelter could be obtained and distributed, while the latter aimed to find and report on missing soldiers and civilians who had become separated because of the war. Headquartered at the Vatican, these organizations raised money, for example, in the Americas, and then worked through Church institutions and personnel at all levels to funnel aid to needy victims. Thousands of people were involved in this work: priests, monks, friars, nuns, lay volunteers, military chaplains, and others. The networks established by and through these organizations would also prove to be instrumental in hiding Jews or helping them to escape.

From the outset Pope Pius insisted, "It is our ardent wish to offer to the unfortunate and innocent victims every possible spiritual and material succor—with no questions asked, no discrimination, and no strings attached...."[22]

In other words, the assistance specifically provided by the pope and the Church to the Jews was rendered to them along with the aid provided to other wartime victims.[23]

This raises a further question, though, of why the anti–Pius authors generally give so little attention to the actual wartime relief and rescue efforts that the church did carry out, however inadequate that they may have been in comparison with the enormity of the Holocaust against the Jews. These efforts are pretty consistently downplayed or even ignored by most of the anti–Pius authors, even while they go on at length about the inaction of Pius XII and his supposed negative attitudes toward the Jews.

On the other hand, all of the pro–Pius authors strongly emphasize the church's relief efforts. All of them quote the estimate of Israeli diplomat and pro–Pius author Pinchas Lapide that "the Catholic Church, under the pontificate of Pius XII, was instrumental in saving at least 700,000 but probably as many as 860,000 Jews from certain death at Nazi hands."[24]

The anti–Pius authors themselves, however, with the exception of Susan Zuccotti, ignore Lapide's statistics completely, not merely as inaccurate, but as if they did not even exist. Relying on these authors alone, it would be hard to learn that Pius XII did anything or helped anybody, and this represents a serious failure on the part of these authors to deal with all the facts of the case.

Susan Zuccotti represents a special case here (as, to a lesser extent, so does Michael Phayer), since she does cover many instances of Jews being helped by Catholics and church institutions and personnel. But her concern is almost invariably to show that they received such aid apart from — and perhaps even in spite of — anything that Pius XII may ever have said or done. She even mentions Lapide several times, only to charge his work with "being replete with egregious mistakes and distortions" (of which she actually cites only two misattributions in newspaper articles). She goes on to characterize Lapide's methodology as "flawed and the results unreliable."[25] She does not document or show this, however, but merely asserts it.

So what is the case then? Did the pope, or the church under his leadership, help to save any Jews in their hour of need, or not? If so, how much help? How many Jews were hidden or saved? If Lapide's frequently quoted figure is so "flawed," then what were the numbers, approximately, if any numbers are obtainable at all? There is certainly plenty of anecdotal evidence of Jews being aided. Should not these questions at least be addressed by those trying to make the case against Pius XII, even if wholly accurate answers might understandably be difficult to come by?

Alas, these questions are basically not addressed by anti–Pius authors.

Unless and until they are addressed their case against the pope can hardly be considered made. If the pope who is accused of being culpably silent and passive in the face of the Holocaust was, in fact, quite active in helping the Jews—just as he was far from entirely silent, as well, — how are the charges going to hold up? What is the Pius XII controversy all about?

As Robert Lockwood points out.... even if Pinchas Lapide's figures represent "an exaggeration by half, it would (still) record more Jewish lives saved than any other entity at the time."[26]

Beginning with Rolf Hochhuth, a recurring idea among the anti–Pius authors is that merely by speaking, Pope Pius XII could somehow have compelled "devout Catholics "to do his bidding. That he is apparently thought to have possessed such power seems to be one of the strongest reasons for condemning him for not having spoken out in the way that his critics wished. The whole notion that Catholics are somehow more than others disposed simply to "follow orders" from the church can no more be verified by reference to the church during World War II than it can by reference to the contemporary church. Nevertheless the idea persists.

Yet this idea is in conflict with another dominant idea found among the anti–Pius authors, most notably, Susan Zuccotti, and to a lesser extent, Michael Phayer, namely: that such help, rescue and shelter work as was carried out by Catholics on behalf of the Jews in Nazi-occupied Europe was largely done on their own initiative, and not in response to any Vatican "policy" or "orders" issued by the pope. This is believed to be the case because the scholars in the anti–Pius camp, after diligent searches, have failed to turn up any "orders" issued by the silent and passive pope. As we shall see, Zuccotti is literally obsessed with the need to find "written" directives before Pius XII can be credited with anything.[27]

This conflict is never resolved: on the one hand, Pope Pius XII, culpably, it is charged, never issued any orders to help Jews: on the other hand Catholics within the authoritarian Church structure — who manifestly did on many and varied occasions help or shelter Jews— would have so acted, it is also maintained, only if the pope and other church authorities had told them to: that, after all, was the very reason why the pope was so urgently required to speak out.

Common sense might suggest a different answer, which probably comes closer to the reality: namely, that many Catholics, clerical, lay, and religious, often did extend help to Jews where they were able to do so (even in spite of the often extremely dangerous consequences for them if caught); at the same time, from the top of the church's authority structure, the pope and (at least in some countries such as France) the bishops both created an atmosphere and in various other ways let it be known that help was indeed to be extended to Jews where possible, even while the church herself was struggling to carry on under a totalitarian regime that was also engaged in persecuting her in various ways.

Probably there is no answer that will satisfy everybody to the questions of what credit should go to church leaders for those actions by Catholics that did result in helping Jews; nevertheless, it does seem that if Pius XII is to be held responsible for what the church failed to do, then he at least ought to be given some credit for what the church did do.

The Popes Against the Jews: The Vatican's Role in the Rise of Modern Anti-Semitism (David Kertzer). David Kertzer's project ... is to go all the way back to 1814 and try to show the papacy and virtually all of the popes from them to the election of Pius XII in 1939 thought and acted in strict continuity with the wartime pope as regards anti–Semitism.

Kertzer expressly links his case to that of John Cornwell's *Hitler's Pope,* in which, according to him, "Pope Pius XII's 'silence' is linked to his personal antipathy to the Jews, along with his larger conservative political agenda, which privileged maintaining good relations with the Nazi regime." Kertzer endorses this characterization, even as he goes on to ask: "But what if we find that Pius XII's benevolent predecessor shared the same stridently anti–Semitic views?"[28]

What, indeed, if we find that virtually all of the popes from 1814 on are guilty of the same prejudice, evidenced by their successive failures to eschew the prejudice or abolish the disabilities suffered by the Jews in their domains? — and later, after the end of the Papal States by their acceptance and cooperation with anti–Semites and anti–Semitic parties in the various European countries?

This is what this book is all about. The author, thought, is almost schizophrenic in his approach to his subject. On the one hand, he shows himself to be conscientious in handling his sources, including the Vatican archives (open for most of the period he is covering), his providing an interesting narrative about some little known historical occurrences. On the other hand, his superficial and labored efforts to link the popes themselves with anti–Semitism that was spreading in Europe during the period are not convincing and are sometimes even laughable (if the accusations were not so serious).

Historically, of course the popes were traditional defenders of the Jews against popular and state violence against them in Europe. Kertzer fails to show this attitude was substantially changed in modern times.

He admits that the popes never espoused anti–Semitism in their public teachings and pronouncements; and, indeed, he correctly notes that they scarcely ever even mention the Jews at all. He ascribes this to expediency, and charges the popes with promoting anti–Semitism "out of the limelight."[29]

It would be closer to the truth to say that throughout the nineteenth century and well into the twentieth, the Jews and anti–Semitism were at the extreme margin of the popes' attention — often not on the radar screens at all. For more than a century, during the precise period covered by Kertzer, the popes were engaged on the political level in fighting what turned out to be a largely losing battle against liberal, secularizing, and anti-clerical European governments—what Pope Pius IX in his famous *Syllabus of Errors* so disastrously described (from the point of view of the Church's public relations) as "progress, liberalism, and modern civilization."

But for the most part, the Jews were not a central concern of the popes until their unhappy situation was forced upon them with the rise of violent, modern racial anti–Semitism. This relative inattention to the affairs of the Jews generally probably even explains more of the conduct of Pius XI and Pius XII than most post–Holocaust writers could ever imagine or admit.

David Kertzer's aim of turning the popes into anti–Semites anyway, however, fails in virtually every instance. Let us take just a couple of examples.

Pope Leo's Secretary of State, Cardinal Mariano Rampolla, sent back a routine courtesy form letter to an anti–Semitic French writer thanking the latter for sending complimentary copies of his book to the Vatican for both the pope and for the cardinal himself; the cardinal wrote that the pope "has asked me to thank you for it in his name, adding that he sends you a heartfelt apostolic benediction."

This form letter is supposed to "prove" the personal anti–Semitic sympathies of both Pope Leo XIII and Cardinal Rampolla himself. It proves nothing of the sort. Anyone who has ever served on the staff of almost any high public official, as I have, has written many such letters with almost identical wording ("asked me to thank you in his name") in response to unsolicited material sent in. As for the "apostolic benediction," routine Vatican mail contains dozens— or hundreds— of them regularly. I suspect that if David Kertzer sent this book in to the pope, he might get a similar courtesy form letter from the Vatican back in reply!

Nevertheless, he is quite serious about his conviction that papal anti–Semitism is in play here. He elaborates further on his "proof," as follows:

> The secretary of state's later claim, when news of the letter became public, that the Pope had this letter sent without having any idea

what the book was about is clearly untrue. Cardinal Rampolla and Leo XIII knew exactly what kind of book it was, and what its purpose was. There is no question that they approved of both.[30]

The reason he is so sure that both pope and cardinal knew and approved is that the journal *La Civiltà Cattolica* was printing a series of anti–Semitic articles at the same time, and surely, it goes without saying that the pope and the secretary of state always knew about and approved of everything that appeared there.

But interpretation is a stretch, if it does not actually border on guilt by association. Pope Leo XIII issued no less than 86 encyclicals in which his official teaching is set forth in great detail; there is no evidence in David Kertzer's book that he has read a single one of them, yet he feels able to deduce anti–Semitism from the pope's associations and routine correspondence.

Pope Pius XI in 1938 memorably declared "anti–Semitism is a movement in which we Christians can have no part whatsoever.... Spiritually we are Semites."[31] Although delivered to a small group of Belgians, the statement was widely publicized at the time, and has been even more widely publicized since. Convincing the author of this statement of anti–Semitism would seem to be a pretty difficult task, and David Kertzer does not even come close. The wonder is that he thought it necessary to try.

Like Leo XIII, Pius XI wrote a large number of encyclicals, 30 in all, setting forth his official teachings. Once again, there is no evidence in this book that David Kertzer has read any of them except *Mit Brennender Sorge*; still he feels quite able to expatiate on the pontiff's views. The principal "proof" he provides of the pope's alleged anti–Semitism has reference to the mission of the then Archbishop Achille Ratti, the future Pius XI, as papal nuncio in Poland in 1919. Popular anti–Semitic pogroms had broken out in a couple of places. Archbishop Ratti's own anti–Semitism, according to Kertzer's account, seems to have consisted of his forwarding to Rome various reports about this violence which he had received from local sources ascribing the problems to "provocations" by the Jews. Kertzer provides no real direct evidence that the future pope endorsed this view; the evidence he does cite shows that, for the most part, the Vatican envoy came to no definite conclusions at all, though in one case he makes what seems to be an eminently sensible comment that "the Jews blame the Christians, and the Christians blame the Jews." Kertzer nevertheless seems to think that he has clinched his "proof" by observing that the "the depths of anti–Semitism among the Catholic clergy of Poland at the time could hardly be overstated, yet Monsignor Ratti saw nothing amiss."[32]

A contemporary biography, published before World War II and the Holocaust, tells a very different story about Achille Ratti's dealings with the Jews during his 1919 mission to Poland:

> He gave numerous signs of his charitable nature and also of the Holy See's determination to frown on any possibility of Jewish pogroms, for wherever he went he took care to be as friendly to Polish Jews as he was with the Christians. On no occasion would he allow anybody to recognize the difference.[33]

In summary, David Kertzer's notion that most of the popes of the last couple of centuries were anti–Semites seems to be based mainly on the fact that they continued to have relationships with some of the members of their flocks who — unfortunately — were themselves anti–Semitic in varying degrees. This is a pretty slender basis on which to convict an entire institution — the modern papacy — of the very serious charge of anti–Semitism. This book fails to prove its thesis.

The Catholic Church and the Holocaust, 1930–1965 (Phayer). Among the various anti–Pius books under review here, this book by Michael Phayer in many respects appears to be the most genuinely serious and scholarly.... His book is carefully written and meticulously documented. He draws on wide sources, including some very considerable Holocaust literature in German.

This is no crude hatchet job in the vein of John Cornwell's *Hitler's Pope*. Still, it reflects a number of the received ideas common in the anti–Pius camp: 1) that Pius XII was indeed "silent," 2) that even when he did speak out, his words were so vague and indirect that they were not understood as specifically condemning persecution of the Jews; and 3) that Pius XII was so obsessed with Communism that he was unwilling to condemn the Nazis outright.

Generally speaking, Phayer provides no significant new evidence for these contentions; he seems to take it for granted that they are already established truths; meanwhile, much or most of what he says is based on material that has been around for a good while now. He uses the *ADSS* collection only sparingly.

Another feature that pervades the book is the author's steady disapproval, and even seeming personal dislike, of Pope Pius XII. Though he grudgingly gives the pope credit from time to time, it almost seems to be a rather forced concession for him. Thus, even if the book is no crude hatchet job, it manages instead to administer a fair amount of poison in successive, small doses.

As its title makes clear, the book covers the decade before the accession of Pius XII, and extends through the 20 years following the Second World War to the close of the Catholic Church's Second Vatican Council.

One of the author's themes is that the prewar and wartime anti–Semitism found among Catholics was not fully exorcised and excluded from respectability among Catholics until Vatican II enacted its Declaration *Nostra Aetate*, both strongly condemning discrimination, and exonerating the Jews as a people for any presumed guilt for the death of Christ. There is truth in this, of course, although Phayer tends to exaggerate the degree to which Catholics were, in fact, "anti–Semitic" up until *Nostra Aetate*.

Another one of his themes is summed in a statement of his already quoted earlier, namely, that Pius XII attempted "to use a diplomatic remedy for a moral outrage." According to Phayer, as a result of this papal choice of a diplomatic rather than a moral approach, "the ethical credibility of the papacy fell to its lowest level in modern times."[34] It is pertinent to ask, though, what other effective means the pope had besides diplomatic ones? He possessed no material or military power, nor should the idea of attempting to incite Catholics to fight against a totalitarian juggernaut really have commended itself to any sensible and responsible spiritual leader in the conditions that prevailed in Nazi-occupied Europe, especially considering that the consequences for any who responded to any such papal appeal could very likely have been concentration camps or death for them.

It will not do simply to dismiss the explanation the pope several times quite earnestly offered for not speaking out, namely, that he did not want to make the situation worse. At the time, the pope could see a lot more clearly than many can apparently see today that that could well have been the likely result of any dramatic public challenge to the Nazis at the height of their power.

So Michael Phayer's proposed alternative to the diplomatic means that he deplores, then, proves to be nothing else than the same one that has fueled the Pius XII controversy from the beginning: the pope should have "spoken out." What else? In a particularly impassioned passage, he writes:

> Pius XII's priorities put Jews at mortal risk. Thousands, perhaps tens of thousands, of additional Jews would have eluded Hitler's death camps had the Holy See accelerated rather than decelerated information about genocide. Did Pope Pius think the church so fragile that, should he speak out, it would not survive the war, even though it had survived the fratricidal Great War intact? Should the possible bombardment of Rome have been Pius's primary concern, or, as Bishop Preysing pointed out, should not the

moral issue of the murder of the Jews have taken precedence? Were the churches and other structures of Rome and the Vatican really the nerve center of Catholic faith that Pius believed them to be? Was the possible future clash between Christianity and atheistic communism more important than the slaughter of the Jews who were being murdered in eastern Europe, and who would continue to be murdered, while Pius hoped for a negotiated settlement to the war that would favor a genocidal Germany, the Church's defender against Russian communism?[35]

It would be difficult to state the anti–Pius case any more clearly or strongly than this. Yet the entire paragraph rests on the initial, totally hypothetical assumption that, "thousands, perhaps tens of thousands" of additional Jews would indeed have been saved, if only the pope had spoken out. Michael Phayer does not know this; nobody could know it; it is unknowable. It nevertheless provides the basis of the charges against the pope that since *The Deputy* have transformed him into a moral leper in the public mind. Yet apart from this wholly hypothetical supposition formulated years after the fact, all the other base motives attributed to the pope here for not speaking out immediately fall to the ground.

Phayer's case against the pope, then, is completely unknowable, a hypothetical case entirely removed from the possibility of any kind of empirical verification. In a very important sense this is not "history" at all; and at a certain point we really have to begin to wonder how scholars can go on year after year producing volumes such as this one about what did not happen in history. While it is both legitimate (and inevitable) that moral judgments will be made about the behavior of historical figures, including popes, such judgments should be made on what they verifiably did, not on speculations about what people think they should have done.

The evidence for the World War II period and the pope's role in it has long since been substantially in. What purpose is served to go on imagining that the pope, or anyone else in his position, was morally obliged to act differently than he did? There were always good reasons during the war for any pubic figure within the striking power of Hitler to be careful about what he might do or say. The pope plainly said that he was not going to speak out as he was urged even at the time because he did not want to make the situation worse. He believed that, and he had good reasons for believing it. It was at least as likely that swift and ruthless retaliation would have followed any papal protest as that the Nazis would have been affected or deterred in any way by anything the pope might have said.

Nor was it simply a matter of fearing for the physical destruction of the art treasures or the churches of Rome. Rome remained the headquarters and nerve center of whatever efforts the church was making on behalf of war victims, and for the pope to risk its destruction would have to jeopardize that work as well as to abandon his responsibility to his own faithful.

Nor was it a matter of fearing the church was too fragile to survive a confrontation with Hitler; the pope had responsibilities also to the Catholics who were largely helpless under Hitler's sway. We have already seen that the idea that he wanted a "negotiated peace" that favored Germany will not hold up.

To give Michael Phayer credit, the three chapters following the paragraph of his just quoted are devoted to describing many of the efforts that were accomplished by Catholics working within the church's structures. Nevertheless his careful research is vitiated by his overall unproven thesis concerning the moral failure of Pius and the church in the face of the Holocaust. The church had no answer for the Holocaust. Nobody did. But the church still went on trying to be the church to the extent possible....

Michael Phayer certainly demonstrates at times the ability to write history, but he seems so consumed by his antecedent conviction about the moral failure of Pius XII that he is unable to manage it consistently. More could be said about this book, not all of it as bad as this. Still it cannot be said the book makes the case against the pope and the Catholic Church that it apparently sets out to make.

More than that, it is a very serious thing in the post–Holocaust climate to accuse someone of being anti–Semitic or of having helped Nazi war criminals to escape. Phayer and the anti–Pius authors are going to have to do a much better job if they really expect such charges to stand.

In the end, Michael Phayer seems to be a prime example among our authors of what Michael Burleigh, in his recent, *The Third Reich: A New History*, thinks is not needed when writing about Nazi Germany, that is, "ex post facto outrage from armchair moralists...."[36]

Papal Sin: Structures of Deceit (Wills). Gary Wills is not only a professional writer and historian, who teaches at Northwestern University; he is also the winner of the 1993 Pulitzer Prize for his Lincoln at Gettysburg. He writes often for the leftist New York Review of Books.

However, it is pretty hard to imagine this book attracting the attention of the Pulitzer Committee. In it (*Papal Sin*) he aims to expose what he calls "structures of deceit" in the modern papacy. By this term Wills seems to mean the dishonesty and hypocrisy that he thinks are habitually employed by the popes and their Curia and others in their entourages to try to maintain — against the plain evidence, as he sees it — that the papacy is never wrong and is always justified in what it decides and does.

Other observers, even those disagreeing strongly with or rejecting the papacy, might not put it quite that bluntly, but Wills' tone throughout is confidently argumentative and polemical. He regularly gets away with saying things that in others would be seen as extreme, insulting, and outrageous; he gets away with this because, after all, he is speaking about his own church "from the inside," and as a "practicing Catholic." It is doubtful that any reputable publisher would publish like this if Wills were not a practicing Catholic.

In a second chapter entitled "Towards the Holocaust, "he describes a draft papal encyclical commissioned by Pope Pius XI, which was supposed to serve as a solemn condemnation of anti–Semitism by the church; but which was apparently put on the shelf by the general of Jesuits and never delivered to the pope for his approval and signature (after consultation, Wills speculates, with Cardinal Pacelli — another "proof" of the latter's anti–Semitism!).

While blaming the Church for never issuing this draft encyclical formally condemning anti–Semitism, Wills at the same time sees no contradiction in quoting examples of supposed church anti–Semitism from the text of the same draft encyclical! It never occurs to him that perhaps the draft was never issued because it proved inadequate and did not accurately reflect the church's mature and considered view on the subject. The discussion essayed by Wills in this chapter about anti–Semitism in the church and among the Popes is a shorter version of the thesis expounded by David Kertzer in the book reviewed above, and now adopted by Daniel Jonah Goldhagen, to the effect that anti–Semitism is actually endemic to the Catholic Church and to the popes....[37]

In his third chapter entitled "Usurping the Holocaust," Wills credits the complaint that the beatification (and eventual canonization) of the Jewish philosopher and convert to Catholicism, now St. Edith Stein, was really a kind of cynical manipulation by the church "to give Catholics a claim that the Holocaust victimized Catholics as well as Jews."[38] Seemingly oblivious to the fact that indiscriminate Nazi murder did also victimize millions of others besides Jews, as we noted above, Wills denies that Stein was any kind of Catholic martyr at all; according to him, she was deported to Auschwitz and gassed solely because she was Jewish.

The facts are that as a Catholic religious, though converted, Edith Stein was for a time exempt from deportation. But after the Catholic Archbishop of Utrecht publicly denounced the Nazi deportation of the Jews, this exemption for Jewish converts to Catholicism was promptly cancelled and the Nazis then rounded them all up and loaded on trains for Auschwitz. During this particular deportation, "Protestant Jews and those of partial Jewish descent" — whose leaders agreed not to denounce the deportations publicly — "were quickly released, but the Catholic Jews remained under arrest, together with approximately a thousand other Jewish prisoners."[39]

Thus, St. Edith Stein was martyred because she was Jewish and because she was Catholic. She was a legitimate martyr in the traditional Catholic understanding of the term. Gary Wills got it wrong here (one is tempted to add: again!).

Only in the fourth chapter does Gary Wills deal with Pope Pius XII as such. His treatment consists pretty much of a rehashing of some of the usual "particulars" against the pope by now familiar to us. Wills accepts them uncritically. As an illustration of the level at which this Pulitzer Prize historian is capable of operating, it should be noted that, with one sole exception, his only source for what he says about Pius XII is none other than — John Cornwell! (The one exception is a citation from the nearly 40-year-old and biased work by Guenter Lewy, *The Catholic Church and Nazi Germany*.)

This book by Gary Wills powerfully supports the contention of those who hold that one of the principal motivations continuing to drive the whole Pius XII controversy is the need to discredit the authority of the papacy, and the Catholic Church generally, not just to "get" Pius XII.[40]

The ... books reviewed here would seem to demonstrate that the long Pius XII controversy is still at high tide and unlikely to recede any time soon. This is too bad. There is very little new in any of these books that has not been available for a good while now....

Not even the publication of the 12 volumes of actual Vatican wartime documents in the *ADSS* collection seems to have brought the questions any closer to settlement — anymore than the opening to scholars of the rest of the Vatican archives for the period is likely to do so. Whatever new is found there will probably only be used to further the controversy along the same lines as before....

In a different world, it might have been possible to disagree, even strongly, with the decision of Pope Pius XII to employ diplomatic rather than prophetic means in trying to guide his Church through the perilous waters of World War II and the Holocaust without ending up with the actual defamation and discrediting of the man. Perhaps a better or more effective course of action was available to him. The Catholic Church certainly claims no "infallibility" for the prudential and practical judgments made by the popes. But we are not dealing here with such mere disagreements about how the pope spoke and acted.

We are dealing with how his speech and actions, such as they were, have caused him to be placed in virtually the same category as the Nazis who carried out the Holocaust as well as to be considered a moral leper and labeled an evil man.... Everybody agrees that the Nazis were evil, and hence it is apparently also fair to characterize as evil anybody thought to be "associated" with them, however tenuously. Even though the association in question has not been established — rather, the contrary has been established — it is still widely considered quite legitimate and natural to label Pius XII as evil simply because he has been accused of favoring the Nazis; if he did not come out strongly enough against them, then he must somehow have been for them.

This is the view of him that, in fact emerges not only from the polemical works by disaffected Catholics such as Cornwell and Wills ... it emerges also from the books with greater claims to scholarship such as those by Kertzer, Phayer, and Zuccotti; although their books are not as shoddily researched and written as those by Cornwell and Wills, they are every bit as agenda-driven by the animus of these authors against their subject(s).

No doubt these authors sincerely believe that they are merely trying to get at the truth, but his does not make their books any less agenda-driven....

CHAPTER 8

Interventions by the Pope and the Nuncio[1]

by Jenö Levai

Taking as our point of departure the course of the Final Solution, let us put the authentic documents alongside of Hochhuth's assertion, "It remains incomprehensible that his Holiness could not summon himself up to protest against Hitler even when Germany was clearly defeated yet the daily murder rate at Auschwitz had not yet reached its peak."[2]

On the 14th of March 1944, in accordance with a plan ... worked out in detail in advance, Hitler's troops marched into Hungary.

On the 22nd of March the pro–Nazi Sztójay government appointed by the Regent Nicholas von Horthy was formed. On the very next day, the 23rd of March, Monsignor Angelo Rotta, papal nuncio since 1939 and doyen of the diplomatic corps, made an urgent request for an interview with the prime minister, who had received the portfolio of foreign affairs.

During the following months the Papal Nuncio — in accordance with instructions from the Vatican — protested many times and in every way against the measures directed against the Jews and the merciless way in which these measures were being put into effect.

On the 24th of March, as the representative of the Pope, the Nuncio recommended moderation in the measures planned against the Jews.

On the 30th of March he visited the foreign minister and pointed out how much inhumanity the regulations then in force contained.

On the 18th of April and several more times in the next few days he spoke personally to the prime minister and strove to make him see reason.

On the 24th of April the Nuncio sought out the special ambassador Arnóthy-Jungerth ... and informed him that "the Holy Father deeply regretted the events, because he could see from them that Hungary ... was taking the path that brought it into conflict with the teaching of the Gospel."

After several interviews and oral protests, made either by the Nuncio in person or by the secretary of the Nunciature, Gennaro Verolino, the Nunciature finally handed over on the 15th of May an energetic note of protest (reference number 1058/44)....

The note was handed to the prime minister and to the foreign minister; the foreign minister's copy was accompanied by a letter which ran (in part) as follows:

> The mere fact that human beings are being persecuted simply because of the race to which they belong is in itself a violation of the natural law. If God gave them life, no one is entitled to take it from them....

By the beginning of June the secretary of the Nunciature therefore visited ... the minister for home affairs, and in the course of a long discussion explained to him the standpoint of the Holy See.... A few days later the Nuncio and the secretary also visited the German Ambassador, Veensenmayer. They asked him to act as a moderating influence to secure the suspension of the deportations and to see that the position of the Jews in Hungary became more tolerable.

However, in his (Veensenmayer) telegram No. 301 of the 6th of July, he did report that Horthy had referred to the Pope's telegraphic intervention and told him that he considered it necessary to do something about the Jewish question.

On the 6th of July the Papal Nuncio, Rotta, again called on Döme Sztójay. He spoke at length about the Jewish question and declared that what was happening in this field in Hungary was disgusting ("abominable") and a disgrace ("déshonneur") to Hungary. Now they could see, he told the prime minister, where the application of the racial theory led.... He particularly criticized the methods of the gendarmerie as "crude and humiliating." Sztójay protested against all these observations.

The Nuncio held fast to his views. He pointed to the removal of old people, children and sick persons, who could not be workers.

The Pope's Open Telegram to Horthy and the Regent's Reply

The Nunciature sent detailed reports of all its interventions to the Holy See, as it was in duty bound to do so. When the Holy Father realized that the steps taken so far had been unsuccessful he decided to go to the extreme. On the 25th of July he sent Horthy an open telegram with a personal message which ran (in part) as follows: "We have been requested from several sides to do everything possible to ensure that the suffering which have had to be borne for so long by numerous unfortunate people in the bosom of this noble and chivalrous nation because of their nationality or racial origin shall not be prolonged and made worse.... Therefore, I am turning personally to your Excellency and I appeal to your noble feelings, in full confidence that your Excellency will do everything in your power to spare so many unfortunate people further suffering."

The Regent replied to the Holy Father's message on the 1st of July, likewise in an open telegram, which ran (in part) as follows: "...I beg you to be convinced that I am doing all in my power to see that the demands of Christian and humane principles are respected."

In connection with this telegram it must be emphasized that the general post office, where foreign telegrams and telephone calls came into the country, was under the control of the German censorship from the first minute of the German occupation.

There can be no doubt that both the papal telegram and the Regent's answer to it could not escape the attention of the German censors and that the latter naturally reported them at once to their superiors. The Nunciature, too, was aware of the activities of the German censorship and certainly brought them to the notice of the Vatican.

The Nunciature then sent the Regent copies of the most important notes and informed of the situation, even after the many representations made by the Nuncio.[3] In his telegram Pope Pius XII says that his intervention was requested "from several sides."

In May of that year two Czecho-Slovakian prisoners, Rudolph Wrba and Alfred Wetzler, succeeded in escaping. Their reliable and detailed report was taken down in Silin (Zsolna) and transmitted to the Nuncio in Bratislava. Even before that a copy was sent to Hungary.

At the same time the Papal Nuncio in Berne, Filippo Bernardini, was requested to pass on this "Auschwitz Deposition" to the Vatican. It was thus from Monsignor Bernardini that Pius XII first received authentic information. A copy of the Auschwitz statements was sent to the World Jewish Congress, which itself had not asked the Pope to intervene. Soon afterwards the "Auschwitz Deposition" also reached Stockholm, where the Stockholm nuncio was requested to arrange for similar intervention.

This is the explanation of the Pope's remark that he had been asked to intervene "from several sides."

The Pope's telegram of protest to Horthy was reported in the press all over the world.

Anthony Eden, the British Foreign Minister, also referred to it in the House of Commons. The Germans naturally also took notice of this speech....

Immediately after receiving the papal telegram Horthy summoned a meeting of the Crown Council the following day, the 26th of June, ... at which he announced the Pope's intervention and, basing his case expressly on this, called on the members of the government to put an end to the cruelties of the deportations. No decision was reached about actually stopping the deportation.

The upshot of this meeting of the Crown Council was naturally also made known to Veesenmayer, the German ambassador and plenipotentiary. Sztójay himself and other ministers, too, informed the Germans regularly of all important events.

Veesenmayer passed on Sztojay's news to Ribbentrop, from whom he swiftly received — on the 3rd of July — the following instructions (top secret):

> I beg you to inform the Hungarian government that it is not opportune to agree to the various foreign offers in favour of the Jews there. I beg you to ensure appropriate handling of the affair.
>
> Ribbentrop[4]

This is new and very important evidence that Hitler showed no respect at all for the intervention of the Pope and the nuncios on behalf of the Jews. This telegram alone refutes Hochhuth's thesis that Hitler would have listened to an appeal from the Pope. When the Pope's intervention was not proclaimed "urbi et orbi" and Hitler thereby branded a murderer, the Germans were content to instruct their representative in Hungary, Veesenmayer, to prevent Horthy, who was growing bolder and bolder, from complying with the Pope's wishes in his own sphere of influence.

The Germans never stopped pressing Horthy and the Hungarian government, requesting agreement to further deportations....

The Pope's protest occupied the Nazi government for a further period. For example, Goebbel's official bulletin, "Die Lage," mentions it again in the edition of 23 August (Docs. 5/6/7). Obviously the Nazis were not in the least frightened by it either earlier or later and carried on energetically demanding the deportations of the Jews!

In accordance with normal practice the papal telegram of protest was communicated to all nuncios throughout the world. The Apostolic Delegate in London brought it to the notice of the World Jewish Congress on the 15th of July in the following terms:

I have just received a telegram from the Holy See. The Holy Father
has made a personal appeal on behalf of your people to the Regent
of Hungary and he has been assured that the Regent is willing to
do everything possible to help.

The Death March to Hegyeshalom

From the beginning of November 1944 onwards thousands and thousands of unhappy people who had to wear the yellow star were robbed,
tortured and taken to the brick-works of Buda. The victims were robbed
and beaten up, mostly in the cellars of the Arrow Cross offices. Here those
courageous persons who claimed the protection of the neutral embassies
and protested against the treatment accorded them had their documents
torn from their hands.

At last came the departure, which has attained a melancholy fame as
the death-march to Hegyeshalom. More than twenty thousand persons, in
groups of a thousand were driven on to the road which runs through Györ
(Raab) to Vienna. They were forced to cover 15 to 20 miles every day on
foot — as far as Hegyeshalom, where they were taken over by SS officers.

This march was organized by Adolf Eichmann. His official purpose
was to procure labour for the erection, ordered by Hitler, of the so called
"East Wall." Eichmann wished to use this opportunity for the deportation
of the Budapest Jews....

Rescue of Many Jews by Blank Letters of Safe Conduct from the Vatican

An official of the International Red Cross, Sándor Ujvári, was sent to
the Nuncio, Angelo Rotta, with one particular suggestion, namely that the
Nuncio should issue uncompleted letters of safe conduct signed by himself in advance, in other words, blank letters.... Ujvári admitted openly
that they would work with forged identity-cards and baptismal certificates,
whereupon the Nuncio, according to Ujvári, made the following reply:
"What you are doing, my son, is pleasing to God and to Jesus, because
you are saving innocent people...."

The Bishop of Györ (Raab), Baron Vilmos Apor, who was aware of
these dreadful happenings, did all he could to help. He organized a collection and gave his clergy instructions to try everywhere to give help to the
deportees as they passed through.

The Nuncio's special group strove to hand out the medicines and food which they had brought with them to the deportees as they were driven on to Hegyeshalom.

This was not so easy. The Arrow Cross men and the gendarmes wanted at all costs to prevent the rescue team from helping the unhappy deportees and the helpers often got into dangerous situations. In the end efforts were made to arrest them, on the grounds that they were "hirelings of the Jews."

In Hegyeshalom town hall a Lazarist father called Köhler fought for the deportees. Inspired by his task, this priest devoted all is time and energy to rescuing people in the last stages of despair.

After discussing the situation with Father Köhler, the members of the Nunciature's "rescue commission" pushed bravely into the throng and picked out those who were most clearly incapable of bearing the deprivation and suffering any longer. For these people the blank letters of safe conduct were filled in.

But for the support of the Nuncio the rescue operation would never have reached such proportions as to cause alarm in the highest circles.

CHAPTER 9

To Halt the Dreadful Crime

by Patrick J. Gallo

On October 6, 1943, a tall SS captain came to Rome and immediately went to the Gestapo chief. The gangly, awkward 30-year-old man with the violent facial tic that shook his head from one side to the other was Theodore Dannecker. Dannecker was a ferocious anti–Semite who had impressed his superiors with the roundup of the Jews in Paris. His directive was to round up Rome's Jews and deport them to Auschwitz. Dannecker, the "Jewish" expert who was sent by Adolf Eichmann, presented Herbert Kappler, Rome's Gestapo chief, with a written directive and then stressed that the Judenrazzia was to be completely secret.

In the long list of charges leveled against Pius XII the revisionists (John Cornwell, James Carroll, Robert Katz, and Susan Zuccotti) charge that the Pope knew of the planned roundup beforehand, and did nothing to stop it or to prevent the deportation of the Jews to Auschwitz.[1] Katz explains: "Moreover, that the strategy of 'neutrality' lay behind his already controversial policy of silence in the face of the Holocaust. Now, in occupied Rome, the most crucial test of that silence was at hand. He had not protested the distant slaughter of Europe's Jews, but should the Nazis lay the terror at his front door, could he still ignore it?"[2]

Zuccotti and Katz are solidly in the prosecution's camp. Katz chooses to ignore the fact that the Third Reich felt that the Pope was definitely pro–Allied, that the Vatican provided the Allies with information regarding troop movements, and that it was in contact with the anti–Hitler conspirators within Germany. His thesis is that official neutrality provided Pius XII with the excuse to remain silent without taking into account that this was the historic official policy of the Vatican. Katz also fails to understand that despite the official stance the Pope could and did accomplish more under the cloak of official neutrality.

Katz's current volume and his earlier books are replete with errors of fact and interpretation. Katz also maintains that no work on the German occupation of Rome has been published in the English language in the last 20 years. That statement alone reveals his limited knowledge of the literature and his sloppy research. This author's work on this subject, *For Love and Country: The Italian Resistance,* was published in 2003 and he might well consult my notations for additional publications and new documentation.[3]

Zuccotti's text contains a litany of phrases such as "surely he knew," "it was not enough," "that was all," "it was very little," "lamentable," "he was wrong," "should have," phrases "that repeatedly raise questions about the author's intellectual, as well as moral, vantage point."[4] Zuccotti's relentless spin and omissions of evidence are evident throughout her book, *Under His Very Windows.*

Katz maintains that earlier books did not have the benefit of now complete and nuanced big picture.[5] He promises to present the big picture but instead provides a series of fuzzy snapshots. I have argued elsewhere the importance for historians to immerse themselves in the context of the times, to evaluate the testimonies on all sides, and to use all available documentation. The failure to do so by the revisionists, and in this case Katz and Zuccotti, is particularly striking.

On July 10, 1943, American and British forces landed in Sicily. Nine days later Hitler summoned Mussolini to meet with him in Feltre. During that morning Rome was under heavy bombardment. Fourteen hundred Romans were killed and another 6,000 were wounded. The ancient Basilica of San Lorenzo Fuori Le Mura sustained heavy damage. The San Lorenzo district was particularly hit hard. Pius XII went to San Lorenzo, "...plodded through the smoking rubble of charred houses where more than five hundred victims were strewn, while survivors struggled to touch his white cassock. Then a laborer spread his jacket on the cobblestones and the Pope knelt to pray."[6] Italians gathered to hear the Pope speak and to receive his blessing. The Pope blessed those who had gathered, the wounded, and the dead. He also arranged for direct relief to be distributed to those who were affected by the bombing. Prior to the July 10 bombing Pius XII and the Vatican had brought spiritual and material comfort on a number of occasions to the stricken. The Pope would become an important referent for all of the people in Rome and throughout Italy.

Sicily fell in 38 days and in the interim, events accelerated within Italy. On July 25, 1943, Victor Emmanuel III forced Mussolini to resign. The following day, the first German troop trains came through the Brenner pass, a strategic entry point that Pietro Badolglio, the new prime minister, should have secured. Shortly thereafter Hitler set in motion plans to occupy Italy, Rome, and the Vatican. Josef Goebbels's diary entry of July 26 recorded Hitler's state of mind and his plan: "I will go right into the Vatican. Do you think the Vatican disturbs me? We will take it immediately. It's all the same to me. That rabble is in there. We will get that bunch of swine out of there. Later we can make the apologies." What Hitler had in mind was the kidnapping of Pius XII. Nazi agents had already been spying on the Vatican. Hitler's mind-set was influenced by the collapse of the eastern front and his fascist ally to the south.[7]

The royal-military dictatorship that replaced the Fascist regime made no plans to extricate Italy from the war. Secret negotiations were initiated with the Americans throughout August of 1943. Rome was bombed again on August 12, and the Basilica of San Giovanni in Laterno barely escaped being damaged. Pius XII rushed to the scene to comfort the survivors, as he had done before. The Pope arranged for the distribution of aid and prayed for those who had perished. He returned to the Vatican in a blood-stained cassock.[8] German units were ordered to prepare to disarm Italian forces. The American generals knew that Italy's surrender was crucial to the success of an invasion of the mainland. On the other hand the Italians were certain they would face the wrath of the Germans as soon as the armistice was concluded. For their part the Italians wanted to know if the Allies could secure Rome and protect the Italians from the Germans.

During these talks the Allies presented a plan (Giant II) to drop airborne troops on Rome's airfields, to be coordinated with Italian forces.[9] The Italians thought an allied landing north of Rome was essential for the defense of the capital. Eisenhower had already set September 9 and Salerno as the date and place for the invasion; however, this information was withheld from the Italians. Italian officials in Rome were basing their policies on acting three days later than the Allies intended. They also expected the landing north of Rome with a very large force. General Maxwell Taylor concluded that Giant II had to be aborted. Thirty-two planes were already airborne but were called back.

A number of historians believe the Allies missed a great opportunity and Giant II could have succeeded. Had the invasion been at Civitavecchia, just 30 miles north of Rome, and had Giant II been implemented Rome would have been in Allied hands. According to Field Marshall Kesselring, "An air landing on Rome and a sea landing nearby, instead of Salerno, would have automatically caused us to evacuate all of the southern half of Italy."[10] Robert Katz deals with this in a superficial manner and does not link this with the fate of Rome's Jews.[11] Rome could have been seized and it would have saved Rome's Jews from the terrible fate that awaited them when the Germans occupied the city.[12]

On September 8, Allied and Italian radio broadcast the news of Italy's surrender. That same day 135 B-17s bombed Frascati, outside of Rome. The landing at Salerno on the following day proved to be of no help in the defense of Rome, which fell to the Germans on September 10.[13] The armed resistance began in Rome soon after the German occupation.

The day before the fall of Rome the royal family and their entourage, Pietro Badoglio and key military officers, fled Rome with the hope of reconstituting the government to the south. Not only did Badoglio fail to provide leadership and instructions to the Italian armed forces, he failed to issue orders as to who was to take charge of Rome and the armed forces.

Also on September 9, Israel Zolli, the chief rabbi of Rome, contacted Dante Almansi, the national president of the Union of Italian Jewish Communities, warning him that the Germans would be in Rome the next day. The rabbi proposed that the two of them should meet with Ugo Foà, the president of the Jewish community in Rome, and decide how they could best protect the Jews. Almansi rejected Zolli's plea as well as his warnings. Zolli had also urged Almansi to close down his office and to advise the Jews to leave their homes and go into hiding. Almansi argued that they should avoid panic and that Jewish life should continue uninterrupted.[14] For his part the 62-year-old Zolli and his family fled their home to a Catholic friend of theirs. Meanwhile 2,000 members of the dreaded SS and Gestapo entered Rome.

On September 11 German bombs landed near the University of Rome, Vatican City, and other parts of Rome. This was Germany's answer to the armistice. The Pope appealed to Harold H. Tittmann, urging him that Rome be declared an open city. Tittmann rejected this appeal, telling the pontiff, "The president has said ... the Germans alone would be responsible for any destruction wrought in Rome."[15] Pius XII held his ground and would continue to argue his position with the belligerents. Cornwell faults Pius XII with what he terms the obsessive concern with the bombing of Rome. Michael Phayer falsely claims the Pope did not condemn the German bombing of England during 1940 and 1941, but then spoke out against the bombing of civilians when the Allies had aerial superiority. Is Phayer insinuating that the Pope was not officially neutral and thus pro–German? The revisionists again fail to do their homework because the record shows that the Pope repeatedly condemned the bombing of civilian centers, starting in 1939, shortly after the 10-day bombing of Warsaw. He also condemned the bombing of Rotterdam, London, Coventry, and other civilian centers by both parties.

In Rome four German authorities converged. Ernst von Weizsäcker was the ambassador to the Holy See, and General Kurt Mälzer, the commandant of Rome, ran the city like a prison. SS Lieutenant Colonel Herbert Kappler, the head of the Gestapo-SD in Rome, was by temperament ruthless and sadistic. Waffen SS Colonel Eugen Dollman served as Heinrich Himmler's personal representative in Rome. Both Kappler and Dollman shared a mutual distrust and hatred of each other. Field Marshall Albert Kesselring was the commander in chief of the Wehrmacht in Italy, and he was completely loyal to Hitler. SS General Karl Wolff was the head of the SS in Italy and had been chief of Himmler's personal staff. By title he ranked second to Himmler in the SS. The SS had honorary members and Waffen (fighting members), the latter were crack assault or shock troops. The SD (Sicherheitsdienst), or intelligence branch of the SS, and the Gestapo to some extent had merged. All six of these men were ultimately responsible to Adolf Hitler. Four of them, including Kappler, Wolff, Mälzer, and Dollman, were also responsible to Heinrich Himmler. Weizsäcker detested Hitler and tried to encourage the British government to take a strong stand against him while officially urging moderation with the Führer.

Immediately after the fall of Rome the Germans unleashed their vengeance on Italian soldiers, who were immediately shot or rounded up and sent to Germany for forced labor. In Italy from 547,000 to 600,000 Italian soldiers and 25,000 officers were captured, deported to Germany and placed in camps. Outside of Italy another 450,000 were deported to Germany. German brutality was also unleashed against the Italian people. The roundup of Italian males was a routine occurrence. Edicts and proclamations were posted daily. Anyone possessing weapons or explosives, or who committed acts of violence against the Wehrmacht or harbored enemy forces, would be executed. The Germans posted a set of punishments for civilians:

> For harboring of escaped prisoners of war: death;
> For making contacts with them: hard labor for life;
> For printing or publishing or circulating news derogatory to
> The prestige of the Axis: Life imprisonment;
> For owning a wireless transmitter: death;
> For looting in evacuated areas: death;
> For desertion of work, or sabotage: death;
> For not fulfilling labor obligations: death;
> For taking photographs out of doors: hard labor for life.[16]

On the day that Rome fell, German troops were posted around Vatican City. On September 12 additional German paratroop units surrounded the Vatican and were stationed there around the clock.[17] The official explanation was that they were there to protect the Vatican from "irresponsible elements."[18] When Victor Klemperer learned that troops were positioned around the Vatican he recorded in his diary: "The Pope (Pacelli!) will regard himself as a prisoner."[19]

Robert Katz, Susan Zuccotti, and Michael Phayer briefly discuss a plan to kidnap Pius XII but do so in passing and attach no real importance to it. Nor do they place this plot on a chronological time line and connect it to the subsequent roundup of the Jews. David Kertzer avoids the subject and Daniel Jonah Goldhagen devotes a few inconsequential paragraphs to the subject.

Katz incorrectly states that the Vatican's anxiety with regard to the placement of troops around the Vatican quickly subsided because they were given strict orders "never to step across the boundary line." He points to the fact that motor vehicles with Vatican license plates could move freely, and that Vatican Radio "remained operational."[20] We have already discussed how dependent the Vatican was for its supplies from the outside, which could have been cut off at any moment. In addition we have discussed how the Nazis monitored all of the Vatican's communications, which necessitated the placement of a secret transmitter in the St. Callistus catacombs.

Katz's lapses in his research are evident in his failure to even mention Monsignor O'Flaherty, who operated a rescue network within Vatican City. O'Flaherty was able to obtain passes from Ernst von Weizsäcker's office signed by the ambassador to the Holy See. These passes allowed the Vatican's staff to move about Rome after curfew. The Vatican printing presses were able to reproduce these valued passes, providing them not only for the Vatican staff and clergy, but for others who were in hiding in Rome. In addition thousands of hunted men were supplied with Vatican identification cards. Harold Tittmann assisted the rescue of American prisoners of war and worked with Father Joseph McGeogh, who operated as his "leg man." Tittmann was also involved in the rescue of Jewish refugees working with Monsignor Herissé. Contrary to Katz's contention, the anxiety within the Vatican and diplomatic corps did not end in September of 1943. It persisted throughout the German occupation, at times to the point of paranoia. John Conway corrects Katz: "The pope and his officials were imprisoned within the Vatican boundaries, surrounded by German troops. Their offices were infiltrated with Nazi spies and their communications were censored. At any moment, they feared the pope might be carried off into captivity and exile. This claustrophobic nightmare was only in part moderated after Rome was liberated."[21]

Both Zuccotti and Katz place the plot to kidnap Pius XII in September of 1943, while in actuality it began much earlier. In April 1941 Ribbentrop had asked Count Galeazzo Ciano, his counterpart in Italy, to remove the Pope from Rome. This was in reaction to Pius XII's Christmas message that the Nazis correctly interpreted as directed at them. Ribbentrop also instructed Diego Von Bergen, then ambassador to the Holy See, to threaten the Pope with physical retaliation. At first Pius XII did not respond to Von Bergen's threat but then very calmly said, "he did not care what happened to him; that if there were a struggle between Church and state, the state would lose." Ciano recorded in his diary: "The Pope is even ready to be deported to a concentration camp but will do nothing against his conscience."[22] The Pope was informed that Ribbentrop and Ciano had talked about his removal from Rome and took the matter as a serious threat. Papal representatives were given special powers in the event of the Pope's abduction. Katz conveniently ignores these facts.

SS Chief Heinrich Himmler and Martin Bormann, the head of the Nazi Chancellery, either independently or together originated the concept before 1943. Bormann was violently opposed to Christianity. Both Himmler and Bormann felt that by seizing the archives they would have certain proof of the Vatican's role in Mussolini's ouster. With this proof in hand and Pius XII in custody, Hitler would be the true spiritual leader of German Catholics, and he would be one more step along the road of eliminating all religious competition.[23]

On September 11 Joseph Goebbels wrote in his diary, "The Vatican has inquired of our Ambassador [Weizsäcker] whether its rights would be safeguarded in the event of our occupying Rome. The Führer has sent an affirmative reply."[24] This was a cover because the Führer had other plans. Robert Katz falsely states that Hitler gave this assurance in October.[25] Katz does not consider that this was intended as a way of lulling the Vatican into a false sense of security, since the assurance was really given on September 11, the day before the abduction plan was formally initiated. Though it was not his intention, the decision to "guarantee the Vatican's rights however, was to allow it to use all of its properties to hide Jews and non–Jews."

On September 12, 1943, two days following the fall of Rome, Hitler summoned General Karl Wolff to Wolf's Lair (Wolfsschanze) in East Prussia. Wolff had established his headquarters in Fasano on Lake Garda. He had served on Himmler's personal staff as the liaison between him and Hitler. Wolff's other titles placed him second only to Himmler in the SS hierarchy. He had arranged for the deportation of 300,000 Jews to Treblinka.

The Nazis were facing defeat despite the occupation of Italy, a short-term solution at best. Hitler lacked the manpower or resources to contain his enemies. Wolff understood the reality of their situation, but the Führer expressed his full confidence in the ultimate victory of the Third Reich and put forth the theory that the Allied alliance would inevitably crumble. At this point in the war Hitler had probably returned to the use of amphetamines. His physician had taken him off the drugs after he diagnosed the Führer with progressive heart disease. This led to severe withdrawal symptoms and deep depression. He didn't exude the supreme confidence that he had often expressed, which led Leonard and Rennet Heston to conclude "...he had resumed taking amphetamines, or possibly cocaine, starting each day with an injection and maintaining an equilibrium that maximized optimism and confidence."[26]

We have already documented Hitler's and the Nazi radical elite's obsession with the Catholic Church and their need to destroy it.[27] Hitler was convinced that the Pope had been part of the plot to overthrow Mussolini. He also believed, correctly, that the Pope was pro–Allied and was plotting with the anti–Hitler conspirators in Germany. At the meeting, Wolff was ordered to devise a plan to raid the Vatican and to abduct the Pope and the Curia. The Vatican's archives and art treasures were also to be seized. At one point Hitler raged that he wanted the SS to level the Vatican with "blood and fire."[28] Hitler told Wolff, "Bring the Pope north so he does not fall into the hands of the Allies if possible, or depending on political and military developments to neutral Liechtenstein. How soon can you carry out this assignment?" According to Albrecht von Kessel, "If the Pope were to oppose this measure, there was even the possibility that he would be killed 'while trying to escape.'"[29] Wolff offered a four- to six-week time frame for the implementation of the mission, citing technical difficulties as an excuse for the delay. He also told Hitler that the abduction would incite all of the Italian people. Hitler thought that this was unacceptable, and ordered Wolff to report on his progress every two weeks. Privately, the blond SS chief thought the whole idea to be ridiculous. Before he left, the Führer admonished Wolff, "...because of its worldwide implications, I am personally conveying to you and you alone. I make it your duty to speak to no one about this matter without my concurrence. Himmler, whom I have just initiated, is the one exception."[30]

On the day of the Wolff-Hitler meeting, Operation Oak, the rescue of Benito Mussolini, was successfully completed. Mussolini was flown to Wolfsschanze and was told that he was to form a new Fascist regime. The Italian Social Republic (RSI), a German puppet regime, was established. Also on September 12 Himmler ordered SS Lieutenant Colonel Herbert Kappler to proceed with the deportation of the Jews of Rome.

There was, of course, historical precedent for a papal adduction. Napoleon had removed Pope Pius VI, who subsequently died in captivity. He repeated this in 1809 with the abduction of Pius VII. Goebbels had referred to raiding the Vatican and seizing the Pope in his diary entries of July 25–26 and July 27, 1943, two months prior to the Wolff-Hitler meeting. Katz makes no mention of this.[31] Goebbels also referred to the belief that Pius XII was fully involved in the overthrow of Mussolini's regime: "again and again reports reached us that the Pope is feverishly at work during this entire crisis."[32]

In August 1943, Admiral Wilhelm Canaris, head of the Abwehr, met with Cesare Amé, chief of military intelligence of the Italian Military High Command, and warned him of the Führer's intention to kidnap the Pope and the king of Italy.[33]

Despite his inner doubts, Wolff went ahead with the abduction plan based on Himmler's guidelines. Approximately two thousand handpicked men would descend on Rome and control all exits from Vatican City and the Vatican itself. Most of the men would be selected from South Tyrol, and would be capable of reading and writing Latin, Italian, Greek, French, and English. They were to proceed to arrest the Pope and the cardinals and take them immediately out of Rome to Munich and perhaps Liechtenstein. Speed was essential so that the Allies would not be able to provide any help to the Pope. Meanwhile some units would remain in Rome and were to search the Vatican for political refugees and Jews. A specialized unit would collect and pack for export documents, art treasures, and money. There was to be a thorough sacking of the Vatican.

Martin Bormann dispatched Ludwig Wemmer to Rome to assist in the papal abduction plot. He was also there to spy on Ambassador Ernst von Weizsäcker, to prevent him from leaking any hint of the abduction to Pius XII and to prevent him from conspiring with the pontiff. Weizsäcker detested Hitler and the Nazi leadership. Before the war he covertly tried to encourage Britain to take a strong stand against Hitler while officially urging moderation. In 1939 he covertly informed the British of a potential Nazi-Soviet pact. Weizsäcker pinned his hopes for some time on effectuating an end to the war. In his mind Pius XII was the principal instrumentality of accomplishing this objective.

Throughout September 1943 Pius took several precautions with reference to the threatened papal abduction. He had his personal archives sealed up in false floors, and had the documents of the Secretariat of State scattered in obscure corners of the Vatican. Papal representatives were given special powers if the Pope was removed. Allied diplomats living in Vatican City were told to be ready to leave, and began burning their official papers. Harold Tittmann records, "At a meeting on September 14, the Allied diplomats decided to follow the cardinal's advice [Maglione] by destroying all documents that might possibly be of use to the enemy. Osborne and I had already finished our burning, and the others completed theirs without exception by September 23, when I reported to the State Department." Meanwhile 10 Swiss guards with rifles were placed outside of the papal apartments on a 24-hour basis. The cardinals had already been told that a strike against the Vatican was likely and could occur at any time. The Pope made it abundantly clear that he did not intend to leave Rome and said, "Rumors of Nazi intentions to kidnap me are not flights of fancy. But must be taken seriously. However, I will never leave Rome or the Vatican unless chained and taken away by force."[34] Meanwhile all extraterritorial properties throughout Rome had a placard posted on their doors alerting all in both Italian and German: "Property of the Holy See."

Robert Katz's conclusion that the Vatican was safe from any German intrusion is preposterous. Prior to the Nazi occupation, Pius XII left the Vatican to go to other parts of Rome or to Castel Gandolfo, his summer residence, but he never left Vatican City once they occupied Rome. During the German occupation the papal guards were increased from 100 to 4,000 and were assigned to protect the Vatican and its extraterritorial properties. Many of the guards in Vatican City were armed with submachine guns.

Here again Katz's haphazard research is apparent. The Vatican, its personnel and all the clergy, as well as its extraterritorial institutions were not secure as long as the Germans occupied Rome and as long as the Fascist authorities remained on the scene. Six groups that specialized in the capture of Jews operated with the approval of the Germans and Italian Fascists. They cooperated with the Germans by raiding the Holy See's extraterritorial properties. The Germans could claim that these acts were committed under the auspices of an independent government. One of the most notorious groups, consisting of 65 men and 10 women, was led by the ruthless Pietro Koch. Koch's group specialized in the capture of partisans, Jews, and escaped prisoners of war. They received a bounty for every person turned over to the Germans. They brutally tortured their prisoners before handing them over to the Germans for payment. On December 21, 1943, Koch led a raid on the Lombardo Seminary at Piazza Maggiore. There he found 47 refugees and beat them on the spot.

Koch enlisted Pietro Caruso, the Fascist chief of police in Rome, in a plan to invade St. Paul's Outside of the Walls and the adjoining monastery. Koch suspected that Jews and Italian soldiers were hidden in the basilica. He was also certain that the priests within were working with the partisans.

Three hundred of Caruso's men surrounded the basilica and the lone Palatine guard was inadequate to stop them from gaining entrance. Sixty-seven Jews and Italian soldiers were discovered and carted off to prison. During the raid a papal representative arrived on the scene and confronted Caruso and Koch, informing them that this was extraterritorial property under the Vatican's jurisdiction. Hadn't they seen the placards indicating that this was off-limits? This was to no avail, and the Germans would claim they had no part in this affair. The Vatican lodged a vigorous protest with Ambassador Weizsäcker. Eitel Möllhausen, the acting head of the German Embassy, reminded Weizsäcker that a letter bore his signature that said religious institutions and property were to be protected and that this extended to the Italian police. It was obvious to the Vatican that if this continued those whom they hid throughout Rome were vulnerable.[35] The leadership of the Rome resistance movement was in hiding in the Seminario of St. John Lateran. With one raid the resistance would be crippled.

The Germans worked with Fascist authorities in other ways. In the fall of 1943 a German broadcast stated: "If in the heat of combat, bombs should fall on Vatican City, we should not be accused of wishing to murder the Pope, whereas in reality we would be defending Rome." The day following this broadcast a lone plane without markings flew over Vatican City several times and dropped four bombs. Roberto Farinacci, the former secretary of the Fascist Party, ordered the bombing that was instigated by the Germans.

There are two additional examples that Katz conveniently omits in attesting to the security of Vatican personnel and the extraterritorial properties. The first example was a plan devised by Herbert Kappler to have Monsignor Hugh O'Flaherty, organizer of the Vatican escape network, shot. Two of his Gestapo agents in plain clothes were to enter St. Peter's Basilica and follow O'Flaherty as he left Mass and crossed from Vatican territory. Kappler told his men, "When you get him away and into a street free him ... for a moment. I don't want to see him alive again.... He will be shot while escaping." O'Flaherty was actually warned by Weizsäcker that he would be arrested if he was found outside of Vatican property. The Gestapo agents joined the worshippers in St. Peter's as directed, but were surprised when two armed Swiss guards flanked the would-be assassins and escorted them out of Vatican City.[36]

The second example involves Father Anselmo Musters, a Dutch priest. The priest was a member of the O'Flaherty escape network. SS policemen in plain clothes followed Musters, ordering him to stop or he would be shot. Musters ignored the warning and took refuge in the sacristy of Santa Maria Maggiore Basilica. A squad of heavily armed SS surrounded the basilica and six of them entered and dragged the priest the full length of the church and down the steps. His head hit every step as they descended. The SS believed Musters to be a British officer in disguise. He was taken to the dreaded Via Tasso prison and escaped while en route to a German concentration camp.[37]

The abduction of Pius XII would certainly have stiffened and broadened the resistance movement in Italy and it would have received worldwide condemnation. It appears that Goebbels and Ribbentrop helped to calm things down. Goebbels wrote in his diary, "I regard such a measure as exceptionally unfortunate because of the effect our measures would have on the whole world opinion."[38] The Führer grew impatient with Wolff's delay in implementing his orders. In December of 1943 Wolff argued that the plan should be canceled because the abduction of the Pope would result in a popular insurrection throughout Italy. Such a development would damage the military effort, since Field Marshall Kesselring's troops would have to be deployed to contain the Italian people. Hitler agreed and put the plan on hold. However, throughout the occupation of Rome German military officials were convinced the order to occupy the Vatican could arrive at any time. Given Hitler's volatile nature this was a realistic expectation. Zuccotti is forced to admit that the Vatican was "completely vulnerable and without defenses," to an invasion. She then makes the astounding conclusion, "the truth of these rumors is less relevant here than the fact that the Vatican officials feared them." As we have demonstrated these were not just rumors; the planned abduction was grounded in fact and this has important contextual relevance to the events of 1943. However, Zuccotti and like-minded revisionists remain in denial.

Rome's Jews were lulled into a false sense of security. The leaders of the Jewish community did not heed Zolli's warnings. Many Jews even dismissed the Nazi massacre of Jews at Lago Maggiore. Italian Jews felt that the RSI would serve as a moderating force on the Germans. Adding to their cautious optimism was the fact that the Allies were not far from Rome. The Italians in Rome had little accurate information regarding the conduct of the war. On September 13, Rabbi Zolli met with Ugo Foà and urged him to close the temple and the offices of the Jewish community. This would send a strong signal to all Jews of the danger they faced. Foà rejected this advice.[39]

In mid–September Weizsäcker and Albrecht von Kessel, his embassy secretary, concluded that the SS was prepared to strike directly at the Vatican and at the Jews. Albrecht von Kessel proposed and Weizsäcker agreed that the leaders of the Jewish community should be told that their members should go into hiding or flee Rome. Von Kessel met with Alfred

Fahrener, the Swiss secretary general of the Institute for International Law, and told him that police measures were going to be taken against the Jews. Kessel urged that he warn the leaders of the Jewish community that their members should leave their homes immediately. Fahrener made contact with the leaders, who greeted the warning with skepticism and said that there was nothing to worry about. According to von Kessel, he and his superior were shocked that their warnings had not been taken seriously and "that leading Jews wanted to make an arrangement with the SS." To some extent even Fahrener felt that the "Germans were behaving correctly."[40]

Both Almansi and Foà had connections to officials in high places. Almansi had been vice-chief of police in Rome. Foà had joined the Fascist Party in the thirties and became a magistrate in the Fascist government. Both counted on their connections to protect the community. They thought that the Jews should go about their business as if things were normal. According to Miriam Zolli: "He [Israel Zolli] did not trust the SS and previously suggested to the leaders of the community that they burn the registers and make the people flee the city. They thought his fears exaggerated, and that he was a prophet of doom. This was in part because they received assurances from the chief of Rome's police, Carmine Senise." By 1943 there were 37,100 Italian and 8,100 foreign Jews in Italy.[41]

On September 25, Herbert Kappler received another communication from Himmler, directing him to proceed with the arrest and deportation of Jews "for liquidation."[42] In part Himmler's directive stated: "It is known that this nucleus of Jews has actively collaborated with the Badoglio movement and therefore its speedy removal will represent, among other things, a necessary security measure guaranteeing the indispensable tranquility in the immediate rear of the Southern front. The success of this undertaking is to be ensured by means of a surprise action...." The directive also stated, "The recent events impose a final solution to the Jewish questions in the territories occupied by the forces of the Reich." Kappler was told that all Jews regardless of age and sex were to be rounded up and deported for "liquidation."[43]

Kappler calculated that if the Jews were to learn of the impending roundup they would surely, "Seek sanctuary in the hundreds of churches, monasteries, and convents throughout the city."[44] The vast majority of Jews followed the example of their leaders and did not go into hiding. They returned to work while others kept their shops opened. This would make it much easier to implement the planned roundup.

The September 25 directive was intended only for Kappler's eyes, but General Rainer Stahel, the military commander of Rome, had read it as well. Contrary to the Zuccotti and Katz account, Stahel first approached Ernst Weizsäcker to enlist his aid to abort the deportations of the Jews. Weizsäcker then let it be known that he "unfortunately could not be helpful," at this time. General Stahel then went to Eitel Fredrich Möllhausen and showed him the directive, declaring he would have nothing to do with the matter. He left Möllhausen with the decision to abort the order. Möllhausen concluded that the order was politically and morally indefensible. He then decided that he would try to convince Kappler to see Field Marshal Kesselring, commander in chief of German armed forces in southern Italy. Möllhausen calculated that if Kesselring opposed Himmler's directive, Kappler would interpret his ruling as a basis for countermanding it.

On Sunday September 26, Kappler went to Kesselring's headquarters in Frascati. The field marshal turned down Kappler's request for a motorized unit to assist in the forthcoming operation. Kesselring argued that it was needed at the front and that the Jews could be used instead to complete defensive fortifications around Rome. Kappler returned and informed Möllhausen of Kesselring's position.[45]

Upon his return from Frascati, Kappler sent for Ugo Foà and Dante Almansi to meet with him at his office in the German embassy. Kappler was initially courteous with the two of them. A scar ran down one side of the black-booted Gestapo chief's face. Kappler was a "vicious Jew hater" and a dedicated Nazi. He was calm at the start of the meeting but then he said angrily, "We regard you only as Jews and as such our enemies ... we regard you as a distinct group, but not wholly apart from the worst of our enemies against whom we are fighting." Kappler proceeded to accuse the Jews of being disloyal. He asserted that the Jews changed their loyalties and nationality as the situation demanded. Kappler went on to blame the Jews for all wars. As his anger grew, the scar across his face reddened. He then got to the point and bellowed, "It is not your lives or the lives of your children that we will take if you fulfill our demands. Within 36 hours you will have to pay 50 kilograms of gold. If you pay, no harm will come to you. If not, 200 Jews will be arrested and deported to Germany...." The 110 pounds of gold would have to be delivered by noon Wednesday September 28. After a brief discussion the leaders sought to determine that if they could not meet the demand would his threat be directed only against those Jews who were not formally part of the community, including those who had converted to Catholicism or the offspring of mixed marriages. Kappler snapped, "I don't make any distinction in the community of disassociated, baptized or mixed, they are all the enemy." Kappler's extortion of gold was most likely an effort to mask his and Himmler's real objective. Kappler's gold extortion demand served to distract the Jews as well as to dry up the financial resources that individual Jews could use to escape Rome.[46]

Foà and Almansi immediately issued an appeal for the Jews to contribute any gold objects in their possession. Both leaders felt that the Germans only wanted their gold. On Monday they met with other members of the community, but not with Rabbi Zolli. It was decided that the council hall of the synagogue on Lungotevere Cenci would serve as the collection center. Most of the donations came from poor Jews since many who were rich had gone into hiding. Thus, the Jews came forward and also "a great many Catholics including not a few priests— a fact which made a deep impression on the Jewish leaders."[47]

What if they could not obtain the amount required from the community? Two separate overtures were made to the Vatican on that same Monday. The first involved two intermediaries, Adriano Ascarelli and Renzo Levi, who went to the monastery of the Sacred Heart. They returned and told everyone that if they could not meet Kappler's demand the Pope would provide the balance as a loan with no time requirement for repayment. Rabbi Zolli, unaware of the Ascarelli-Levi mission, decided to meet directly with two papal representatives in the Vatican. Zolli also received the assurance that the Vatican would place the amount that was lacking at the community's disposition. A cable from the Irish minister in Rome to the foreign office in Dublin reported Kappler's gold extortion demands. The cable, which was intercepted by "Magic," the United States code decryption device, went on to state that the Vatican offered to help meet the demand if the Jews could not raise the required amount of gold.

At this critical juncture a serious rift occurred when Foà decided to fire Rabbi Zolli. The rabbi had little faith that Kappler's demand for gold would save any Jews. Zolli once again told the leaders to urge the Jews to go into hiding. Rabbi Zolli had often reminded the members of the community that Foà and Almansi had been officials in the Fascist government. This only exacerbated the rift, which widened at this crucial moment.

In the final analysis the Vatican's offer was not necessary because the Jewish community met their goal, and they delivered the gold on September 28 to Kappler's headquarters at Via Tasso.[48] Zucccotti's account of Kappler's gold extortion is at best superficial.[49] She does not hold Foà or Almansi accountable at any point for the predicament of the Jewish community. After the delivery of the gold Foà and Alamansi continued to believe that the Germans would honor their word. One member of the community confronted Foà, "Mr. President, need we fear?" Foà replied, "The authorities have no interest against the people, and the people must be tranquil. When people are tranquil, the authorities do not intervene."[50]

The day after the gold had been delivered to Kappler, a cordon of SS surrounded the synagogue and blocked all of the exits. The Jewish community's administrative offices were located in the synagogue. They proceeded to search for incriminating documents perhaps tying Jewish leaders to "enemy agents." They carted off file cabinets, the minutes of meetings, and, most importantly, the records of contributors containing their names and addresses. These lists should have been destroyed. Foà's failure to do so was to have tragic consequences. The events of that day should have convinced Foà and Almansi to warn the community that they were in serious danger but they did not. For his part Zolli sought refuge in the Vatican.

On October 2 the Germans returned to the synagogue and then left. The Jews were relieved to learn that the Allies had entered Naples and as a result the small Neapolitan Jewish community was safe. "Almansi quietly changed apartments ... no one was told."[51] Several other prominent Jews left their homes without telling anyone. Foà did not change his residence and went about his business as usual.

SS Captain Theodore Dannecker came to Rome on October 6 and presented Kappler with a written order to carry out the Judenrazzia. He brought with him a team of 44 SS "reliable veterans of the Death's Head Corps. They were part of an experienced and ruthless Einsatgruppe. They would form the nucleus of his raiders, to be supported by the SS police or Wehrmacht troops—but not Italian."[52] Contrary to most accounts the Judenrazzia was to extend over a two-day period, not one day as most report.

Möllhausen learned of Dannecker's arrival and immediately cabled Ribbentrop arguing against the deportation of the Jews. He presented Field Marshal Kesselring's position that they be used for fortification work. Ribbentrop's reply came quickly and Möllhausen was told not to interfere in this matter. Möllhausen claims that he passed on Ribbentrop's reply to Weizsäcker, who according to Zuccotti and Katz informed the Vatican of the impending roundup. They provide no conclusive proof to back up their charge.

When Pius XII received an earlier assurance that the extraterritorial properties and enclaves would be off-limits he ordered them opened to give refuge to the Jews. Sir Martin Gilbert notes that before the roundup: "A few days earlier, Pope Pius XII had personally ordered the Vatican clergy to open the sanctuaries of Vatican City to all 'non Aryans' in need of refuge." Some 4,500 to 5,000 were hidden in the monasteries, churches, convents, and extraterritorial properties within Rome. Thousands were hidden in Castel Gandolfo, the papal summer residence. Fearing a German raid at any moment, no records were kept of those hidden within by these church institutions. The Germans were particularly ferocious in their reprisals against any member of the clergy whom they suspected of help-ing Jews and partisans. The Nazis executed 170 Italian priests.[53]

On October 7, 1943, the Germans rounded up 1,500 carabinieri and shipped them to Germany. This insured that they would not interfere in the forthcoming operation. Four days later two Gestapo officers came to the synagogue accompanied by SS troops. One of the officers was an expert on Semitic philology and browsed the libraries of the rabbinical college. They read and identified ancient texts, but before leaving they removed catalogues and indexes.

Six days later the Germans placed two freight railroad cars on trol-ley tracks, rolled them to the front door of the synagogue and began the removal of the contents of the libraries. While the Germans went about their assigned tasks, Foà and others gathered the temple's artifacts from the treasury and hid them. Some were hidden in the homes of Catholic neighbors. After several hours in the synagogue, the Germans left with nearly 200 years of Jewish history in Rome.

On the same day the Germans were raiding the synagogue the *New York Times* carried a report that Ambassador von Weizsäcker had advised the Pope to go to neutral Liechtenstein for his own protection. The news-paper report did not indicate that a plot was being hatched, but that Liecht-enstein would provide a safe haven for the Pope.[54] It is significant to note that the report had once piece of Hitler's abduction plan. Though Wolff had been ordered to keep the papal adduction plan a secret, word of it made its way to Weizsäcker. In a papal audience in October, Weizsäcker confirmed that such a plot existed when the Pope confronted him with what he knew about the matter. It cannot be determined how the *New York Times* obtained the Liechtenstein report.

On October 15 additional German parachute troops were added to the force "protecting" the Vatican. That evening German guards fired at the Vatican Palace when a light blinked at regular intervals. The guards thought that a secret signal was being sent to partisans, allied planes or whomever.[55]

Theodore Dannecker methodically compiled a comprehensive list of the names, addresses, and the residential patterns of the Jews. The Juden-razzia began at 5:30 A.M. on October 16, 1943. The Jews that lived in the old ghetto, Trastevere, and elsewhere were taken and placed in the Colle-gio Militare. The roundup tapered off at noon and ended around 2 P.M. It took 365 SS to seize 1,259 Jews, most of them women and children. A tenth of the 12,000 Roman Jews were arrested in nine hours. For every Jew caught in Dannecker's operation, 11 escaped to nearby homes, churches, monasteries, or convents. Martin Gilbert records that while the roundup was in progress, "A total of 477 Jews had been given shelter in the Vatican and its enclaves." Thousands of Jews fled to convents, monasteries, and churches for protection. The Italian clergy was at the center of the rescue efforts not only on the 16th but thereafter.[56] According to Princess Enza Pignatelli Aragona Cortes, Karl Gustav Wollenweber drove her to the Vatican while the roundup was in progress. Wollenweber, who was attached to Weiszäcker's staff, confirmed her account. Pignatelli told the Pope what she had seen. Pius XII was stunned but immediately called Cardinal Maglione.

While the roundup was in progress Cardinal Maglione called Weizsäcker to his office and told him, "It is painful for the Holy Father, painful beyond measure that in Rome itself and under the eyes of the father of us all so many people are made to suffer for the simple reason they are members of a particular race." The cardinal then stated that the Holy See would be forced to protest even if retribution followed. The Pope also sent his nephew, Carlo Pacelli, to Alois Hudal and "had him relay a message to General Rainer Stahel, military governor of Rome, that the deportation of Jews from the Holy City had to be stopped, if a protest from Pius XII was to be avoided."[57]

Weizsäcker had assigned Gerhard Gumpert to German military headquarters and placed him at General Stahel's service. Gumpert, who served as legation secretary at Villa Wolkonksy, was a good friend of both von Kessel and Weizsäcker. Shortly after the roundup began Gumpert phoned von Kessel. He devised a plan whereby an official of the Vatican would present a letter of protest to Stahel. Weizsäcker approved the idea and von Kessel went to Padre Pankratius Pfeiffer with the plan. Pfeiffer, known throughout Rome as Padre Pancrazio, had been selected by Pius XII to serve as his personal intermediary with German headquarters. Pfeiffer went to the Pope with the Weizsäcker-Gumpert plan. The Pope agreed to intervene on this basis. Alois Hudal, the rector of the Collegio dell' Anima in Rome, composed and signed the letter of protest. On the evening of October 16 Pfeiffer delivered Hudal's letter to Stahel.[58] The letter read in part:

> A high Vatican authority has told me that this that arrests of Jews of Italian nationality had begun. I strongly request that in the interest of peaceful relations between the Vatican and the German military authorities, which relations are due primarily to Your Excellency's political farsightedness and kindness will go down in the history of Rome, the order be given for these arrests to be stopped immediately both in Rome and its environs forthwith; I

fear otherwise the Pope will openly oppose it, thus providing anti–German conspirators with a weapon to use against us.[59]

The intent of the letter was to obtain Stahel's support and throw doubt in the minds of those in Berlin. Hudal had made it clear that all actions against the Jews were to be suspended. Weizsäcker sent a copy of Hudal's letter to Ribbentrop. Stahel forwarded a copy to his superiors and one to Himmler in a phonogram. To underscore the prospect of a papal protest he called for a halt to the roundup. "This kind of violent action against the Italian Jews disturbs my military plans to reinforce the German divisions far south of Rome, and can also create serious problems here in Rome."

On the morning of October 17 Weizsäcker reported to the foreign ministry and warned that a papal protest could be forthcoming. Himmler followed with the order to suspend all further arrests in Rome, which he said was, "out of consideration for the special character of Rome." Weizsäcker functioned in a dual role by outwardly conforming to Nazi policy in his official role as representative to the Holy See. At the same time he sought to sabotage and resist Nazi policies. Meanwhile, Cardinal Maglione and Padre Pfeiffer were only able to save 252 of the 1,259 Jews who were held in the Palazzo Salviati. Meanwhile, "Pius XII ordered the extra-territorial monasteries and convents in Rome to open their doors even wider to Jews seeking asylum, and allowed a number to take refuge in Vatican City itself." Adolf Eichmann wrote in his diary:

> The Church was vigorously protesting the arrest of Jews, requesting that such actions be interrupted immediately throughout Rome and its surroundings. To the contrary, the Pope would denounce it publicly.... The objections given and the excessive steps necessary to complete the implementation of the operation, resulted in a great part of Italian Jews being able to hide and escape capture.[60]

On Monday October 18, shortly after 2 P.M., 20 freight cars left Rome and headed for Auschwitz. By the evening of October 23, 800 Jews had been sent to the gas chambers. Of those deported as a result of the October 16 Judenrazzia only 16 survived.

Zuccotti, as we have noted, asserts that the Pope knew about the forthcoming deportations well in advance. She points to October 9 when Möllhausen informed Weizsäcker and says, "Those officials certainly notified the Pope." This is consistent with her firm conviction of the culpable silence and passivity of Pope Pius XII with regard to the Holocaust. Zuccotti's evidence rests solely on Robert Katz's 1987 interview with Möllhausen, who never stated that he had conclusive proof that this information was conveyed to the Vatican. In addition, in light of Weizsäcker's actions before and after the roundup it is equally unlikely that he passed this on to the Vatican. Albrecht von Kessel has gone on record stating that it was unclear if this information was ever handed over to Vatican officials. Zuccotti is forced to admit, "Others equally informed could have warned Jewish leaders directly. Möllhausen himself, or one of his assistants, could have done so." She proceeds to ask: Why didn't the Pope issue any warning to the Jews? "Did he disbelieve Möllhausen and others?" Zuccotti leaves the reader with the impression that Möllhausen went directly to the Pope with this information. Möllhausen did not do so, nor did Weizsäcker for that matter; both men had direct access to the Pope if they chose to go to him. Zuccotti appears to be unaware of the latest documentation that shows the OSS had information beforehand of the impending deportation.

All of the revisionists from Cornwell to Goldhagen take the Katz-Zuccotti account of the October 16 roundup. In essence they quote one another and recycle the same account.[61] What is their conclusion? The October 16 roundup was the pope's fault. What the revisionists don't tell their readers is that the original Judenrazzia was to extend over a two-day period; it was halted by papal intervention and confined to one day, allowing more Jews to be saved.

Zuccotti is obsessed with "her steady insistence that Pius XII is not to credited with any action, initiative, or interpretation unless she can find written documentary evidence for it which she generally does not find. Although she is willing to assert without any documentary evidence that the pope must 'certainly' have known in advance about the roundup of the Roman Jews."[62] She rejects all testimonies and eyewitness accounts that state otherwise and accepts those that only prove her case. Michael Tagliacozzo, one of Italy's leading historians and director of the Center of Studies on the Shoah and Resistance, offers just one of many examples of personal testimonies: "Monsignor Giovanni Butinelli, of the parish of the Transfiguration, told me that the Pontiff told him that parish priests were to be told to shelter Jews." Tagliacozzo was saved on October 16 along with other Jews who were hidden in St. John Lateran, which is the Pope's seat as the bishop of Rome.[63] Is it conceivable that the Vatican and the Pope were unaware of O'Flaherty's escape network and that he was just a loose cannon? How do the revisionists explain the cooperation and instruction given to that network by Vatican officials or the work of Father Benoît and the hundreds of other priests and nuns?

The thousands of Jews sheltered in church institutions were in constant fear that the Nazis would raid these sanctuaries. On October 25, 1943, the Vatican secretary of state wrote to all the superiors of religious orders urging then to help all refugees. That same day the Vatican distributed placards to be placed on all church institutions that declared that even under martial law they were immune from being searched. Wasn't this providing sanctuary to the Jews? Not according to Zuccotti: "That placard ... was distributed ... regardless of whether [an institution was] harboring illegal fugitives." Therefore according to Zuccotti's spin, its intent was "to affirm and protect the special prerogatives of the Church rather than to protect fugitives." Instead, according to her logic, rescue houses — and rescue houses only — should have received large "No Jews Hidden Here" placards! She then asserts that refugees were pressured by the Vatican to leave these properties after an SS raid. Then Zuccotti coyly admits, the departing refugees "could be and were, referred to convents and monasteries."

Zuccotti claims that Pius XII did not personally order the opening of church properties to shelter the Jews. She maintains that the clergy at their own initiative undertook all rescue activities. Zuccotti is obsessive in finding a written order from Pius XII, and rather than trying to account for the lack of one she cites this as proof of her assertion. Did the possible penetration of the Vatican have a bearing on the avoidance of documentation? Is it possible that the Vatican's communications were being intercepted and monitored by the Germans? Why did the Vatican resort to placing a transmitter in the catacombs? Pius XII often dealt with his aides such as Leiber, Pfeiffer, and Müller, on a one-to-one basis and transmitted directives verbally, not in writing. As we have noted earlier (chapter V) Pius XII dealt with the anti–Hitler conspirators' plan through intermediaries and did not commit his actions to paper nor did he inform his own secretary of state.

Zuccotti dismisses out of hand the personal testimonies even from such people as Archbishop Roncalli (John XIII), Giovanni Montini (Paul V), Cardinal Pietro Palazini, Cardinal Paolo Dezza, and Cardinal Pierre Gerlier, among many other church officials, who in sworn depositions have stated that they and those under their authority engaged in the rescue of Jews and said they did so on direct orders from Pius XII. She also dismisses the testimonies of those Jews who have testified that they were rescued and survived because of papal intervention. These are only a few examples but Zuccotti will not be deterred from her preconceived judgments that support her claim to be the bearer of "the terrible truth." Jenő Levai, one of the foremost Jewish scholars of the Holocaust has written that it was a "regrettable irony that one person in all of occupied Europe did more than anyone else to halt the dreadful crime and alleviate its consequences." Levai went on to state that the attacks on Pius XII by the revisionists are "demonstrably malicious and fabricated.... The archives of the Vatican, of diocesan authorities, of Ribbentrop's ministry, contain a whole series of protests—direct and indirect, diplomatic and public, secret and open. The nuncios and bishops of the Catholic Church intervened again and again on the instructions of the Pope." Sir Martin Gilbert has stated: "The Pope has also played a part ... in the rescue of three quarters of the Jews of Rome, at very short notice, when the SS came in and tried to round up [the Jews] ... at least 4,000 of whom were given shelter in the Vatican itself and other Catholic places ... the Catholic Church, on his direct authority, immediately dispersed as many Jews as they could." We have the testimony of two popes (John XXIII and Paul VI), five cardinals, and a number of bishops who said they acted on the direct instructions of Pius XII to save Jews.

Zucccotti lauds both Ugo Foà and Dante Almansi, who went into hiding after October 16, "but continued to work actively and courageously for their people throughout the occupation."[64] Zuccotti absolves these two men and other leaders who failed their community in their hour of need. There is no need to recount their roles since we have already documented their failures.[65] None of the revisionists mention or assess the fact that in the fall of 1943 the OSS was reviewing Nazi messages resulting from "Ultra" and the British code-breaking operation. The messages revealed that the Germans had planned to seize the Jews of Rome. They had the decrypted orders from Berlin to Kappler prior to the October roundup. Should the Allies have broadcast a warning to the Jews? Would this have affected a decision to hide or to flee the city? Would such a broadcast compromise their code-breaking operation? OSS documents reveal that United States officials were fully aware that the Vatican was hiding Jews.

The Pope's disapproval of the roundup was contained in the October 25, 1943, issue of the *L'Ossveratore Romano*. Those Romans reading between the lines understood that Pius XII wanted all Catholics to "do all they possibly can, to hide and save Jews." Weizsäcker misled his superiors in Berlin by toning down the position that the Pope had taken in the Hudal letter and in the October 25 article.

> Weizsäcker's communication was a deliberate misrepresentation in an effort to head off a more violent reaction from Berlin ... the Nazi government had reacted sharply to Papal statements even the very so-called mild or oblique criticism. The gist of Weizsäcker's-report was that the possibility of a papal condemnation had made the Germans discontinue the arrests and further deportations from Rome and in return the pope made no formal condemnation.... He had misled and calmed Berlin.[66]

The final solution was intended for all of Italy, not just Rome. Dannecker left Rome and extended the Judenrazzia to Florence and Milan and other Italian cities. In January 1944, Friedrich Bosshammer replaced Dannecker and continued with the ruthless roundup of Italian and foreign Jews. The Italian people and the clergy hid large numbers of Jews. By the end of the war a total of 6,816 foreign and Italian Jews had been deported. Eighty-five percent of the entire Jewish population in Italy had been saved.[67]

What accounts for Pius XII's actions? The Pope had an acute understanding of power — its possibilities and limitations. He had little use for plans, no matter how idealistic, if there was no power to effect their actualization or to ensure success. Though Hitler temporarily abandoned the plan to abduct the Pope in December 1943, he still toyed with the idea until the liberation of Rome. As Richard Breitiman discovered in recent OSS documents, "Hitler distrusted the Holy See because it hid Jews." The occupation of the Vatican was a constant threat. Ambassador Rudolf Rahn made several trips to Berlin in order to forestall any such attempt.

A strong public protest would not have halted the Final Solution in Italy or, for that matter, anywhere else. This view is shared by Dr. Marcus Mechior, the chief rabbi of Denmark, and by a number of diplomatic and military officials. If he broke the "official silence" there would have been even greater reprisals against Jews and Catholics. The Jews hidden in extraterritorial properties were at grave risk. Pius XII understood all too clearly the mindset and personalities of the Nazi radicals. He was guided by what had occurred in the Netherlands. In July 1942, the Catholic bishops joined with the Reformed Church of Holland and protested the deportation of Dutch Jews. At that time, they threatened that they would make their protest public if the deportations were not terminated. The Reformed Church accepted the German offer not to deport baptized Jews and did not go forward with a public protest. The bishops followed through with their threat and went public. The Catholic bishop of Utrecht released a strong letter to all Catholic churches protesting the deportations of the Jews. The Nazis reacted violently to this protest by increasing the deportations. In fact they revoked the exception that had been given to Jews who had been baptized and they too were arrested. One in this latter group was Edith Stein, a Jewish convert who had become a nun. She and her sister and 600 Catholic Jews were transported to Auschwitz, where they died. Though the Dutch Catholic Church publicly protested, about 110,000 Jews—79 percent of the entire Jewish population in the Netherlands— were deported to the death camps.

Likewise in July 1944, the Pope appealed to the Hungarian premier to stop the deportations of the Jews in that country. Jenö Levai, in his study of Hungarian Jewry, has shown that Hitler ignored this appeal and maintains that an open protest would have had no effect on the Nazis.[68] News of the deportations in Hungary produced international denunciation, which led to the protests from the Pope, the International Red Cross, and the United States and British governments. On July 7, 1944, Admiral Horthy, the Hungarian premier, ordered a halt to further deportations, thus saving almost 200,00 Jews in Budapest.

Before the October 16 roundup, the Pope wrote to Cardinal Konrad Preysing on April 30, 1943, with these instructions:

> We give to the pastors who are working on the local level the duty of determining if and to what degree the danger of reprisals and of various forms of oppression occasioned by Episcopal declarations — as well as perhaps other circumstances caused by the length and the mentality of the war — seem to advise caution, a majora mala vitanda [to avoid greater evil] despite alleged reasons urging the contrary.... In spite of good reasons for Open intervention, there are other equally good reasons for avoiding even greater evils by not interfering. Our experience in 1942 when we allowed the free publication of certain Pontifical documents ... justifies this attitude. This is one of the reasons why We ourselves are imposing limits to our declarations.[69]

The Pope was telling Preysing that local church officials could assess the situation since they were closest to the problem. According to Meir Michaelis, "In sum Pius XII was a diplomat who thought it his duty to keep silent ad majora mala vitanda [to avoid greater evils] ... if he was guilty of an error of judgment, it does not follow that his silence was due to unworthy motives; nor is it likely that in 1943 a 'flaming protest' would have saved the life of a single Jew." Jenö Levai has assembled impressive documentation that supports the view that the Vatican was in fact working to save Jews at the height of the Nazi Holocaust.[70]

Should Pius XII have resorted to the use of excommunication? Excommunicate whom? James Carroll states in hindsight that the pontiff should have excommunicated Hitler but does not pursue its effects on Hitler, Heydrich, Himmler, or Eichmann.[71] Would excommunication have deterred any of the Nazi elite? The Pope admitted: "I have often considered excommunication, to castigate in the eyes of the entire world the fearful crime of genocide. But after much praying and many tears, I realize that my condemnation would not only fail to help the Jews it might even worsen the situation.... No doubt a protest would have gained me the praise and respect of the civilized world, but it would have submitted the poor

Jews to an even worse persecution."[72] Jonathan Luxmoore and Jolanata Baubiuch point out that Pius XII's protest and excommunication did not help Catholics against the Communist regime after the war.[73] A papal protest or the threat of excommunication has to be placed within the context of the war against those who planned and implemented the Final Solution. Pius XII understood the mentality and mindset of these racial fanatics. The threat of a papal protest or excommunication would have little or no impact on stopping the deportations, and those revisionists who argue otherwise are merely speculating. Guenter Lewy, an early critic of Pius XII, conceded that the threat of excommunication would have had no effect on Hitler. José Sánchez comments on the limitation of excommunication:

> Another, and more serious form of protest would be to excommunicate persons guilty of crimes against the defenseless. But, excommunication in such broad terms in the circumstances of modern wars are difficult to administer.... Moreover, only in a totally Catholic society which accepts the concept of excommunication does such punishment work. Neither Germany nor any of the states under its control or allied with it was totally Catholic.... Years of clerical threats against anticlerical legislation in countries such as Italy had proved the futility of such threats. Furthermore, the coercive power of the modern secular state is great, and few believers can make the choice to obey the Church against the state.... Excommunication as used in the distant past was primarily against monarchs to bring them to heel, because excommunication of a ruler absolved his subjects from obeying him. Would such a threat work against a modern leader like Hitler...? Would German Catholics refuse to follow an excommunicate?[74]

All of the major Jewish communities of northern Italy remained under German subjugation until April 1945. On August 2, 1944, Heathcote Smith, representative to the Inter-Governmental Committee on Refugees, who was based in Rome, reported to Myron Taylor that the Pope, "will ... request the German Government to ... stay all further deportations and to communicate to His Holiness the probable number of Jews and others in North Italy still awaiting deportation, possibly Italian Jews. He will further suggest that the Axis should permit these people to reach some haven or refuge."[75] Berlin at first delayed then responded that the RSI was a sovereign government, and the problem of the Jews in Italy was within its jurisdiction. In short, Germany would not and could not interfere in the RSI's internal affairs. This was pure fiction, since the RSI was a German satellite, and the Reich had already disregarded the territorial integrity of many countries.

Harold Tittmann, chargé d'affaires of the United States to the Vatican during the war, states:

> Personally, I cannot help but feel that the Holy Father chose the better path by not speaking out and thereby saved many lives. Who can say what the Nazis would have done in their ruthless furor had they been further inflamed by public denunciations coming from the Holy See? To the wealth of information in the archives on similar information garnered by the Vatican over the centuries, and the help of expert historians using these archives, Pope Pius XII was able to add his unusual personal knowledge of the Nazi and German character. There was much inside information available to the Pontiff from secret sources. Who could have been more qualified than this Pope to decide under the circumstances?

Albrecht von Kessel maintains:

> All we could do ... was to warn the Vatican, the Curia, and the Pope against rash utterances and actions ... if Pius XII had assumed the martyr's crown even without achieving any practical results.... Perhaps such a politically senseless sacrifice might have sown seeds that would be yielding the rich harvest which we miss today. Pius XIII ... was a great personality. But I was convinced then and am still convinced today that he almost broke down under the conflicts of conscience ... he struggled to find the right answer, but who can now maintain that he found the wrong answer when he avoided the martyrdom? And who dares, if the answer was indeed the wrong one, to cast the first stone.[76]

Renzo De Felice concludes:

> ... Pius XII's fundamental principle was to save lives, that is to say, to give concrete aid to persecuted Jews without, however, permitting himself to adopt positions which were liable to exasperate the Nazis and end up by unleashing their bestiality.... The highly noteworthy and ever increasing help accorded, apart from individual Catholics, by all Catholic institutions and very numerous priests, to Jews hunted by the Germans after September 8, 1943, fully tallies with this line of the Holy See....[77]

CHAPTER 10

Zuccotti's Lack of Evidence

by Ronald Rychlak

In her book, *Under His Very Windows: The Vatican and the Holocaust in Italy*, Susan Zuccotti reports on research that took her into diocesan archives that others had not yet mined.[1] What she found — time and time again — was that Catholic clergy and laypersons defied the Nazis and the Fascists by providing food, clothing, and shelter to Jews and other refugees. As a result of these efforts, while approximately 80 percent of European Jews perished during World War II, 85 percent of Italian Jews survived Nazi occupation. Despite this evidence, Zuccotti gives little credit to the leader of the Catholic Church, Pope Pius XII.[2] In fact, she also faults Pope Pius XI.

In addition to the archives, Zuccotti reviewed the Vatican's published documents on the Holy See and the Second World War (Actes et Documents). In her introduction, she explained her belief that all of the good evidence about Pope Pius XII appears in these published documents.[3] Failing to find a written order from Pius among those documents, she assumed that he did not participate in rescue efforts. She thus rested her case on the absence of documents, not the existence of evidence. Nowhere in the book did she cite a single Italian priest, nun, or bishop who criticized Pope Pius XII by name for an alleged failure to assist Jews. In fact, despite her strained arguments, the actual evidence that Zuccotti has uncovered demonstrates the heroic leadership of the Nazi-era popes.

Zuccotti's argument that Pius XII was not supportive of rescue work is based upon the lack of an existing, written order from the Pope. She writes that if there were a papal order to help Jews, it "would almost certainly have been preserved by someone clever enough to understand that it might someday help the Pope's reputation." In making this argument, she severely underestimates the danger of life in a Nazi-controlled nation.

It was extremely dangerous to keep papers related to anti-Nazi efforts, and few who worked underground did. Italian Senator Adriano Ossicini, founder of the "Chrisitian Left" in Italy, was arrested by Mussolini's Fascists in 1943. Upon his release, he thanked Pius for his intervention with Mussolini and apologized to the Pope because one of the reasons for his arrest was that he was carrying a document that showed how strongly Pius opposed racial laws.[4]

Similarly, in the spring of 1940 there was a group of German generals who wanted to oust Hitler and make peace with the English. The negotiations took place with the Vatican's mediation and the direct cooperation of Pope Pius XII. However, there are no documents on this in the Vatican's published collection. The documents were found only in the British archives.[5] During Pius XII's pontificate, and particularly during the war, important matters were not kept on paper:

> For every form of communication used within the Roman Curia —
> Memo, letter, phone call, encyclical, Papal bull and smoke signal —
> the whispered word outranks them all. Millions of words are put
> to paper or sent over wire. But urgent and hot gossip go out by
> whisper, shot anywhere from two inches to one foot from the ear
> of the listener.[6]

Any Vatican papers related to the planned coup, like any relating to other anti-Nazi or rescue efforts, were undoubtedly destroyed. This direct involvement by the Pope in an attempted coup is far more telling than mere words ever could have been. Zuccotti, however, barely mentions it.[7]

Anyone who cared for the Pope would have destroyed written instructions for him. More importantly, no one at the time thought Pius XII's reputation would need to be protected.[8] In his earlier book, John Patrick Caroll-Abbing wrote of being inspired by the "luminous sublime example of the Holy Father."[9] He also reported assistance being given to Jews, and the Pope's order that "no one was to be refused shelter."[10] In fact, in an interview given shortly before his death, Carroll-Abbing said: "I can personally testify to you that the Pope gave me direct face-to-face verbal orders to rescue Jews." Asked about Zuccotti's thesis that the rescuers like him acted without papal involvement, he denied it and added:

> But it wasn't just me. It was also the people I worked with: Father
> Pfeiffer and Father Benoît and my assistant, Monsignor Vitucci,
> and Cardinal Dezza and Pallazzini, and of course Cardinals
> Maglione and Montini and Tardini. We didn't simply assume
> things; we acted on the direct orders of the Holy Father.[11]

Another author wrote: "Any direct personal order would have had to be kept very quiet to protect those who were actually sheltered." This other author is Zuccotti, in her 1987 book, *The Italians and the Holocaust*.[12]

Zuccotti's failure to understand what life was like under Nazi rule is revealed in two of her other arguments. In 1943, the Vatican and its properties in Rome would be regarded as extraterritorial, not part of German-occupied Italy. Signs were posted on the buildings to warn German soldiers that they should not search them.

Zuccotti complains that the Vatican put protection notices on all of its building, instead of just the 160 or so where refugees were hiding. From this she concludes that the church was protecting its property, not the refugees. She suggests that the warnings should have been put on only those churches, monasteries, and schools that contained Jews or other refugees. That, however, would have been nothing but a clear indication that refugees were hidden therein. If the Nazis had been provided with such information and they used it to deport more Jews, the Vatican would indeed have been responsible. Besides, by posting signs on every building, refugees were informed that these buildings were safe, and they could be entered on a moment's notice.

Zuccotti also treats her readers to an extended discussion of an order that went out to expel refugees from church properties. Only after a long, speculative discussion about pressures put on refugees to leave Vatican properties, does she explain that the order was not enforced within the Vatican and had virtually no impact anywhere (those affected by it were referred to other church properties).[13] It is obvious to anyone giving it a fair reading that the unenforced order was nothing more than a means of appearing to comply with Nazi orders while still protecting the Jews. Such deception was necessary at the time.

Pius used deception effectively. Zuccotti suggests that all or almost all effort was directed toward converted Jews, leaving unconverted Jews to fend for themselves. Joseph Lichten, director of the Inter-Cultural Affairs Department of the Anti-Defamation League of B'nai B'rith, recognized this argument as a red herring as early as 1987. "There is an element of naiveté" on the part of those who make such allegations, he wrote, because the Catholic Church issued tens of thousand of blank and forged baptismal certificates during the war."[14] With these documents, any Jewish person could avoid deportation by the Nazis as long as converted Jews were protected.

New documents discovered only since the Vatican opened archives in 2003 show that Pope Pius XI and Secretary of State Pacelli were concerned about Jewish victims, regardless of whether they were baptized.

Peter Godman, who reviewed these documents for his forthcoming book explains, "both Pius XI and his second-in-command (Pacelli) recognized the Church's duty to intervene in order to alleviate the suffering of German Jews. Not only Jews converted to Catholicism but all people — irrespective of race, rank, or religion — in need of Christian charity."[15] Godman further explains that by 1936 (well before the Kristallnacht pogrom) "the Vatican understood that Nazi treatment of the Jews violated 'the law of justice toward all races' which the Supreme Tribunal of the Roman Catholic Church regarded as a binding principle."[16]

Zuccoti claims that there was a great deal of criticism of Pius XII during and after the war. Almost no one else sees it that way. Peter Novick wrote: "As far as I know, the only comment on Pius's silence during the Holocaust that was made at the time of his death came from a writer for the French Communist newspaper *L'Humanité*."[17]

> ...The Communist official organ L'Humanité accused the late Pope of allowing his doctrinal condemnation of Marxist atheism "to be transformed into an arm of anti–Soviet policy in Europe and the world. "...The origin of the false accusation that Pope Pius XII had been silent concerning the Holocaust, was Soviet Russia. It was propaganda for Communist ends.[18]

The church used its legal standing to object when the Nazis brutalized Catholic Jews. When non-Catholics were brutalized it had only the moral authority, which was not respected by the Nazis. Pius and his church made the best arguments that were available and tried to have those arguments cover everyone. That was certainly a reasonable way to proceed and perhaps the best way to proceed during the period of Nazi terror.

In a case built not upon evidence, but upon a lack thereof, it is imperative to review all of the evidence that is known and to give it appropriate consideration. Time and again Zuccotti fails to do this, which results in the complete failure of her thesis.[19]

In arguing that Pius cannot be associated with Catholic rescue efforts because she cannot find existing written documents in the Pope's handwriting, Zuccotti is violating the Talmudic rule "not to have seen is not yet a proof."[20] This has also been called rule one of archaeology: "Absence of evidence is not evidence of absence."[21] The same maxim applies to legal analysis.[22] No honest historian should make the argument that Zuccotti makes.

One problem with her argument is that in order for it to be valid, the researcher must have scoured every potential source. Zuccotti assured her readers that she did just that, but subsequent discoveries have established that she did not find all the evidence.

In southern Italy, Giovanni Palatucci was known as the "Policeman Who Saved Thousands of Jews." He was named by Yad Vashem as a "Righteous Gentile" for helping save 5,000 Jewish lives.[23] Palatucci worked in close cooperation with his uncle, Giuseppe Maria Palatucci, bishop of Campagna. In 1940, Bishop Palatucci received two letters from the Vatican.

The first letter, sent to the bishop on October 2, 1940, reported that Pope Pius XII has agreed to grant to him a sum of 3,000 lire. The letter, which was signed by Cardinal Maglione, Pius XII's secretary of state, then stated, "The sum is preferably to be used to help those who suffer for reason of race." The choice of language at this point in history was a clear reference to Jews.

In a second letter, the future Pope Paul VII, Giovanni Battista Montini, then an official in the Vatican's Secretariat of State, notified Bishop Palatucci that Pope Pius XII had granted him the sum of 10,000 lire "to distribute in support of the interned Jews." These two letters are very clear, and they completely contradict Zuccotti's thesis.[24]

Between 1967 and 1974, 98 witnesses who knew Pope Pius XII personally gave sworn testimony, under oath, about his life. This evidence, unlike the published documents, focuses directly on Pope Pius XII's personal efforts on behalf of Jews and others. In other words, these transcripts contain exactly the type of evidence that Zuccotti was seeking, but she did not review them for her book.[25]

No less than 42 witnesses, including five cardinals, spoke directly of Pius XII's concern for and help given to Jewish people. Some witnesses spoke of papal orders to open buildings. Others testified that Pius knew of and approved of the sheltering of Jews in church buildings. The vice-director of the Vatican newspaper testified that Pius personally opened Vatican buildings, and he authorized convents and monasteries to welcome outsiders.

It may be understandable that a researcher would not consult the deposition transcripts. They have not been translated or widely published. One cannot, however, legitimately overlook this most relevant testimony and then turn around and build a case upon an alleged lack of evidence.

In a related matter, Zuccotti leads her readers to believe that none of the rescuers credited Pius for supporting their work. Again, she is mistaken. Pius has a long list of very credible witnesses on this matter, including two popes.

In 1955, a delegation from Israel approached Archbishop Montini, the future Pope Paul VI, to determine whether he would accept an award for his work on behalf of Jews during the war. He declined the honor: "All

I did was my duty," he said. "And besides I only acted upon orders from the Holy Father. Nobody deserves a medal for that."[26]

Angelo Roncalli (the future Pope John XXIII) made a similar statement when he was offered thanks for his efforts to save Jewish lives in Istanbul: "In all these painful matters I have referred to the Holy See and simply carried out the Pope's orders: first and foremost to save human lives."[27]

Cardinal Pietro Palazzini, then assistant vice-rector of the Seminario Romano, hid Italian Jews there in 1943 and 1944. Palazzini stressed that "the merit is entirely Pius XII's, who ordered us to do whatever we could to save Jews from persecution."[28]

Jewish historian Michael Tagliacozzo, head of the Center on Studies of the Shoah and Resistance in Italy, told about how he was rescued from the Nazis and hidden in the Pope's building in Vatican City. He also said that Pius himself ordered the opening of convents and that Pius was the only person to intervene when the Nazis rounded up Roman Jews on October 16, 1943.[29]

Hungarian rescuer Tibor Baranski was honored by Yad Vashem as a Righteous Gentile for his rescue work in Hungary during World War II. As executive secretary of the Jewish Protection Movement of the Holy See, Baranski officially saved 3,000 Jews. He worked closely with Angelo Rotta, papal nuncio in Hungary during the war (who was also recognized by Yad Vashem as a Righteous Gentile). Baranski makes clear that these lifesaving activities were not the lone actions of himself or Nuncio Rotta: "I was really acting in accordance with the orders of Pope Pius XII." Baranski reports that he personally saw at least two letters from Pius XII instructing Rotta to do his very best to protect Jews but to refrain from making statements that might provoke the Nazis.[30]

Another witness to Pius XII's orders to help Jews was Righteous Gentile Don Aldo Brunacci. Zuccotti spoke to him as part of her research. He told her that the Vatican sent a letter instructing Catholics to assist Jews during the Nazi occupation of Italy, but she discounted his testimony because he did not read the letter of instruction that came from the Vatican; it was read to him by Bishop Giuseppe Nicolini of Assisi. Brunacci, interviewed after Zuccotti's book was published, disputed her analysis: "...Signora Zuccotti ... cannot accept that this letter was sent out, and she has to invent the story that the bishop deceived me to explain it away. But the letter was sent out. I saw it with my own eyes, in my bishop's hands, as he read it to me. It was a letter from the Vatican asking the bishop to take measures to help protect the Jews. And we took the measures."[31] Italian Senator Adriano Ossicini and Sister Maria Ferdininda Corsetti, both told similar stories.[32]

Karl Otto Wolff, SS chief in Italy, testified to having received orders to invade the Vatican from Hitler himself.[33] The German ambassador to Italy and an aide to the German ambassador to the Holy See both confirmed that Hitler had such plans.[34] In fact, in 1944 before the Allies liberated Rome, Wolff approached Pius XII to discuss a possible peace treaty. At that time Wolff provided Pius with documents regarding Hitler's plans to invade the Vatican.[35]

When the Germans occupied Rome, they sought a ransom from Jewish leaders in exchange for the promise not to deport Jews. Unfortunately, the ransom merely bought a bit of time. Shortly thereafter, Colonel Kappler received an order to arrest the 8,000 who were living in the ghetto and send them to northern Italy, where they would face eventual extermination.[36]

Without written evidence to back up her suppositions, Zuccotti speculates that Pius knew of the roundup before it took place, and she argues that the Pope did virtually nothing while most of the captured Jews were deported.[37] The only recorded witness to the Pope's reaction upon learning of the roundup, however, tells a very different story. Italian Princess Enza Pignatelli went to the Pope to seek help. She reported that Pius was "furious" when he learned of the roundup.[38] "Let's go make a few phone calls," he said.[39]

Pius immediately filed a protest through Cardinal Secretary of State Maglione with the German ambassador, demanding that the Germans "stop these arrests at once."[40] The result, according to British records, was that "large numbers" of the Jews were released.[41] Most of this evidence was available to Zuccotti as she wrote her book, but she either ignored it or explained it away. It is harder, however, for her to dismiss the recently released memoirs of Adolf Eichmann. Eichmann wrote that the Vatican "vigorously protested the arrest of Jews, requesting the interruption of such action."[42]

Zuccotti admits that the raid on Roman Jews ended abruptly at 2 P.M. on October 16, 1943, after the Nazis seized about 1,200 of the originally intended 8,000 Jews. She refuses to acknowledge that the Vatican played any part in this decision. Indeed, she declares (p. 169) that there is: "no evidence of this position ... Himmler could not have learned of the possibility of a papal protest until ... the evening of October 16...."

According, however, to the sworn testimony given by German diplomat Gumpert for the 1948 trial of Baron von Weizsäcker, Pius XII's personal emissary, Father Pancratius Pfeiffer, delivered a letter of protest to General Rainer Stahel, the German army commander in Rome, "toward noon" on October 16.[43] According to recent testimony of an eyewitness,

Nikolaus Kunkel, a former German lieutenant who served as an assistant to General Stahel, the general contacted Himmler shortly after receiving this message.[44] There was therefore plenty of time — two full hours — for Stahel to contact Himmler and for Himmler to order Kappler to end the raids. Indeed, Bishop Alois Hudal reported that on October 17 he received a phone call from General Stahel who assured him that he had "referred the matter at once to the local Gestapo and Himmler." Himmler ordered that "in view of the special character of Rome these arrests were to be halted at once."[45]

Zuccotti's claim that "clearly, there were no plans for continuing the [roundup] action" by the Nazis is made without supporting documentation and is flatly contradicted by Jewish historian Michael Tagliacozzo.[46] At Eichmann's trial, Israeli Attorney General Gideon Hausner, in his opening statement, said "the Pope himself intervened personally in support of the Jews of Rome."[47] Documents introduced in that trial also show Vatican efforts to halt the arrests of Roman Jews.[48] In rejecting Eichmann's appeals, the Israeli Supreme Court noted the Pope's protest regarding the deportation of Hungarian Jews.[49] Such evidence overwhelms Zuccotti's argument regarding an alleged lack of papal involvement.[50]

Zuccotti also completely overlooks Vatican Radio. A 1941 profile of Pope Pius XII reported: "Rumors of accord with the Reich have repeatedly been smashed by new outbursts against Nazi persecution from the Vatican radio or the semi official Vatican newspaper, *L' Osservatore Romano*."[51] Zuccotti suggests that the only versions of Vatican Radio available to researchers today are the rebroadcasts of the BBC, which she says are unreliable. In this she is clearly wrong. Accounts exist in many languages and from many sources and they are consistent with the BBC transcripts.[52] The late Father Robert Graham described Vatican Radio's role in detail: "Research into the broadcasts during the crucial period 1940–1941 reveals a massive denunciation of persecutions and oppressions in Germany and in the German occupied territories...."[53]

Vatican Radio explicitly condemned "the immoral principles of Nazism" on October 15, 1940, and the "wickedness of Hitler" on March 30, 1941.[54] Broadcasts like this regularly prompted vigorous protests from Mussolini and the German ambassador to the Vatican.[55] Goebbels vowed to silence Vatican Radio, and it was a capital crime to listen to it in Nazi Germany.[56] The Nazis called it the "Voice of the Pope."[57] They were right. Pius XII was behind many of the anti-Nazi statements that were beamed around the world.[58]

Author Antonio Gasparri recounts several instances of Pius XII intervening in his personal capacity, through the Vatican secretariat, to save

Jews.[59] In one case, 1,000 German Jews wanted to emigrate to Brazil, and the pontiff paid out of his own pocket the $800 each needed for the trip. Regarding Zuccotti's central thesis that Catholic rescue activity took place without papal support, Gaspari expressly says, "This is a thesis that is impossible to defend."[60]

So how does Zuccotti argue that Pope Pius XII had no role in rescue efforts when so many witnesses testified that he did? The answer is that — time and time again — she discounts or dismisses testimony of people who were there.

On page 264 she discusses a bishop who claimed to have been holding a letter from Pius in his hands, but she suggests that the bishop falsified this claim because he "may have considered it useful to make his assistants believe that they were doing the Pope's work."

On page 193 Zuccotti suggests that nuns who credited the Pope for having ordered their convents opened to Jewish refugees were "eager that Pius XII receive credit for the work of their order." (She does, however, concede that Pius probably knew these nuns were sheltering Jews.)

On Page 143 she discusses a letter from A. L. Eastman, of the World Jewish Congress, thanking the Pope for helping free imprisoned Jews. Zuccotti, however, dismisses this testimony, saying, "Eastman must have known better."

On page 301 she discusses gratitude from Jewish people to the Pope following the war. She attributes their attitude to "benevolent ignorance."[61]

Zuccotti does not show a lack of papal involvement in rescue efforts. All she has shown is that she does not believe the limited amount of evidence that she has reviewed. Her failure to discuss Castel Gandolfo is worth particular note. Castel Gandolfo, the papal summer home, was used to shelter hundreds and perhaps thousands of Jews during the war. In fact, photos from Castel Gandolfo show people not only sleeping in the halls, but even up and down staircases.[62] The director of the papal villa at Castel Gandolfo during the Second World War, Emilio Bonomelli, wrote a book in 1953 in which he discussed the caring for Jews and other refugees during the war.[63] According to another account, about 3,000 Jews were sheltered there at one time.[64] The papal apartments were opened up to shelter pregnant women nearing the days of childbirth, and some 40 children were born there.[65]

A wartime U.S. intelligence document reported that the 'bombardment of Castel Gandolfo resulted in the injury of about 1,000 people and the death of about 300 more. The highness of the figure is due to the fact that the area was crammed with refugees.[66] Intelligence reports also indicate that Pius himself protested the bombing.[67]

This information — from U.S. archives — shows a great deal of papal involvement in Jewish rescue operations. No one but Pope Pius XII had the authority to open these buildings to outsiders. At least one witness (P. Guglielmo Heintrich) testified under oath that the orders came from the Pope.[68] Again, in a case built not on evidence, but on alleged lack of it, Zuccotti's failure to address this clear papal intervention is inexcusable.

In some instances, Zuccotti simply misconstrues the evidence. For instance, she gives considerable attention to a Jewish family's request for permission to stay in an Italian convent.[69] She discusses Montini's note of October 1, 1943, concerning this matter and his efforts on behalf of the Jewish family, but says nothing of Pius XII's own involvement, which is confirmed at the bottom of that note (Ex. Aud. Ssmi. 1.X.43)[70] In fact, below this indication that the matter was discussed with the Pope is a further notation: "Si veda se possible aiutarlo." The phrase means roughly "See if he or they can be helped." Following the notation of the meeting with the Pope, this is an indication of his permission for the convent to admit a male Jew, despite a normal prohibition on men in the convent. Again, one cannot overlook or fail to understand written exhibits like this and build a legitimate case arguing that there is a lack of evidence.

There are several quotations in Zuccotti's book that seem to have been truncated so as to eliminate any evidence that might show the Pope in a favorable light. For instance, she drops the first and last paragraph of Maglione's memo about meeting with Weizsäcker, thereby eliminating several express comments about Jews.[71] She also quotes Nuncio Valerio Valeri's report of August 7, 1942, to Maglione on the Vichy roundup of Jews (p. 103), but she deletes the crucial first line of Valeri's report where he mentions that he used his position to frequently intervene for Jews in the name of the Pope.[72]

Zuccotti also quotes Cardinal Tisserant, who in 1939 questioned whether Eugenio Pacelli was strong enough to be Pope (p. 61). She does not, however, mention that Tisserant later dramatically clarified his position and praised Pius XII's wartime conduct and his "invincible strength."[73]

The full facts are that Cardinal Tisserant wrote a private letter to Cardinal Emanuel Suhard, the archbishop of Paris, in 1940 in which he wrote, "I fear that history will reproach the Holy See for having followed a policy of comfort and convenience." In 1964, at the height of the controversy over *The Deputy* by those seeking to damage the reputation of the wartime pontiff, Tisserant immediately issued a statement unequivocally clarifying his remarks: "The pope's attitude was beyond discussion. My remarks did not involve his person, but certain members of the Curia...."[74] Robert Graham later interviewed Tisserant about the whole affair, and Tisserant admitted that he had written his 1940 letter in anger ("ad irato") and that was perhaps unfair to the people in the Curia whom he was criticizing. He also underscored that it was written in 1940 when he could not "have dealt with the tragedy which was yet to unfold."[75]

Similarly, Zuccotti tells us that the French priest-rescuer Father Pierre Marie-Benoît received virtually no support from Rome, but he is on record of saying just the opposite.[76] Among the published documents, Zuccotti encountered evidence that the Vatican provided money to help Marie-Benoît.[77] She says this is difficult to interpret and supposes that the amount must have been "exceedingly sparse."[78] However, Fernande Leboucher, who worked with Father Benoît as perhaps his closet collaborator, wrote a book about their rescue work. In fact, she called upon him for help in putting the book together.[79] Leboucher estimated that a total of some four million dollars was channeled from the Vatican to Marie-Benoît and his operation.[80]

The evidence is certainly not as Zuccotti would have us believe.

Zuccotti advances an argument that was made by Holocaust denier David Irving. He once offered a reward for anyone who could find a document from Hitler linking him to the extermination of Jews. Serious historians rightfully rejected his argument. A lack of existing written evidence is not sufficient to prove that Hitler lacked responsibility for the Holocaust. Everyone who arrested a Jew, informed on those who sheltered refugees, or helped run a concentration camp knew that Hitler approved of this work.[81]

Unfortunately, like Irving, she rejects overwhelming evidence simply because she could not find the written order. Zuccotti's theory is bad logic for a Holocaust denier and it is bad logic for her. Actually, the Nazis noted the coordinated efforts of Catholic officials in different areas and speculated that they were acting pursuant to a large plan.

When evidence of papal support for the Jews is offered, she demands documentation, but when people say bad things about the pope, she is all too eager to accept it. For instance, in her conclusion (p. 311), Zuccotti repeats an old canard. It is said the Pope was unwilling to speak out against the Nazis because this would create a conflict of conscience for the German soldiers. There is no document to back this up, and no one who has spent any time trying to know Pope Pius XII can believe that this was a primary influence upon him.[82]

Similarly, Zuccotti is all too quick to accept Robert Katz's claim that Pius knew of the October 16, 1943, roundup before it took place.[83] Katz claimed to have talked to a German diplomat (Eitel Möllhausen) who claimed to have told the German ambassador to the Holy See, Baron Ernst von Weizsäcker, about the roundup in advance. Katz then suggests that

Weizsäcker told Vatican officials and they must have told the Pope. Weizsäcker never mentioned it in his memoirs, and Italian princess Pignatelli, who told the Pope about the roundup after it took place, reports that he was shocked when she so informed him.[84]

In other words, all of the best evidence suggests that the Pope was not warned about this roundup. Nevertheless, without written evidence, Zuccotti is quick to accept the theory that Pius could have warned the people, but failed to do so. In her 1986 book, *The Italians and the Holocaust*, Zuccotti acknowledged that the story about Weizsäcker alerting the Pope might be "untrue."[85] In a footnote, she even noted that Weizsäcker's secretary, Albrecht von Kessel, did not know whether the Pope had been informed and that Weizsäcker never mentioned the incident in his memoirs.[86] In *Under His Very Windows*, however, all qualifications and cautionary notes have vanished and Pius XII's foreknowledge is presented as fact. This inconsistent way of measuring evidence is completely unfair and has led Zuccotti to a very unjust result.

Zuccotti has labeled certain authors as being biased, particularly the Jewish scholars Joseph Lichten and Pinchas Lapide. On pages 303–04 she asserts, without evidence, that both men deliberately sacrificed the truth to foster good relations between Israel and the Holy See. On page 67, she asserts that Lichten "wrote without evidence" that the Vatican offered Jewish scholars teaching posts to protect them from Fascist persecution. In fact, his matte was well publicized at the time.[87]

Lapide, a journalist and diplomatic official of the Israeli government, knew both Pope Pius XI and Pope Pius XII. He was the author of at least nine books, and he wrote extensively on religious affairs for journals throughout the world.

Lapide is perhaps best known for the estimate, following months of research at the Yad Vashem archives, that Pius saved 700,000 to 860,000 Jews. Actually, Lapide attributed his number to "The Holy See, the nuncios, and the entire Catholic Church.[88] Seen that way, and recognizing that he was an Israeli diplomat, who spent months researching the issue at Yad Vashem archives, it is not surprising that his figures have become so widely accepted, despite protestations from Zuccotti to the contrary.

Many who try to document historical attitudes cite the *New York Times*. Zuccotti has challenged this as a biased source.[89] While I seriously question her claim about the *New York Times*, positive evaluations of Pius can be found in many other sources.[90]

Zuccotti reveals her bias and refusal to acknowledge beneficial actions for Jews that were taken by the Pope or others from the very start of her book. For instance, she notes that many authors who disagree with her have translated the Italian word stripe, which was used in several official pronouncements including Pius XII's 1942 Christmas statement, as meaning race. On page two of her book, however, Zuccottti explains that stripe does not exactly correlate with the English word race, but should be understood as meaning descent. Her suggestion is that when the Pope or various Church officials used the word stripe, they were not saying race and therefore were not defending the Jewish people.[91]

Cassell's Italian Dictionary (1979) gives the following definition of the Italian stripe: "stock, race, descent, lineage, extraction." ("Race" precedes "descent." The Zanichelli New College Italian and English Dictionary gives: "stock, race, family, lineage, ancestry." ("Descent" is not given as an option.)[92] Of greatest importance, the Nuovo Dizionario della Lingua Italiana published in Milan in 1924 (therefore best reflecting Italian usage when Pius XII was a young man) gives schiatta ("race") as an exact synonym of stripe. It even provides as an illustration of the word's meaning the phrase "la stripe semitica" ("the Semitic race").[93] Stripe was well known as a reference to people of Jewish heritage, and Zuccotti's efforts to dismiss numerous war-time statements with this analysis should be rejected.

One of Zuccotti's most inexplicable charges is that Pius never condemned anti-Semitism during or after the war. He did so many times. After the liberation of Rome, Pius made one of his most fervent pleas for tolerance. "For centuries," he said, referring to the Jews, "they have been unjustly treated and despised ... St. Paul tells us that the Jews are our brothers. Instead of being as strangers they should be welcomed as friends."[94]

In a major address to the College of Cardinals on June 1, 1945, after the surrender of Germany, Pius XII spoke of the background and impact of the anti–Nazi encyclical Mit brennender Sorge.[95] Later that year he expressed his concern over the terrible suffering of the Jews as he addressed a group of Jewish refugees on "the brotherhood of man."[96] When he expanded the College of Cardinals to 70 from 38 he said, "This Church does not belong to one race or to one nation, but to all peoples."[97]

On August 3, 1946, Pius said the following to a delegation of Palestinian Arabs: "We condemn all recourse to force and violence from wherever it may come, as We have condemned on several occasions in the past the persecutions which a fanatical anti–Semitism unleashed against the Jewish people."[98]

On August 16, 1943, Time magazine wrote: "...it is scarcely deniable that the Church Apostolic, through the encyclicals and other Papal pronouncements, has been fighting totalitarianism more knowingly, devoutly, and authoritatively, and for a longer time, than any other organized power."

Following the liberation of Rome, Herbert L. Mathews on October 15, 1944, wrote in the *New York Times*: "under the Pope's direction the Holy See did an exemplary job of sheltering and championing the victims of the Nazi-Fascist regime."

Even Zuccotti agrees that Catholic rescuers "invariably believed that they were acting according to the pope's will."[99] He encouraged, inspired, and authorized them to do what they could to help, but in conformity with the Catholic social doctrines of subsidiarity and solidarity, details were usually left to be decided at the local level.[100] That is not to say however, that Pius was uninvolved in rescue efforts. In August 1944 Pultizer-winning *New York Times* reporter Anne O'Harre McCormick wrote from liberated Rome that Pius enjoyed an "enhanced reputation because during the Nazi occupation he made hiding someone 'on the run' the thing to do" and had given Jews "first priority." Harold Tittmann revealed that Pius XII maintained "personal and secret accounts," as well as special accounts in New York banks. Archbishop Spellman administered the special accounts but knew nothing of the Pope's secret account. These accounts were to be "used exclusively for charitable purposes" and supports the 1966 testimony of Father Robert Leiber that "The Pope sided very unequivocally with the Jews at the time. He spent his entire private fortune on their behalf."[101]

At the end of the day, we have Zuccotti on one side arguing that there is no evidence of papal involvement. On the other side we have a mountain of testimony from rescuers, victims, Germans, Jews, priests, nuns, the *New York Times* (and other papers), seven cardinals, and two popes. We also now have the written, archival confirmation of papal involvement in the rescue of Jews that Zuccotti thought did not exist. In other words, the evidence all weighs in favor of Pope Pius XII. To ignore that evidence is to deny history. With this subject, that is a very dangerous thing to do.[102]

Chapter 11

Via Rasella and the Ardeatine Massacre

by Patrick J. Gallo

After September 1943 the resistance movement increased its activity within Rome and Lazio.[1] On January 22, 1944, Allied forces landed on the shores of Anzio, a small port 30 miles south of Rome. "Shingle" was an improvised operation put together in about three weeks. One part of the invasion plan was to seize the Alban Hills and move tanks into Rome. If they moved quickly and shed their characteristic caution, they would have found little opposition between Anzio and Rome. This was entirely possible since a jeep patrol was sent into the Alban Hills and was able to drive undetected to the outskirts of Rome.[2] In turn a German officer left Rome to inspect the Alban route and found no Allied troops were on the way despite the fact the path was wide open for a mortal assault on the city. The Germans had initially anticipated that an amphibious landing north of Rome was the likely landing site. Field Marshal Kesselring soon realized: "...as I traversed the front I had the confident feeling that the Allies had missed a uniquely favorable chance of capturing Rome ... I was certain that time was our ally."[3]

The Allies, with characteristic caution, failed to take Albano, which would have cut off all German forces and rail traffic to the south. Once again an opportunity was lost that would have led to the liberation of Rome and would have saved thousands of people from Nazi brutality. Robert Katz fails to connect this with the fate of the Romans, the Jews, and the refugees who crowded into Rome.

Hitler dispatched an emissary with orders to round up 300,000 Romans for forced labor in Germany. Ambassador Weizsäcker and Kesselring intervened and were able to stop this insane order. Three thousand men were already on their way before the operation was terminated.[4] Meanwhile Allied bombing raids outside of Rome continued. OSS agent Peter Tompkins in Rome felt that the bombing raids were ineffective:

> ... they miss the target so often, and sometimes by quite a distance, and the people of Rome are angry, and it creates a wave of hatred and bad feeling which isn't worth candle especially as I don't believe that the rail yards and stations of Rome are an effective target, then they could interrupt traffic more effectively, and with no loss of civilian lives (and prestige) outside the city.[5]

In February the monastery at Monte Cassino had been bombed, and the following month the town of Cassino was reduced to rubble. Within the monastery there were approximately two thousand refugees and only a few hundred survived. Cardinal Maglione met with Harold Tittmann and told him that the abbey held no Germans. He added that the attack was a colossal blunder "...a piece of gross stupidity." The bombing of Monte Cassino produced nothing of military value. Nazi diplomats were instructed by the German Foreign Office to exploit the destruction of the Monte Cassino monastery. The bombings of the monastery and Rome affected Italian public opinion and produced an unnecessary obstacle for the partisans to get popular support. Zuccotti, Cornwell, and Katz maintain that the Pope failed to condemn attacks on civilian centers other than Rome. They also conveniently omit the fact that others within Italy and specifically within Rome who were not part of the Vatican also objected to the bombing of the city.

Robert Katz's three books on the events during this period contain significant errors of fact and interpretation. This is evident in his treatment of the Via Rasella attack and the Ardeatine massacre.

Throughout March of 1944 the partisans conducted a total of 75 separate operations against the Nazi and Fascist targets within Rome. Katz seems to downplay the role and effectiveness of the partisans. Kesselring was gravely concerned about maintaining control of Rome and the morale of his troops in the city. In his opinion the situation in Rome was so volatile that it was ready to explode.[6]

On March 12, 1944, thousands of Romans made their way to Vatican City and streamed into St. Peter's Square, which was unable to hold the multitude. This Sunday marked the 187th day of the German occupation, and it was also the fifth anniversary of the coronation of Pope Pius XII. The Pope appeared on the balcony with just one guard and one secretary. The people, as if electrified, came to life and chanted as if on cue, in a rhythmic cadence, "Pace Papa! Viva Il Papa! Viva Il Papa!" again and again throughout the Pope's remarks.[7] During his address the Pope was inter-rupted by cheering and loud applause. It didn't matter if some of what he said was not fully understood or heard by some in the crowd. Katz, in his effort to prosecute Pius XII, does not capture for his readers the love the people had for the Pope. He had been an important symbol of hope, peace, and compassion. Pius XII embodied the deepest longings for peace throughout the world.[8]

The success of partisan warfare depends on popular support. Some historians have contended that the partisans were isolated from the masses and lacked popular support. Mario Fiorentini, a partisan who belonged to a GAP unit in Rome, corrects this assumption: "This was not the case. The vast majority was with us. Some were too afraid and hungry. But the major-ity were not indifferent and supported us." Carla Capponi, another active partisan, reinforced Fiorentini's sentiments, "What helped was the popu-lar support of the people and the solidarity we had with them."[9]

The intense and vicious antipartisan campaign of the Nazis attests to the effectiveness of partisan warfare. Their goal was to drive a wedge between the resistance and the people.[10] To this end the Nazis created the SS Bozen, which consisted of three battalions, and placed them under the command of SS General Karl Wolff. The SS Bozen were recruited from the South Tyrol and had the reputation for being notoriously cruel. The 1st Battalion was sent to Istria for antipartisan duty. In February of 1944, the 2nd Battalion was dispatched to Belluno for the same purpose. This unit engaged in a number of massacres of women and children, and burned villages in reprisal for partisan attacks.

On February 12, 1944, the Polizeiregiment Bozen's 3rd Battalion, con-sisting of 500 men, was transferred to Rome. The 3rd Battalion, under the command of Hellmuth Dobbrick, was made up of the 9th, 10th, and 11th companies, which were attached as SS police to Kappler. In reality they were under the command of General Kurt Mälzer. To keep up the fiction that Rome was an open city, the Germans decided to use SS police instead of soldiers in central Rome. Actually the 3rd Battalion's mission was to rein-force the repression of the Romans, to destroy popular support for the par-tisans, and to crack down on them as well. The 9th Company was deployed south of Rome while the 10th was assigned to combat the partisans in the Castelli Romani. In all of Lazio there were 40 separate partisan forma-tions.[11]

The 11th Company, under the command of Lieutenant Wolgast, marched daily in the center of Rome as they returned to their barracks. The column of 160 men were armed and escorted by a small contingent armed with submachine guns. An armored truck with a machine gun mounted on a platform trailed behind them. The entire formation extended 100 yards, the length of a football field.

In early March of 1944 an idea had germinated in the mind of Mario Fiorentini. The 11th Company followed the same path at irregular intervals. The column passed Via Tritone onto Via Del Traforo and made a left onto Via Rasella. Robert Katz incorrectly states they marched at regular intervals at the same times and days of the week. They didn't march up Via Rasella on March 18, 19, and 21 but did so on March 20 and 22.[12] The partisans kept the SS unit under careful and constant surveillance. Fiorentini calculated that they would return on March 23 and this became the target date for a three-pronged operation.

Fiorentini's plan was to attack the unit as it ascended the narrow Via Rasella. This particular attack was to involve all four squads of GAP centrali, a total of 17 partisans. The attack was carefully planned and involved the placement of a bomb in a street cleaner's cart that would explode in the center of the formation. Some partisans would also attack the column with mortar shells while others would fire on the Germans, blocking any retreat. Each of them had assigned tasks and escape routes.[13]

There were two additional components to the partisans' plan. In addition to the attack on the 3rd Battalion, the second prong of the plan was to attack the Fascist parade that was to culminate at the Teatro Adriano. The Fascists, who were losing all touch with reality, were to mark the 25th anniversary of the founding of the Fascist movement by staging the parade. The third part of the overall plan was to attack the dreaded Via Tasso Gestapo prison. Eitel Möllhausen and Eugen Dollman felt the parade to be "a useless provocation," and they were successful in urging Mälzer to shift the Fascist ceremonies to the more secure Ministry of Corporations.

On March 23, late in the afternoon, Major Helmuth Dobbrick, the commander of the 3rd Battalion, decided to return the 11th Company to their barracks and take the usual route. Many in the company thought this to be too dangerous, to cross in the center of Rome so late in the afternoon. At 3:45 they turned the corner and marched up Via Rasella.[14] Then came the shattering roar of the explosion, which could be heard throughout the center of Rome. Four mortar shells were hurled at the rear of the column. The Germans at the end of the column who attempted to escape were prevented from doing so by the partisans, who opened fire. The attack ended within minutes, leaving 26 Germans dead and another 60 seriously wounded. The remaining members of the Bozen unit were dazed and began firing their weapons wildly in all directions, at open windows and at empty shadows of buildings.[15]

General Mälzer was drunk when he arrived at Via Rasella and began to bark out irrational orders. He wanted to blow up the entire area and wanted to shoot all the civilians who were emptied from the buildings on Via Rasella. Dollman and Möllhausen arrived on the scene and tried to calm Mälzer. Then Kappler arrived and urged Mälzer to return to his headquarters and Kappler took charge. According to Mario Fiorentini: "The Germans at first were sure that this was a military attack. The scope and precision of the Via Rasella attack seemed to be evidence of this."[16]

When Himmler was informed of the attack he ordered what amounted to the deportation of every adult male in Rome. Hitler, when told of the attack, flew into an immediate rage and said he wanted that section of Rome where the attack took place to be blown up, with the people as well. In addition he wanted 30 to 50 Romans executed for every dead German. Eventually a 10 to one ratio was ordered.[17] Later, on March 23, Bruno Cassinelli, a lawyer who defended may of those held in the Nazi prisons, went to Padre Pfeiffer: "I found him immediately and he told me that he had already the task of discerning the moods of the German military commanders and to bring them to a state of calm and understanding...."[18]

Could the reprisals have been avoided? Katz, in his effort to condemn Pius XII at every turn, contends that he could have prevented the reprisals and chose not to do so. He rests his argument on the supposed meeting between Eugen Dollman, head of the SS in Rome, and Padre Pankratius (Pancrazio) Pfeiffer at 6 P.M., which he claims would have prevented the reprisals. Pfeiffer was the abbot-general of the Salvatorian order, "a most loyal and capable man of the cloth who carried out the Holy Father's and the Holy See's admirable work in defense of Rome and Italy."[19] He was the Pope's liaison with the Germans in Rome and reported directly to Pope Pius XII.

Robert Katz contends that Dollman met with Pfeiffer and informed him about the reprisals. This is not true; Pfeiffer already knew of the Via Rasella attack. The purpose of Dollman's alleged meeting was to prevent the reprisals.

According to Katz, Dollman then told Pfeiffer that since he had been away from headquarters: "He did not know at this point in time to what extent the military men would go." If Pfeiffer would pass this on to the Pope it could prevent or delay reprisals since it was "the Germans who were crying for vengeance." Pfeiffer supposedly agreed. Katz proceeds to contend that Pfeiffer endorsed Dollman's alleged plan. The families of the 11th Company who had been killed would be bought to Rome and would participate in a funeral procession, "the victims' widows and children walking behind the coffins." Extra editions of the newspapers would publish pictures of the "victims," and Kesselring and Pius XII would give commemorative speeches. The bells of the churches would ring out during the procession. Kesselring would speak on the radio and announce that the Romans would have to pay families a monetary compensation for those who had been lost.[20]

The Pope then would "speak from the Loggia of San Pietro urging the people of Rome to take advantage of the German act of clemency and to exhort them not to commit any further acts of violence." According to Katz, when Dollman completed the exposition of his plan, Padre Pfeiffer supposedly exclaimed: "Excellent! I am certain that the Vatican will be very enthusiastic. And I will go at once to inform them." Katz erroneously claims that late on the afternoon of the 24th while the massacres were well under way, Dollman telephoned Padre Pfeiffer. Dollman supposedly told Pfeiffer that the plan they had discussed to avoid the reprisals was overtaken by the executions which were in progress. According to Katz, Pfeiffer "could only offer his regrets that he had failed to enlist the Vatican in the scheme."[21] Buried in Katz's notes is the fact that after the war Dollman denied ever making the phone call.[22]

Katz asserts the Pope never responded to Dollman's initiative. Since Katz is predisposed to criticize Pius XII at every turn, he accepts Dollman's version and further charges that the Pope could have prevented the reprisals and chose not to do so. Katz's version of events is filled with many inaccuracies that are accepted uncritically, especially by revisionists. In fact it is beyond fantasy to have expected the Pope and Kesselring to cooperate in such a scheme.

Upon hearing of the reprisals, Monsignor Nasalli Rocca went to Regina Coeli prison at 11 P.M. and remained there until 7 o'clock the morning of March 25. Rocca testified: "I went to the Pontiff Pius XII (we were alone) and I related to him what I had heard in the prison. The Holy Father raised both hands, burying his head in a gesture of astonishment and pain, and he cried, 'What are you telling me? It cannot be, I cannot believe it'— in a way that made it clear to me that he knew nothing about what had happened." Rocca said the Pope, in anguish, repeated this statement several times. Katz fails to complete Rocca's statement in which he said, "Later I went to Monsignor Tardini, Acting Secretary of State, who seemed to be in the dark about everything that happened; frantically he charged me with the task of finding out certain details but I was unable to do so...."[23]

Katz's account of the Dollman-Pfeiffer meeting was fabricated by Dollman. The meeting never took place. Dollman wrote this account after the war when Pfeiffer was dead and Dollman could not be contradicted. Pfeiffer died in a motorcycle accident in 1945. Dollman was Himmler's personal representative in Rome. Dollman wrote this in his own self-defense, given his role in the reprisals and his ties to the SS and the Nazi regime. This is borne out by his actions at the end of the war in his attempt to save himself from prosecution. Katz never mentions any of this and accepts this version uncritically in his determined effort to prosecute Pius XII.[24]

First, Kesselring would not and could not have consented to any part of this scheme. Contrary to Katz's account, Kesselring was not in Rome, but in Liguria on March 23, returning to his headquarters on March 25. Katz would be better served to have used the latest findings on Kesselring's whereabouts during this period instead of repeating the same factual errors he made nearly 37 years ago.[25] He might at least have consulted and evaluated Cassio Brauchle's account.

Secondly, Pfeiffer would not have agreed to such a far-fetched plan and he certainly would not have said it was "excellent." Pfeiffer was an intelligent and talented mediator who knew the mentality of the Germans and who understood his role as the pope's emissary, whom he served so well. Pfeiffer and Pius XII's main objective was to save lives. Pfeiffer and the pontiff would have thought this plan was preposterous.[26]

After the war Cassio Brauchle, a Salvatorian brother and doorkeeper of the Salvatorian house, said under oath before an Italian court: "I do not recall Colonel Dollman's coming on the evening of March 23, 1944. I don't think it could have happened, unless Dollman had telephoned Father Pancrazio (Pfeiffer) beforehand and was personally received by him that night. A possibility that I would exclude since Father never opened the gate himself...."[27] Dollman's supposed plan lacks all credibility. It is naïve at best to think such a plan, if true, would have satisfied Hitler, who wanted to execute 30 to 50 Romans for every dead German and blow up an entire section of Rome. Would it have satisfied Himmler, who wanted the immediate deportation of every adult Roman male?[28] Does Katz really believe that this so-called plan could really have forestalled the horrible reprisals? Why Katz continues to cling to this fabrication and a plan that is so fantastic can only be explained by his deep-seated biases.

Since he received the Via Rasella report Hitler was impatient, and kept intensifying the pressure for the immediate execution of his order. That order, it must be emphasized, was to be implemented in 24 hours. According to Eitel Möllhausen, "There is absolutely no doubt in my mind that no power on earth, naturally with the exception of Hitler himself, could have prevented the ... tragedy considering the atmosphere created after the attack.[29]

Katz's treatment of the October 16, 1943, roundup of Jews in Rome, the Via Rasella attack, and the Ardeatine massacre in all of his volumes are prime examples of Gresham's law of bad history driving out accurate history. Katz or any responsible authors of history should be conversant with the latest research on their subject and they have the obligation to subject their use of eyewitness testimony to rigorous standards of authenticity and credibility. If Katz is pinning his accusation on this fabricated meeting between Dollman and Pfeiffer he should inform his readers about Dollman's character.

Eugen Dollman was the head of the SS in Rome. He was directly responsible to both Hitler and Himmler. Dollman once said of the Führer: "For me Hitler was a great personality, he was a great man." In October 1943, he personally congratulated Mussolini on his return to power though the RSI was a puppet of the regime he served. Dollman was a confidant of Eva Braun and he quickly became a favorite of the Fuhrer. He was devious, cunning, and conspiratorial. He hated Herbert Kappler and General Mälzer, and they him.

At the end of the war Italian authorities issued arrest warrants for Karl Wolff and Eugen Dollman, while the Italian military tribunal filed formal charges contending that they were key participants in the mass executions of civilians. Wolff had been responsible for the deportation of thousands of Jews to Treblinka. A public trial in Italy would have produced either a death sentence or, minimally, life imprisonment. Wolff was accorded protection by OSS Chief Allen Dulles for his role in ending the war in Italy. Dollman was afforded de facto protection by the United States government. He was able to enter Switzerland and worked for the CIA and British intelligence. He was never tried for his role in the extermination of Italian Jews or the Ardeatine massacre. Padre Pfeiffer was tragically killed in 1945 and kept no known records of his work on behalf of Pius XII.[30]

There are other aspects of Katz's accounts that are inaccurate. Though they don't bear directly on Pius XII they do bring into question the reliability of much of what Katz has written on the subject. Let me cite two examples. The first is Kesselring's whereabouts. Katz places him on March 23 at the front and returned to his headquarters at 7 P.M. This is impossible since he had been in Liguria since March 22 and didn't return to his headquarters until the afternoon of the 25th. What was he doing in Liguria? Kesselring feared that with German reserves deployed across Italy the Allies might make a landing on the coast of Tuscany behind the German 10th and 14th armies. He was there to plan for this eventuality. While there an OSS (U.S. army volunteers) team had landed on the Ligurian coast. Their mission, code-named the Ginny mission, was to demolish two railroad tunnel exits.

On March 24 the Germans captured all 15 uniformed men. Before Kesselring left for his headquarters at Monte Soratte on the 25th, General

Anton Dostler ordered the execution of the uniformed soldiers. "It is hardly likely that Kesselring was in La Spezia on March 24 and did not know about the captured Ginny Mission commandos. It is equally unlikely that Dostler would have ordered their executions without first receiving confirmation from Kesselring."[31]

Katz places Dollman at a meeting in Rome on the 23rd and says he remained in the city the following day. Dollman, in an interview in 1975, said he was not in Rome on March 24. Katz is either unaware or chooses to ignore any of these findings and contradictions.

On the evening of March 23 Kappler knew that the number of those he had in prison fell below the number of candidates for death. This was underscored when the German death toll climbed to 32, which meant he would have to draw up a list of 320. SS General Wilhelm Harster told him to include as many Jews as he could to reach the set quota.

Neither Kappler nor any other German in authority made an effort to arrest the partisans. In addition no appeal was made for those responsible for the attack to turn themselves in. Neither Kesselring in Liguria nor Kappler in Rome made any inquiry if any of those responsible for the attack had been found. Mario Fiorentini maintains:

> The Nazis wanted to teach the people of Rome a lesson rather than capturing the partisans. They wanted to turn the people against the partisans. This was not an attack on a single individual or a few of them. This was an attack on an entire formation. Nothing like this had occurred at this point in all of Europe. They could not tolerate this. Our objective was to demonstrate that the Wehrmacht was not invincible. That the Nazis were the padrone of Rome. This is why the action was prepared so carefully and why it had three stages.
>
> They [Germans] were going to move quickly and secretly. If they published an appeal before the reprisal the people of Rome would know what was going to happen. It may have led to a popular uprising. Thousands of Romans would have stepped forward and turned themselves in claiming that they were the ones who took part in the attack. Certainly those who had fathers, sons, husbands in prison would have done so.[32]

There were two additional reasons why they never made such an appeal. This would, in fact, have given Mussolini or the Pope the time and the opportunity to intervene. Then there was the real possibility that the partisans would attack the location where the reprisals were being conducted. They would have been on the lookout to determine where it was to be carried out. Kappler admitted this at his trial after the war. Rosario

Bentivegna, who was a key player in the Via Rasella attack, underscored the fact that no announcement of a reprisal had been made and denied that it could have been prevented had the partisans turned themselves in to the Germans. "That night by 11:30 P.M. the Germans had finalized the reprisals, the type and their application. Less than 24 hours from the time of the attack the first trucks were leaving with their victims...."[33]

On the morning of March 24 one more German from the 11th Company had died. The number to be executed would have to rise to 330 because the number killed at Via Rasella now stood at 33. It was also decided that the caves on Via Ardeatina between the catacombs of Santa Domitilla and Santa Callixtus would be used for the execution and the disposal of the bodies. To hide any trace of the executions all entrances to the caves would be sealed off when all 330 had been killed. Padre Pfeiffer left for Via Tasso on the morning of March 24 to see Herbert Kappler but the Gestapo chief was not there.[34]

Between 1:30 and 2 P.M. German trucks left the various prisons and made their way to the Ardeatine caves. The trucks backed up facing the entrance. Then the back doors were flung open and the prisoners descended with their hands tied behind them. They were taken into the caves in groups of five and brutally executed. During the next five and a half hours the process would be repeated again and again as one truck after another arrived. There were the groans of anguish among some of the victims; some prayed or remained silent, while still others cried out patriotic slogans. The mounds of corpses would reach five feet.[35]

According to Robert Katz, Padre Pfeiffer was "instructed by the Holy See not to go to the German offices that day."[36] This is not true, because sometime between 5 and 6 P.M. Pfeiffer returned to Via Tasso for a second time and encountered Erich Priebke, who had returned briefly from the caves. From the expression on his face and the silence within the prison he knew for sure something terrible had happened somewhere in Rome. Preibke would confirm that Padre Pfeiffer had come twice to the prison on that day. "At about 6 P.M. Father Pfeiffer came to my office who all day had been looking for Kappler, without being able to find him. When the good father saw my state of mind, he understood that there was no longer any hope."[37]

Meanwhile back at the caves Kappler was intent on meeting the 8 P.M. deadline set by Hitler. When the final bullet entered the head of the last victim, a total of 335 men were dead. By error an additional five prisoners had been added to the list so that instead of the 330 there were 335 victims who were massacred. They had been killed like cattle, given no opportunity to communicate with their families or accorded any religious comfort. By 8 P.M. the final victim was dead and the German engineers sealed the caves. After the liberation of Rome only 323 victims would be identified. Their ages ranged from 14 to 75 and included 253 Catholics and 77 Jews.[38]

Robert Katz, among other revisionists, charges that Pius XII could and should have prevented the reprisals. The rapidity and secrecy of the reprisals precluded this. Many of the partisans who took part in these events whom this author interviewed agreed that neither the Pope nor anyone else could have forestalled the reprisals. There is nothing in the Vatican archives about any warning or plan to abort the reprisals. The whole of Rome anticipated some sort of violent German response but nobody knew it would be so violent and so swift. Mario Fiorentini has stated: "When GAP began its war against the Germans, for me there was always the possibility of reprisals. It was like the sword of Damocles. We completed many actions before March 23 and the rule of ten to one was never applied."[39] Fiorentini went on to assert: "It seems to me that the Nazis wanted to teach the people a lesson. The reprisals were automatic and set in motion. There was no way to stop or contradict them."[40] The trucks left Via Tasso at 2 P.M. and Regina Coeli prison between 4:30 and 5 P.M. The first executions began at 2:30 and they were over by 8 P.M. Neither the Pope nor any other Italian could know the scope and extent of the German response. No one could have prevented the Ardeatine massacre except Hitler himself.

There is a close correlation between the intensity of the partisan operations in Rome and Lazio, the state of the German mind within Rome and Berlin, and the decision to put an end to the resistance within the eternal city. Though the Germans had conducted reprisals outside of Rome, the Via Rasella attack was the most audacious attack conducted within a large city perhaps in all of Europe.

Katz is in error in stating that the purpose of the Via Rasella attack was to spark a popular insurrection. This is patently absurd and the partisans understood that a popular insurrection would have caused a bloodbath. The purpose of the reprisals was to drive a wedge between the people and the partisans.[41] Contrary to Katz's assertion, this too failed. The Ardeatine massacre was a major psychological error on the part of the Germans. The barbarity of the reprisal rallied the uncommitted behind the partisans and the Allies. Moreover, contrary to Katz's contention, the Via Rasella attack achieved an important strategic objective in that the Germans never marched in the center of Rome again. They were forced to the peripheral areas, where they were easier targets for Allied planes. Katz is also in error in stating that the partisans were intimidated from continuing their attacks within Rome. In April the attacks on the Germans continued right up to the liberation of Rome. Some members of the GAP units were assigned to join the partisans in Lazio.[42] After the liberation of Rome many of the partisans joined their countrymen in central and northern Italy.

CHAPTER 12

Constantine's Sword:
A Review Article[1]

by Robert P. Lockwood

A former Paulist priest and award winning novelist ... Carroll's stated goal is to present "a history" of the Church and the Jews to show the linkage between Catholic belief and the Nazi Holocaust.[1] "Auschwitz, when seen in the links of causality, reveals that hatred of Jews has been no incidental anomaly but a central action of Christian history, reaching to the core of Christian character. Jew hatred's perversion of the Gospel message launched a history, in other words, that achieved its climax in the Holocaust an epiphany presented so starkly it cannot be denied...."[2]

Carroll's thesis is that anti–Semitism, which resulted in the Holocaust, is central to Catholic theology and derived from the earliest Christian expressions of belief, namely the Gospel accounts themselves. He concludes his book with a call for a third Vatican Council to make a series of changes in basic Catholic belief that he envisions purging the church from this alleged fundamental anti–Semitism.... However, it is important to understand fundamentally, Carroll's purpose is to put forth a laundry list of liberal bromides for church reform and uses the context of anti–Semitism and the Holocaust to push this reform agenda.

Carroll's book is described as "history" of the church and the Jews, but it is a great deal more personal rumination than serious historical, or theological study.... Carroll's main sources from a Catholic perspective are disaffected theologians such as Hans Kung, Rosemary Radford Ruether, or scriptural scholars like John Dominic Crossan from the Jesus Seminar. His primary source on the church and the Holocaust, for example, is Cornwell's *Hitler's Pope*, which he acknowledges in a footnote to have been "controversial," but that he had reviewed it favorably. His knowledge —

162

or at least citation — of mainstream Catholic sources is limited to nonexistent.

Constantine's Sword, at the risk of understatement, is a lengthy book that actually argues little but avers grandly. Like Gary Wills in *Papal Sin*, Carroll makes assertions, backs them up when possible with the assertions of others who share those assertions, then considers the matter settled.[3]

Carroll's goals are worthy: an investigation into the source and history of anti–Jewish acts, atrocities and polemics within the 2,000-year history of the church and within the course of Western civilization. To deny that such a history exists would be to live a lie. Understanding that history, and knowing that it may have been a factor in allowing European Catholics and Protestants to turn a blind eye toward Nazi atrocities against the Jews is to acknowledge a painful, and indeed horrifying, reality. This was central to the Vatican's statement on the Shoah and to that part of the papal apology of March 2000.[4] But to make the assertion, as Carroll does (despite a few protestations that the Nazis did, in fact, carry out the "Final Solution," not the Catholic Church) that Catholic theology, history and belief were fundamental and direct causes of the Holocaust is scurrilous and betrays another agenda more fully spelled out in the concluding section of *Constantine's Sword* when Carroll calls for his Third Vatican Council.

In recent years, of course, it has become part of conventional wisdom that Pius XII was silent in the face of the Holocaust and that the Catholic Church, despite saving more Jewish lives than any other entity at the time, was virtually a collaborator in the "Final Solution."

It is also necessary to make the church the cause of the Holocaust because so much of what passes as contemporary enlightened thought and views have their roots not in Catholicism or Christianity, but in the very secular ideologies that laid the true foundation for the Holocaust. So-called enlightened views on euthanasia or abortion, for example, find their philosophical origins in late 19th century racial eugenics that propagated Hitler's attack on the Jews. That is a reality the chattering classes want to ignore. To scapegoat the Catholic Church as the cause of the Holocaust makes a secular examination of conscience unnecessary.

The roots of Hitler's anti–Semitic racist frenzy, and that of European society as a whole, are found not in Catholic belief but in the cultural rejection of Catholic belief in the Enlightenment and pseudoscientism of the 18th, 19th, and 20th centuries. Rather than a continuum from a beginning in the New Testament, rabid anti–Semitism was born in the stew of competing 19th century liberal ideologies of nationalism, racialism, eugenics, ideologies fought most solely by the church and that still have their impact in the 21st century.

To Carroll, however, these theories were merely part of a whole. Though such theories that led to and created the Holocaust were a fundamental rejection of thousands of years of Judaic and Christian thought, Carroll sees it differently. He sees these enlightenment theories as ideas that grew naturally from Christian origins, rather than an outright rejection. One was merely grafted on the other.[5] ... But it is that fundamental premise that is wrong. Hitler's anti–Semitism was not caused by religious differences between Catholics and Jews, or anti–Jewish outbursts during the First Crusade. His hatred was a fundamental rejection of both Christianity and Judaism. His hatred was of faith in anything but the Aryan race and the German nation-state. His beliefs and his rationalization derived from the stew of anti–Catholic secularist philosophies, not Catholicism. He did not approach the world with a mode of thinking and belief rooted in the 1,900 years of Western civilization. Rather, he was rooted in the 150 years of elitist and racist thought that had abandoned the Judeo-Christian roots of Western civilization.

Constantine's Sword is a slogging journey through history of the church over the two millennia. He touches down here and there when it suits his purpose. For example, while the treatment of the twelfth through the sixteenth centuries is endless, he barely touches on the nearly 800 years from Constantine to the calling of the First Crusade — which leaves a rather sizeable gap in the alleged linkage of anti–Semitism in the church from the Gospels to the Holocaust.[6]

Though Carroll's book can bend a coffee table at 756 pages, his litany of anti–Jewish incidents in Western history is spotty and lacking historical nuance. He touches on various events with Western history such as the Crusades, the Inquisition, the Plague, the Council of Trent and its aftermath, the French Revolution, the Dreyfus Affair, the Kulturkampf and concludes, actually quite briefly, with the Holocaust.

The church and Hitleralism is confined in Carroll's book to less than 70 pages, about the same length that he gives for church reform. He begins by restating his essential charge "however modern Nazism was, it planted its roots in the soil of age old Church attitudes and a nearly unbroken chain of Jew-hatred. However pagan Nazism was, it drew its sustenance from groundwater poisoned by the 'Church,' most solemnly held ideology — its theology."[7] This is, of course, a gross misreading of history. Hitler and Nazism were created by a rampant social Darwinism and ubiquitous European belief that it was a virtual biological imperative that the lower classes be dominated by their racial superiors, the ideology of imperialism, the birth of scientism that would dispel the "myths" of religion, the campaign to radically excise the church from public life, the denial of the sacredness of the individual for the good of the state, or in communism, the good of the class, the creation of the myth of the Nietzsche-like Superman who could undertake any evil for the good of his race, and the replacement of Christianity with neo-paganism. The church was not the progenitor of the beliefs that created Nazism. It was one of the last remaining bulwarks in Europe against it. The Nazis killed the Jews. For reasons of an internal agenda against the church, Carroll would prefer to dismiss that, like a revisionist who would claim the Holocaust never took place, and shift the blame to the church for his own agenda.

Carroll doesn't really spend much time on the Holocaust itself or a detailed look at the entire World War and how the church responded. He states that from the onset of Nazism, the "Church, for its part, had come to a decision it would stick with, almost without exception — that the 'wretched fate' of the Jews was unconnected to its own fate, or that of anyone else."[8] Carroll says such things without any necessity of proving that was church policy. The first formal protest filed by the Vatican under the Concordat was against the Nazi boycott of Jewish businesses. It assumes that a calculated decision by Pius to work behind the scenes through his papal representatives and through the existing vehicles of the church to save as many lives as possible was a callous decision to save as many lives as possible. None of the critics of Pius have yet been able to put forth a concrete alternative that Pius could have developed to save more lives than were saved by the church in that period. Throughout the war years, the church would save more Jewish lives than any entity that existed at the time.

Disagreeing, however, with the tactics of Pius is one thing. Stating that the church abandoned the Jews does not reflect any kind of reality. Which is one of the most frustrating aspects of Carroll's entire "history" of the church and the Jews. It is not history at all, but an amateur's mediation on various historical events skewed to reflect the prejudices of his own thesis. This is not careful scholarship. This is simply a very long anti–Catholic essay.[9]

No one can argue that members of the church throughout the centuries, going to the highest leadership within the church, engaged and endorsed at time in anti–Jewish words, sentiments and actions. At the very same time many within the church officially condemned such actions and it was the very church leadership that Carroll hopes to be abandoned that was most vociferous in that condemnation. It was not the belief of the church, the New Testament, the church centered in Jesus ... that created the Holocaust. It was the rejection of those, and the attempt to substitute for Judeo-Christian civilization a secularist pseudoscientism of race, class and nationalism that generated Nazism and the Holocaust. Nazism and the Nazis killed the Jews, and their philosophies that created them still bubble just below the surface. But not in the Catholic Church.

CHAPTER 13

Goldhagen vs. Christianity

by Ronald Rychlak

Daniel Goldhagen's *A Moral Reckoning: The Role of the Catholic Church in the Holocaust and its Unfulfilled Duty of Repair*, like his essay that preceded it, is noteworthy both for the breathtaking scope of its claims and the air of righteous indignation that Goldhagen uses.[1] Not content to argue that Pope Pius did less to save the Jews that he should have, Goldhagen goes much further—to attack Pacelli as an anti–Semite and the church as an institution thoroughly, and perhaps inextricably, permeated by anti–Semitism. In fact, he even argues that "the main responsibility for producing this all-time leading Western hatred lies with Christianity. More specifically, with the Catholic Church."

In his previous book, *Hitler's Willing Executioners*, Goldhagen asserted the blame for the Holocaust should be placed on ordinary Germans and their unique brand of anti–Semitism.[2] When contemporary historians challenged him on this point, he eventually conceded that he had under-estimated how factors other than anti–Semitism helped lead to the Third Reich's crimes. "I skirted over some of this history a little too quickly," he said.[3] He has skirted again.

Goldhagen claims the Catholic Church provided the Nazis with a "motive for murder" and should be held to a moral reckoning for its sin-ful behavior. He argues that the authors of the New Testament (he calls it "the Christian Bible") inserted anti–Semitic passages into the text decades after the crucifixion in order to serve their own political needs. As such Goldhagen's book is not simply an attack on the papacy or the Catholic Church, but on Christianity itself, especially the New Testament, which Goldhagen says is "fictitious" and "not a reliable rendition of facts and events, but legend."

He goes on to demand that the Catholic Church make reparations to

Jews.[4] He says that money reparations are deserved; political reparations are useful; but above all he stresses the need for the church to admit its moral failings. He asks for apologies, the erection of suitable monuments, an end to the church diplomatic relations with other nations, support for Israel, and repudiation of any claim that Christianity has supplanted Judaism. Instead, the church must embrace religious pluralism....

Goldhagen's argument is not based on original research. He simply culled the worst accusations from authors like Suzan Zuccotti and John Cornwell, without giving any consideration to the serious flaws that have been noted in their work.[5]

Goldhagen's main source for his charges about the Vatican allegedly helping Nazi war criminals escape justice is Michael Phayer's book. Phayer, in turn, draws mainly from Mark Aarons and John Loftus and their discredited book, *Unholy Trinity: The Vatican, the Nazis and the Swiss Banks.* More recently, Loftus has accused the Bush family of establishing a fortune by laundering money derived from the Nazis.

Similarly, Goldhagen relies heavily and uncritically on Susan Zuccotti's *Under His Very Windows* for his analysis of that period of the war when the Germans occupied Rome and northern Italy (1943–4). One of Zuccotti's chief sources is the notorious Robert Katz — who was successfully sued by relatives of Pope Pius XII and publicly condemned by Italy's highest court for defaming the wartime Pope.

Goldhagen also blindly accepted John Cornwell's mistranslation of a letter written in 1919 by Eugenio Pacelli, the future Pope Pius XII, when he was papal nuncio in Munich. This letter was published in its original in 1992. Considering the centrality of this letter to the Cornwell-Goldhagen thesis, one might have expected (and editors should have demanded) they publish it in full. That did not happen, however, perhaps because when the entire letter is read in an accurate translation, it is not anti–Semitic. The tone of anti–Semitism is introduced only by Cornwell's calculated mistranslation.[6]

Several of the dates Goldhagen provided related to the establishment of European ghettoes were wrong (one by more than 50 years). He was also wrong (by three decades) about the beginning of the process for Pius XII's beatification, and he was wrong about the date that the so-called "Hidden Encyclical" was made public.[7] He was wrong to try to portray Pope Pius XII as an anti–Semite. He was wrong in calling the concordat with the Holy See "Nazi Germany's first international treaty." He was wrong to say that the Belgian Catholic Church was silent; it was one of the first national churches to speak out against Nazi racial theories. He was way off base to suggest that German cardinals Michael von Faulhaber and

Clement August von Galen were insensitive to or silent about Jewish suffering. Goldhagen said that Pius XII "clearly failed to support" the protest of French bishops.[8]

Goldhagen also misidentifies the role of Vatican official Peter Gumpel (who is the realtor or judge, not the postulator or promoter, of Pius XII's cause for sainthood). A German court even ordered Goldhagen's book to be pulled from the shelves due to a terribly misleading caption that was beneath a photo showing a Catholic prelate surrounded by Nazis.

Goldhagen argues that the Vatican "endorsed" Italy's anti–Semitic laws. Actually, Mussolini's "Aryan Manifesto" was issued on July 14, 1938. On July 28, 1938, Pius XI made a public speech in which he said: "The entire human race is but a single and universal race of men. There is no room for special races. We may therefore ask ourselves why Italy should have felt a disgraceful need to imitate Germany." This was reprinted in full on the front page of the Vatican newspaper on July 30, 1938, under a four-column headline. Other articles condemning anti–Semitism appeared (1938) on July 17, 23, 30, August 22–23, October 11–18, 20, 23–24, 26–27, November 3, 14–16, 19–21, 23–25, December 25, and January 19, 1939.

As Pope Pius XI said in 1938:

> Mark well that in the Catholic Mass, Abraham is our Patriarch and forefather. Anti-Semitism is incompatible with the lofty thought which that fact expresses. It is a movement with which we Christians can have nothing to do. No, no, I say to you it is impossible for a Christian to take in anti–Semitism. It is inadmissible. Through Christ and in Christ we are in the spiritual progeny of Abraham. Spiritually, we are all Semites.

It is easy enough to find sloppy interpretations of the Bible or hatemongers who bend it for their own purposes, but that is not to be found in the official teachings of the Catholic Church. Unfortunately, Goldhagen appears to be unfamiliar with most of the existing scholarship.[9] He says that Catholic teaching has always "revised" its essential beliefs. That is certainly not true, and it reflects a fundamental ignorance of the topic on which he purports to write.[10]

Those who are interested in learning more about Catholic teaching regarding relations with Jews (which should include every reader who treated Goldhagen's book with any degree of respect) are advised to read *Nostra Aetate*, the Second Vatican Council's renewal of the church's condemnation of anti–Semitism. That is a far better way to approach this subject than by reading *A Moral Reckoning*.[11]

Certainly no one would suggest that Christians and Jews have gotten along well at all times throughout history. Prior to 1970, when popes had real temporal power, Jews were sometimes treated with religious and political contempt.

The incorrect understanding of scripture did indeed breed suspicion and mistrust between Christians and Jews, but even papal critics acknowledge that throughout even the worst periods the popes regularly condemned violence directed against Jews and offered protection when they could. Catholic "anti–Judaism" was a matter of religion, not race. In fact, the more common charges arising out of this history related to efforts directed towards encouraging Jews to covert — to become Catholics.

In *Mein Kampf*, Hitler went to great length about misusing religious imagery to inspire and inflame the masses. Hitler also played to a populist mentality, a racist mentality, a socialist mentality, a chauvinistic mentality ... and just about any other mentality that he could think of. Are they all to be condemned because they were capable of being manipulated by Hitler (who also planned to eliminate largely Catholic Poland)? The answer is equally clear: of course not.

In order to understand the dynamics of the time, one only need to examine Nazi arguments from the 1930s and '40s. Hitler regularly complained about Christian interference with his plan (saying one time that the Pope was blackmailing him).[12] Nazi propaganda often showed Jews invoking Christian imagery or hiding behind church symbols for protection.[13]

Goldhagen's efforts to trivialize and diminish Pope Pius XII's famous 1942 Christmas statement and its clear denunciation of Nazi ideology are representative of the bias that permeates his work. In the 1942 statement, Pius said that the world was "plunged into the gloom of tragic error" and "that the church would be untrue to herself, she would have ceased to be a mother, if she were deaf to the cries of suffering children which reach her ears from every class of the human family." He spoke of the need for mankind to make "a solemn vow" ... that mankind owed this vow to all victims of war, including "the hundreds of thousands who, through no fault of their own, and solely because of their nationality or race, have been condemned to death or progressive extinction."[14]

British records reflect the opinion that "the Pope's condemnation of the treatment of the Jews and the Poles is quite unmistakable, and the message is perhaps more forceful in tone than any of his recent statements."[15] The Dutch bishops issued a pastoral letter in defense of Jewish people on February 21, 1943, making express reference to the Pope's statement.[16] Moreover, a well-known Christmas Day editorial in the *New York Times* praised Pius XII for his moral leadership in opposing the Nazis:

> No Christmas sermon reaches a larger congregation than the mes-
> sage Pope Pius XII addresses to a war-torn world at this season. This
> Christmas more than ever he is a lonely voice crying out of the
> silence of a continent.... When a leader bound impartially to nations
> on both sides condemns as heresy the new form of the national state
> which subordinates everything to itself ... when he assails violent
> occupation of territory, the exile and persecution of human beings
> for no reason other than race or political opinion ... "the impartial
> judgment" is like a verdict in a high court of justice.[17]

A similar editorial from the *Times* of London, commenting on the
Pope's statements in general, said: "He condemns the worship of force and
its concrete manifestation in the suppression of national liberties and in
the persecution of the Jewish race."[18]

An American report noted that the Germans were "conspicuous by
their absence" at a midnight Mass conducted by the Pope for diplomats
on Christmas Eve following the papal statement. German Ambassador
Diego von Bergen, on the instruction of Ribbentrop, warned the Pope that
the Nazis would seek retaliation if the Vatican abandoned its neutral position. When he reported back to his superiors, the German ambassador
stated: "Pacelli is no more sensible to threats than we are."[19]

Goldhagen asks rhetorically: "Why, as a moral and practical matter,
did (Pius XII) speak publicly on behalf of the suffering of Poles, but not
Jews? No good answer."[20] He then quotes a Vatican Radio broadcast of
January 1940, trying to make the point that the Vatican was concerned
only about Polish Catholics and could not spare a good word for Jews. In
doing this he badly misrepresents the truth.

As an initial matter, the quote cited by Goldhagen does not limit itself
to Christian Poles. It merely refers to "Poles." Of course, writings of that
time sometimes distinguished "Poles" and "Jews," using the former des-
ignation to refer to Polish Christians, but this was far from always the case.
Moreover, Goldhagen implies that Jews were never mentioned on Vatican
Radio. This is simply false.

Goldhagen seems to have taken his Vatican Radio quote from Pierre
Blet's book. This book presents itself as a synopsis. Had Goldhagen actually researched the Vatican Radio transcripts from January 1940 (the month
upon which he focuses) he would have found that Jews were indeed
expressly and clearly identified.[21] On October 15, 1940, Vatican Radio
denounced "the immoral principles of Nazism," and on March 30, 1941,
explicitly condemned "the wickedness of Hitler."[22] These broadcasts were
among the first to break the news of the Nazi persecutions, but they were not
the only such stories on Vatican Radio. They continued throughout the war.

The Catholic faithful heard these broadcasts and reacted accordingly. French priest-rescuer (and later Cardinal) Henri de Lubac paid tribute to the Pope's radio station in his book *Christian Resistance to Anti-Semitism*, describing the profound impact it had upon the French resistance.[23] Similarly, Michael Riquet, SJ, an ex-inmate of Dachau who was recognized for saving Jewish lives, stated: "Pius XII spoke; Pius XII condemned; Pius XII acted ... throughout those years of horror, when we listened to Radio Vatican and to the Pope's messages, we felt in communion with the Pope in helping the persecuted Jews and in fighting against the Nazi violence.[24]

Of all of Goldhagen' outrages, none is less compressible than his depiction of the great encyclical *Mit brennender Sorge* (*With Burning Anxiety*) — the Vatican's powerful denunciation of German fascism and racism — as an anti–Semitic screed. *Mit brennender Sorge*, issued by Pope Pius XI when Pacelli was his secretary of state, is one of the strongest condemnations of any national regime that the Holy See ever published. It condemned not only the persecution of the church, but also the neopaganism of Nazi racial theories.[25]

The persecution of Jews, unfortunately, did not lessen; it got worse following the release of *Mit brennender Sorge*. This reaction is but one of many examples of Nazi retaliation — against Jews and Christians— that Goldhagen denies ever happened.

Goldhagen also misrepresents Pope Pius XII's encyclical *Mystici Corporis Christi* (*On the Mystical Body*).[26] The impact of the encyclical was expanded as it was repeated. Vatican Radio, in fact, used the encyclical as the basis for a broadcast that stated: "he who makes a distinction between Jews and other men is unfaithful to God and in conflict with God's demands."[27]

Like many other papal critics, Goldhagen claims that the Pope favored the Germans in their war against the Soviet Union. The historical record does not support this charge. After the Allied victory the Soviets expanded their spheres of influence (and their persecution of the church) throughout most of Eastern Europe, including half of Germany. They murdered millions of people.

Despite his concern over the spread of communism, however, Pius was neither blind to other threats nor unable to recognize the virtue of the Soviet people. As early as 1926, at the direction of Pope Pius XI, then–Nuncio Pacelli attempted to secure a concordat with the Soviet Union.[28] In 1942, Pius told Father Paolo Dezza (made a cardinal in 1991): "The Communist danger does exist, but at this time the Nazi danger is more serious. They want to destroy the Church and crush it like a toad."[29] When the Axis sought to have him bless the German "crusade" into the godless Soviet Union, he refused.[30] In fact, by cooperating with Franklin Roosevelt's request to support the extension of the lend-lease program to the USSR, Pius actually gave economic and military aid to the Soviets.[31] (Later, his appeals on behalf of Ethel and Julius Rosenberg again revealed his ability to look beyond the "Communist" issue.)[32]

The recently failed Catholic-Jewish study group found that the evidence does not support the conclusion that Pius favored the Germans over the Soviets. It is no longer surprising that Goldhagen fails to mention this.

It does, however, seem shocking that Goldhagen quotes the notorious pro–Nazi Bishop Franz-Justus Rarkowski without mentioning that (1) he was virtually forced upon the church by the Nazis (under the threat of having no military ordinary or military chaplains), (2) the church banned Rarkowski from participation in the German episcopacy, (3) Vatican Radio under Pius XII explicitly denounced Rarkowski,[33] (4) Vatican Radio declared that: "Hitler's war is not a just war and God's blessing cannot be upon it."[34] Catholic clergy were among the first people in Germany to recognize the threat posed by the Nazis.

In 1945, Fabian von Schlabrendorff, a Protestant member of the German resistance, wrote a memorandum to U.S. General ("Wild Bill") Donovan, in which Schlabrendorff reported: "Because of the hierarchic organizations of the Church, the denunciation of Hitler was propagated by the majority of Catholic clergy in the land. The result of this was the enmity toward Hitler was promulgated not only by the high clerics but was also carried to the masses by the low clerics."[35]

Donovan, in his own report for the OSS War Crimes Staff, which was approved by the Prosecution Review Board, examined the relationship between the German Catholic leadership and the Nazis as they came to power: "In several pastorals, they expressly warned the faithful against the danger created to German Catholicism by the party."[36]

In a recent, detailed study of Nazi attitudes towards Christianity, Richard Steigmann-Gall detailed the attitude of the German clergy towards National Socialism:

> For its part, the Catholic Church opposed the Nazi party for (attacks by the Nazis against the Church), but also for the Nazis' racialist dogma and extreme nationalism.... Those isolated Catholic Churchmen who publicly supported Nazism ... were the exceptions that proved the rule....[37]

Hitler certainly did not see the Catholic clergy in Germany as his allies. On August 11, 1942, he expressed his frustration:

> I'll make those damned parsons feel the power of the State in a way they never would have dreamed possible! For the moment I am just keeping my eye on them; if I ever have the slightest suspicion that they are getting dangerous, I will shoot the lot of them.... The Catholic Church has but one desire, and that is to see us destroyed.[38]

He also called Christianity one of the two great scourges (along with the pox) in history, and said that "the priests continue to incite the faithful against the State."[39] In 1934, SS Chief Heinrich Himmler circulated a 50-page memorandum complaining about hostile clergy.[40] The previously mentioned report from the Nuremberg prosecutor's office outlines dozens of cases where Catholic priests were persecuted due to their opposition to the Nazis.[41]

Goldhagen's specific targets from among the German clergy are very poorly chosen. Declassified documents from the OSS show that American intelligence during the war knew well that two of the German Catholic leaders Goldhagen focuses upon (Cardinal Faulhaber of Munich and Bishop von Galen of Munster) were particularly strong in their opposition to the Nazis.[42] In the 1930s, Cardinal Faulhaber wrote Secretary of State Pacelli, describing the persecution of the Jews as "unjust and painful." In 1935, at an open meeting, Nazis called for him (Faulhaber) to be killed.[43] In late November 1938, after he had given a speech, a uniformed detachment arrived in front of his residence and threw stones at the windows. They shouted "Take the traitor to Dachau" and shattered window frames and shutters.[44] In May 1939, demonstrations against Faulhaber took place throughout Bavaria, and posters were hung saying "Away with Faulhaber, the friend of the Jews and the agent of Moscow." After the war began, Faulhaber cited Pius XII's encyclical *Summi Pontificatus* (*Darkness over the Earth*) in an address condemning Nazis, resulting in a headline reading "Cardinal Faulhaber Indicts Hitlerism" in the *London Tablet*.[45]

After the war, Rabbi Stephen S. Wise, one of the leading American voices for the Jewish cause, called Faulhaber "a true Christian prelate" who "had lifted his fearless voice" in defense of the Jews.[46]

Bishop (later Cardinal) Clemens August Graf von Galen also took a leading role in opposing Nazi racial laws. His reputation for standing against the Nazis became international when news of three "amazingly bold" sermons denouncing Nazi principles filtered to the international press in 1942.[47] Later, Pius XII sent Galen a letter praising his "open and courageous pronouncements" and telling him that letters he had mailed to the Holy See laid the groundwork for the 1942 Christmas message.[48]

Goldhagen notes Galen's protests against the euthanasia program, but he argues that the Nazis did not retaliate against him and asks why the

German bishops and the Vatican did not "rally behind Bishop Galen."[49] In fact, on December 2, 1940 — well before Galen's famous sermons against euthanasia — Pius XII published an official Vatican statement in the Catholic press that unequivocally condemned the killing of "life unworthy of life."[50] This decree went into every diocese in Germany and was favorably and publicly commented on by the German bishops. On March 9, 1941, in a public sermon, then–Bishop Konrad von Preysing (whom Goldhagen wrongly portrays as a critic of Pius XII) made reference to Pius XII, "whom we all know — I should say from personal experience — as a man of global horizons and broadmindedness (who) has reaffirmed the doctrine of the Church, according to which there is no justification and no excuse for the killing of the sick or the abnormal on any economic or eugenic grounds."

To compound his errors, Goldhagen charges that Galen's protests were successful in ending the euthanasia program and that the Nazis did not retaliate. In fact, the euthanasia campaign was not ended, but continued under greater secrecy until the end of the war.[51]

Goldhagen asserts that the Polish ambassador pleaded with Pius in vain for the Jews, and that by 1944 Pius XII was so "sick" of hearing about the Jews that he got angry with the ambassador. Goldhagen gives no documentation for this charge. This is hardly surprising since it is untrue. Pius XII was upset about reports the ambassador was receiving from people outside of occupied Poland who, relying on erroneous information, complained that the Pope was doing too much for Jews, but not enough for Poles.[52] The Polish ambassador to the Holy See during the war was Casimir Papée, whose 1954 *Pius XII e Polska* (*Pius XII and Poland*) discussed Pius XII's wartime policies and said he agreed with them.[53] That record is comprehensively analyzed — and supported — in Papée's book, of which Goldhagen makes no mention.

In 1942, following the deportations of Jews from occupied France, the French bishops issued a joint protest.[54] Goldhagen says that Pius XII "clearly failed to support" this protest. This is yet another falsehood. At the direction of the Pope, the protests were broadcast and discussed for several days on Vatican Radio.[55] Statements such as "who makes a distinction between Jews and other men is unfaithful to God and is in conflict with God's commands" were broadcast into France, in French, on Vatican Radio. Pierre Cardinal Gerlier, a French Catholic bishop who condemned Nazi atrocities and deportation of the Jews, explicitly stated that he was obeying Pius XII's instructions when he made these statements.

When the deportations began from France, Pius protested to Head of State Marshall Henri Pétain, instructed his nuncio to issue another protest, and recommended that religious communities provide refuge to Jewish people. In fact the Associated Press reported that the Pope protested to the Vichy government three times during August of 1952.

Rabbi Steven S. Wise, perhaps the leading Jewish voice in the United States during the war, wrote in 1942: "It appears to be more than a rumor that his Holiness Pope Pius XII urgently appealed through the papal nuncio to the Vichy government to put an end to deportations from France, and the appeal is said to have been reinforced by petition and protest from the Cardinal Archbishops of Paris and Lyons...."[56]

Even Godhagen has to admit that Pius XII intervened in Hungary, but he attempts to diminish the importance of the Pope's actions by suggesting that his famous open telegram protesting Jewish deportations was isolated and late. Again, the facts are against Goldhagen, Jenö Levai, the great authority on Hungarian Jewry, who had direct access to primary archival evidence, documented the Church's rescue efforts.

On June 25, 1944, Pius sent the well-known open telegram to the regent of Hungary, Admiral Nicholas Horthy. Pius XII also sent a telegram to Hungarian Cardinal Justinian Serédi asking for support from the Hungarian bishops. Serédi responded by issuing a statement of his own. This strong statement, issued pursuant to a request from the Pope, was read publicly in the Catholic churches until Nazi authorities confiscated all copies.

Admiral Horthy complained to the Germans that he was being bombarded with telegrams from the Vatican and others and that the nuncio was calling on him several times each day. Horthy agreed to work against the deportations, and he even signed an agreement with the Allies. The Germans arrested Horthy in October, put Hungary under the control of Hungarian Nazis, and the deportations resumed.

The World Jewish Congress, at its December 1944 war emergency conference in Atlantic City, sent a telegram of thanks to the Holy See for the protection it gave "under difficult conditions to the persecuted Jews in German-dominated Hungary." Similarly, the American Jewish Committee sent an expression of deep thanks to Pius and Cardinal Luigi Maglione for having helped stop the deportations from Hungary.[57]

In attempting to implicate Pius XII in the atrocities carried out in the Nazi satellite states of Slovakia and Croatia, Goldhagen again makes many inexcusable errors. Goldhagen suggests that the Vatican action in Slovakia came only after it was clear that the Allies would win the war. In fact, the Nuremberg race laws were introduced in that country on September 9, 1941. Two days later the Vatican's charge d'affairs in Bratislava went to see President Jozef Tiso to stress "the injustice of these ordinances which also violate the rights of the Church."[58] Shortly thereafter, Slovakia's representative to the Vatican received a written protest from the Holy See that these laws were "in open contrast to Catholic principles."[59]

When Jews were deported from Slovakia in 1942, the Vatican secretary of state immediately filed a protest.[60] Between 1941 and 1944, the Vatican sent six official letters and made numerous oral pleas and protests regarding the deportation of Jews from Slovakia.[61] A letter sent from Pius himself, dated April 7, 1943, could not have been more clear: "The Holy See would fail in its Divine Mandate if it did not deplore these measures, which gravely damage man in his natural right, merely for the reason that these people belong to a certain race."[62]

Like most papal critics, Goldhagen fails to give important details about the deportation of Jews from Holland. Dutch bishops had warned their followers about the dangers of Nazism as early as 1934, and in 1936 ordered Catholics not to support Fascist organizations or they would risk excommunication.[63] In the summer of 1942, as Jews were being deported from Holland, the Nazis warned Christian leaders not to interfere. Despite the warning, on July 26, 1942, the Catholic archbishop of Utrecht had a letter read in all of the Catholic churches, condemning the treatment of Jews. In a direct response to that statement, the Nazis began to deport even those Jews who held a Catholic baptismal certificate. The language from the Nazi officials makes clear that the deportations were made in direct response to the bishop's letter.[64]

Goldhagen also asserts that Pius did not privately instruct cardinals, bishops, priests, and nuns to save Jews. Catholic rescuers— including such people as Cardinal Pietro Palazzini and Tibor Baranski, who were later recognized by Israel as Righteous Gentiles— testified that they received precisely such orders from the Pope.[65] Several other witnesses also testified that such instructions were sent out in the form of letters.[66] Still others, including Father Marie-Benoît, Caroll-Abbing, Pope John XXIII, and Pope Paul VI, all testified that they received such instructions from Pope Pius XII in face-to-face meetings, or through other direct channels.

Goldhagen even tries to link the Vatican and Pacelli with the notorious anti–Semite Julius Streicher. Streicher's venomous writings tell a different story. He railed against the Pope's support of the Jewish people: "The Jews have now found protection in the Catholic Church, which is trying to convince non–Jewish humanity that distinct races do not exist. The Pope has made his own the false conception of racial equality — and the Jews, with the help of Marxists and Freemasons, are doing their best to promote it." Pacelli's opposition to Streicher's worldview was well known. In *Three Popes and the Jews*, Pinchas Lapide cites a public address by Pacelli in Rome which repeated Pope Pius XI's eloquent statement that "spiritually we are all Semites."

Following the arguments of Zuccotti and Michael Phayer, Goldhagen asserts that even after the liberation of Rome, Pius remained "silent" about Jews and anti–Semitism. Actually, on August 3, 1946, in a statement that Goldhagen mentions only to belittle (he also ignores or dismisses Vatican condemnations of anti–Semitism in 1916, 1928, 1930, 1942, and 1943), Pius declared: "we condemn all recourse to force and violence, from whatever it may come, as also we have condemned on several occasions in the past the persecutions which a fanatical anti–Semitism unleashed against the Jewish people." He also made many other statements condemning anti–Semitism, even after the war.

One of the most amazing parts of *A Moral Reckoning* is where Goldhagen attempts to construe the U.S. bishops' 1942 statement as a slap at Pius XII. At their annual meeting in November 1942, the U.S. bishops released a statement on the plight of the Jews in Europe. Goldhagen tries to turn this statement into a slap at the Pope and an "all but explicit rebuke of the Vatican." Actually, the American bishops repeatedly invoked Pius XII's name and teaching with favor.[67] ("We recall the words of Pope Pius XII"; "We urge the serious study of peace plans of Pope Pius XII"; "In response to the many appeals of our Holy Father.") Moreover, in a letter written at this very time, Pius expressed thanks for the "constant and understanding collaboration" of the American bishops and archbishops.

Goldhagen's lowest blow is directed at Father Peter Gumpel, SJ. An official of the Congregation of the Causes of Saints, Gumpel is the relator, or independent, investigating judge — by papal appointment — for the cause of Pius XII's sainthood. In what is arguably the most shameful sentence in his polemic magazine article, Goldhagen writes: "Perhaps the Church protects Fr. Gumpel in his post because only an anti–Semite and a historical falsifier can be counted on to present Pius XII in the glowing manner required for canonization."

That Goldhagen would disregard the facts and call this good man an anti–Semite is depressingly unsurprising. (Witness the way Godhagen twists Pacelli's 1933 promise not to interfere "in Germany's internal political affairs" is converted into "the Church's intention to let the Germans have a free hand with the Jews.") His evidence in this case comes from truncated quotations that have been taken out of context. In fact, Gumpel has repeatedly condemned anti–Semitism and affirmed his allegiance to the teachings of Vatican II.[68] The charge that Gumpel is a "historical falsifier" is perhaps even more outrageous than calling him an anti–Semite. Goldhagen provides no evidence to support it. Indeed, he leaves the reader entirely in the dark about what it is Gumpel is alleged to have falsified.

Goldhagen seems to want nothing less than a renunciation of Christianity. He accuses Pope Pius XII of collaborating with the Nazis and treats the cross as a symbol of oppression. He lectures about how portions of the New Testament were fabricated and asserts that the very term "New Testament" is offensive.

The main thing for Goldhagen about Pius XII seems to be that he thinks the Pope should have set aside all of his intelligence and adopted a confrontational approach to the Nazis—in each and every location. That, of course, would have been foolish. He had the example of Holland. He has sent an express condemnation into Poland to be read but the Archbishop of Krakow, Adam Sapieha, burned it, saying that it would bring too many reprisals. In fact, the Nuremberg report documents case after case of retaliation against the clergy (Catholic and Protestant) following statements or other agitation against the Nazi regime.[69]

Rather than endangering others with grand public gestures, Pius used churches, convents, monasteries, seminaries, and the Vatican itself to run a rescue operation for all victims, without any distinction based on race, religion, or nationality. The last thing a rescue operation wants is attention, particularly when it is likely to bring about reprisals. Goldhagen focuses only on potential reprisals against the Jewish people. Such reprisals occurred; but the Pope was also concerned about Catholics. For one thing, Catholic rescue efforts could be harmed, causing further suffering for Jews. More importantly, as Pius said, martyrdom cannot be imposed on someone, but must be voluntarily accepted.[70] Catholic doctrine would not permit the Pope to sacrifice some lives to save others, even if a utilitarian equation might suggest that would be appropriate. The church did not, however, vary its approach based upon the identity of the victim. Goldhagen's speculations notwithstanding, the Vatican under Pius XII acted in the same way whether the victims were Catholic priests or Jewish peasants.

Marcus Mechior, the chief rabbi of Denmark during the war, well understood his situation. He explained that Pius had no chance of influencing Hitler: "I believe it is an error to think that Pius XII could have had any influence whatever on the brain of a madman."[71] He added that if he had been more confrontational, "Hitler would have probably massacred six million more Jews and perhaps ten times ten million Catholics, if he had the power to do so." Similarly, the chief rabbi in Rome during the German occupation, Israel Zolli, said, "no hero in all of history was more militant, more fought against, none more heroic, than Pius XII."

Goldhagen naively suggests cookie-cutter approach to resisting the Nazis. The historical facts show that sometimes a confrontational approach worked with the Nazis, but at other times it did not. Robert M. W. Kempner, the deputy chief U.S. prosecutor at the Nuremberg war trials, explained that a public protest against the persecution of the Jews could only lead to "partial success when it was made at a politically and militarily opportune moment."[72] He added that Pius made such protests through nuncios when and where possible. Confrontation would not, however, have been advisable with Hitler. "Every propaganda move of the Catholic Church against Hitler's Reich," he wrote, "would have been not only 'provoking suicide' ... but would have hastened the execution of still more Jews and priests."[73]

Pope John Paul II frequently reached out to his Jewish "elder brothers." The Holy Father has called upon Jews and Christians to "work together to build a future in which there will be no more anti–Jewish feeling among Christians, or any anti–Christian feeling among Jews. We have many things in common." Let us hope that many Catholics and Jews heed those words. Goldhagen, unfortunately, is doing precisely the opposite.

The End of the Pius Wars[1]

by Joseph Bottum

The Pius War is over, more or less. There will still be a few additional volumes published here and there, another article or two from authors too slow off the mark to catch their moment. But, basically, in the great argument that has raged over the last few years about the role of Pope Pius XII during World War II, the books have all been written, the reviews are in, and the exchanges have all simmered down. It was a long and arduous struggle, vituperative and cruel, but, in the end, the defenders of Pius XII won every major battle. Along the way, they also lost the war.

Who, even among scholars in the field, could keep up with the flood of attacks on Pius XII that began in the late 1990s? John Cornwell gave us *Hitler's Pope*, and Michael Phayer followed suit with *The Catholic Church and the Holocaust*. David Kertzer brought charges against Pius XII in *The Popes Against the Jews*, and Susan Zuccotti reversed her previous scholarship to pen *Under His Very Windows: The Vatican and the Holocaust in Italy*. Gary Wills used Pius as the centerpiece of his reformist *Papal Sin*, as did James Carroll in *Constantine's Sword*. So, for that matter, did Daniel Goldhagen when he wrote what proved to be the most extended and straightforward assault on Catholicism in decades: *A Moral Reckoning: The Role of the Catholic Church in the Holocaust and Its Unfilled Duty of Repair*....

The champions of Pius had their share of book-length innings as well—although, one might note, never from the same level of popular publisher as the attackers managed to find. In 1999 Pierre Blet produced *Pius XII and the Second World War According to the Archives of the Vatican* and got the Paulist Press, a small respectable Catholic house, to publish it in America. Ronald Rychlak finished his first-rate *Hitler, the War and the Pope*, but this appeared in presses not quite at the level of distribution, advertising and influence enjoyed by Doubleday, Houghton Mifflin, Knopf, and Viking, the large houses that issued books against Pius.

The commentator Philip Jenkins recently suggested that this disparity in publishers sends a message that the mainstream view is the guilt of Pius XII, while praise for the Pope belongs only to the cranks, nuts, and sectarians. Jenkins' suggestion is worth considering. Still, no one can say that Pius' supporters were crushed or censored. In just six years, Margherita Marchione managed five books in praise of the Pope. (Her views were followed by Ralph McInerny, Justice George Lawler, and José Sanchez).

But it was primarily in book reviews and responses that the defenders of Pius fought out the war — which is something of a problem. Every pope precipitates biographies, hagiographies, and maledictions, like the dropping of the rain; it is part of the job to be much written about, and the works of Eugenio Pacelli that began when he became pope in 1939 seem innumerable.

But no supporter has yet produced a book-length biography in the wake of the recent years of extended blame. Even Rychlak's excellent book is essentially reactive, devoting a 30-page epilogue to a catalogue of the errors in Cornwell's book.

We have seen this pattern before. Hochhuth's play *The Deputy* premiered in Berlin in 1963, and its picture of a greedy pope, concerned only about Vatican finances and silent about the Holocaust, immediately caused the firestorm of comment from the intellectual world. Everyone who was anyone felt compelled to weigh in. Hochhuth himself when he tried to extend his censure to Winston Churchill, which led to a lost libel suit....

Even without Hochhuth, the wide discussion about Pius XII he initiated in 1963 went on for several years. The brouhaha also prompted the Vatican to begin releasing material from Pius' pontificate, which appeared from 1965 to 1981 as the 11-volume series *Actes et Documents du Saint Siège relatifs à la second guerre mondiale*. In part by relying on these new documents, but even more by simply gathering their forces and investigating each of the incidents taken as the core of the indictment, the defenders gradually tamped down *The Deputy's* claims about Pius XII and the Holocaust. Pope John Paul II was a consistent advocate for his predecessor, and even once-popular notions about Pius— that he was, for instance, the great reactionary opponent against whom Vatican II turned — gradually seemed to lose steam by the late 1970s and early '80s. It took more than a decade, but the reactive reviewers appeared to carry the day, and the popular magazine press and major book publishers lost interest....

Most skeptical observers were unprepared when the criticism began again in the late 1990s. To journalists and cultural commentators, Cornwell's

Hitler's Pope seemed almost to come out of nowhere in 1999, and it received almost entirely ecstatic reviews when it first appeared.... Time was needed for scholars to gin up the machine again, double-check the claims in *Hitler's Pope*, and publish the reviews. Some of the results proved deeply embarrassing for Cornwell, particularly the falsity of his boast that he had spent "months on end" in the archives, when he visited the Vatican for only three weeks and didn't go to the archives every day of that. The Italian letter from Pacelli that Cornwell placed at the center of his book as evidence of deep anti–Semitism has been, he claimed, waiting secretly "like a time bomb" until he did his research. In fact, it had been published in 1992 in a book by Emma Fattorini, who— an actual Italian, not working on a partisan translation — thought it meant very little. By the time all this came out, however, *Hitler's Pope* had ridden out its time on the best-seller list.

Pius' supporters were better prepared for Susan Zuccotti and still better prepared for Gary Wills, and David Ketzer, and James Carroll, and, particularly, Daniel Goldhagen, who was especially harried in late 2002. By then, the whole thing had turned into a giant game of "Whack the Mole," with dozens of reviewers ready to smash their mallets down on the next author to stick up his head....

Just as *The Deputy* moved the archivists in Rome to release *Actes et Documents* over the next 16 years, so the current Pius War has prompted an accelerated — by glacial Vatican norms— opening of a few new archives from the pontificate of Pius XI (1922–39), whom Pacelli served as the Vatican's secretary of state. Along with an Italian Jesuit named Giovanni Sale (who has been writing a torrent of articles for the Roman Jesuit journal *La Civiltà Cattolica*), Peter Godman in his *Hitler and the Vatican* is among the first scholars to have used the new documents. And although he looked at only a handful— the title of his book is considerably overblown — he seems to have done so in a relatively reasonable and balanced way, particularly given the standards set by Cornwell and Goldhagen....

In the public mind at the present moment, there is almost nothing bad you can't say about Pius XII. The Vatican may end up declaring him a saint — the slow process of canonization has been winding its way through the Roman curia since the mid–1960s— but the general public has gradually been persuaded that Pius ranks somewhere among the greatest villains ever to walk the earth....

The point is that there is simply no depravity one can put past the man. He suppressed the anti–Nazi encyclical that Pius XI on his deathbed begged him to release. He was deeply implicated in the Germans' massacre of 335 Italians in the Ardeatine Caves. He expressly permitted, even encouraged, the SS to round up Rome's Jews in 1943. At the root of all this lies the fact that Pius XII was, fundamentally, a follower of Hitler, a geno-cidal hater of the Jews in his heart and mind, and once we recognize him as a Nazi who somehow escaped punishment at the Nuremberg trials, we can see the origin of all the rest. He was Hitler's Pope, etc. etc.... In a 1997 essay, the widely published Richard L. Rubenstein concluded, "during World War II Pope Pius XII and the vast majority of European Christian leaders regarded the elimination of the Jews as no less beneficial than the destruction of Bolshevism."

All of these claims are mistaken, of course — and more than mistaken: demonstrably and obviously untrue, outrages upon history and fellow felling for the humanity of previous generations. But none of them are merely the lurid fantasies of conspiracy-mongers huddled together in para-noia on their Internet lists. Every one of these assertions has been made in recent years by books and articles published with mainstream and pop-ular American publishers. And when we draw from them their general conclusion — when we reach the point at which Rubenstein, for example has arrived — then discourse is over. Research into primary sources, argu-ment about interpretation, the scholar's task of weighing historical cir-cumstances; all of this is quibbling, an attempt to be fair to monstrosity, and by such fairness to condone, excuse, and participate in it....

It was here that the Pius War was lost — and lost for what I believe will be at least a generation — despite the victories of the reviewers ... I am con-vinced that we will not achieve anything resembling historical accuracy until all present views have been cleared away — and thus, that the job for every honest writer who takes up the topic now is to correct the slander of Pius XII. A good example was set by Rabbi David Dalin, in an essay which was published in the *Weekly Standard* in February 2001. Dalin concluded that Pius XII deserves recognition among Jews as a Righteous Gentile who saved hundreds of thousands of lives during the Holocaust. The reaction ... was brutal, and the *Weekly Standard* found itself leading the parade only in the sense that a man running for his life leads the mob pursuing him.

But the center-left *New Republic* immediately commissioned Daniel Goldhagen to interrupt the book he was writing and savage Pius XII instead — which he did in what was said to be the longest essay ever pub-lished in the magazine's pages. The neo-conservative *Commentary* was so rankled that it did what it would not have done in nearly any other cir-cumstance: it published a long rebuke of the *Weekly Standard* by a leftist author who had already made many of the same complaints in an article for *Christian Century*....

The attempt to sift through the endless stream of books about Pius XII in recent years was actually carried out by indefatigable reviewers in dozens of magazines and journals, responding to the texts one by one. The controversy also motivated additional research, and new material now seems to arrive every week. As far as I can tell, all this recent information tells in favor of Pius XII. A recently discovered 1923 letter to the Vatican from Eugenio Pacelli, then nuncio to Germany, for instance, denounces Hitler's putsch and warns against his anti–Semitism and anti–Catholicism. A document from April 1933, just months after Hitler obtained power, reveals how Pacelli (then secretary of state) ordered the new German nuncio, Cesare Orsenigo, to protest Nazi actions. Meanwhile, newly examined diplomatic documents show that in 1937 Cardinal Pacelli warned A. W. Klieforth, the American consul to Berlin, that Hitler was "an untrustworthy scoundrel and fundamentally wicked person" to quote Klieforth, who also wrote that Pacelli "did not believe Hitler of moderation, and ... fully supported the German bishops in their anti–Nazi stand." This was matched with the discovery of Pacelli's anti–Nazi report, written the following year for President Roosevelt and filed with Ambassador Joseph Kennedy, which declared that the church regarded compromise with the Third Reich as "out of the question." Archives from American espionage agencies have recently confirmed Pius XII's active involvement in plots to overthrow Hitler. A pair of newly found letters, written in 1940 on the letterhead of the Vatican's Secretariat of State, give Pius XII's orders that financial assistance be sent to Campagna for the explicit purpose of assisting interned Jews suffering from Mussolini's racial policies. And the Israeli government has finally released Adolf Eichmann's diaries, portions of which confirm the Vatican's obstruction of the Nazis' roundup of Rome's Jews. There's more, a regular flow of new material: intercepts of Nazi communications released from the United States' National Archives include such passages as "Vatican has apparently for a long time been assisting many Jews to escape," in a Nazi dispatch from Rome to Berlin on October 26, 1943, 10 days after Germany's Roman roundup. New oral testimony from such Catholic rescuers as Monsignor John Patrick Carroll-Abbing, Sister Mathilda Spielmann, Father Giacomo Martegani, and Don Aldo Brunacci insists that Pius XII gave them explicit orders and direct assistance to help persecuted Jews in Italy. The posthumous publication this year of Harold Tittmann's memoir, *Inside the Vatican of Pius XII*, is particularly interesting, for in it the American diplomat reveals, for the first time, that Pius XII's wartime conduct drew upon advice from the German resistance. Out of all this, one might begin to build a new case for Pius XII. My own sense is that the anti–Pius books are coming to an end....

What we really need now is a new biography of Pius XII during those years: a nonreactive account of his life and times, a book driven not by the reviewer's instinct to answer charges but by the biographer's impulse to tell an accurate story. Before that can be done well, I think, the archives of Pius XII's pontificate will probably have to be fully catalogued and opened. Documents released here and there are useful, but useful is a dangerous word in this context, for the use is always in building an argument: a laying out of evidence to make or rebut a charge, rather than a knowledge of the Pope's day-to-day actions. The Vatican has already begun to open some archives earlier than scheduled under the various time-locks, and it promises to open more. But the reviewers' dilemma remains as well: They won the battles, but how are they going to win the war?

Chapter Notes

Introduction

1. Archivio Segreto Vaticano, AES Germania 1935 "Scatole," fasc.9a 81, 154. (Hereinafter cited as ASV, AES; *New York Times* "Nazis Warned at Lourdes," April 29, 1935, 8. Hereinafter cited as *New York Times*. See also: Gallo, *Enemies: Mussolini and the Antifascists* (PA: Xlibris, 2003), 73. While nuncio to Bavaria, Pacelli wrote Secretary of State Gasparri on November 14, 1923, in which he denounced the Nazi movement as a threat to the Catholic Church and noted that the cardinal of Munich had already condemned anti–Jewish persecution of Jews. Pacelli said this was a "vulgar and violent campaign," aimed directly at Catholics and Jews. ASV. Archivo della Nunziatura di Monaco, Pos.396, fasc.7, 6–7, 75–76.

2. Charles Gallagher, "Personal, Private Views," *America* (September 1, 2003), 9. See also: Harold Tittmann, *Inside the Vatican of Pius XII* (New York: Doubleday, 2004), 40–42; Peter Godman notes, "Pacelli recognized the movement headed by the Fuhrer for what it was." Peter Godman, *Hitler and the Vatican* (New York: Free Press, 2004).

3. Gallagher, 9–10.

4. Gallo, *Enemies: Mussolini and the Antifascists*, 104.

5. Harold H. Tittmann, *Inside the Vatican of Pius XII*, 95. See: Gallagher, 9–10; Andrea Tornielli, *Pio XII: il papa degli ebrei* (Piemme: Casale Monferrato, 2003), 131, 136–39.

6. John Conway, "Pope Pius XII and the Myron Taylor Mission," in David Woolner & Richard Kurial, *FDR, the Vatican and the American Catholic Church in America, 1933–1945* (New York: Palgrave, 2003), 143. Pius was convinced that the Allies would win the war. See: Tittmann, *Inside the Vatican of Pius XII*, 130.

7. John Conway, "The Silence of Pope Pius XII," in Charles F. Delzell, *The Papacy and Totalitarianism Between the Wars* (New York: John Wiley, 1974), 92–93.

8. *New York Times*, December 25, 1941. See: Tornielli, *Pio XII*, 171–78.

9. Richard Lukas, *The Forgotten Genocide: The Poles Under German Occupation* (Lexington: University Press of Kentucky, 1986), 3–5, 37–39.

10. James McPherson, "Revisionist Historians," *Perspectives*, American Historical Association (September 2003), 5–6.

11. Justus George Lawler, *Popes and Politics: Reform, Resentment and the Holocaust* (New York: The Continuum International Publishing Group, 2002), 41.

12. Richard Lukas, "Of Stereotypes and Heroes" (New York: Catholic League), 2.

13. David Jonah Goldhagen, *A Moral Reckoning* (New York: Alfred Knopf, 2002), 12.

14. American Jewish Congress Monthly (November-December 2002.) See also: Frederick Schweizer, "In Pursuit of guilt and accountability," *Journal of Genocide Research*, vol. 5, no. 3 (September 2003), 451.

15. Norman Finkelsten sees this same pattern in Goldhagen's, *Hitler's Willing Executioners*. Norman Finkelstein & Ruth Bettina Birn, "Goldhagen's Crazy Thesis," "Revising the Holocaust," *A Nation On Trial: The Goldhagen Thesis and Historical Truth* (New York: Metropolitan Books, 1998), 1–100, 101–48. See also: José Sánchez, *Pius XII and the Holocaust* (Washington, DC: The Catholic University of America Press, 2002), vii; Richard John Neuhaus, "Daniel Goldhagen's Holocaust," *First Things* (August/September 1996), 36–41; Kirsten R. Monroe, review of *Hitler's Willing Executioners*, *Comparative Politics*, vol. 91 (March 1997), 212–13.

16. Robert Cowley, *What If?* (New York: G. P. Putnam, 2001), 317. See: Goldhagen, *Hitler's*

Willing Executioners: Ordinary Germans and the Holocaust (New York: Vintage, 1976), 444; Finkelsten and Birn, 101–48; Mark Riebling, "Jesus, Jews, and the Shoah — A Moral Reckoning," *National Review* (January 27, 2003).

17. John Cornwell, *Hitler's Pope* (New York: Viking Press, 1999); David Kerzer, *The Popes Against the Jews: The Vatican's Role in the Rise of Modern Anti-Semitism* (New York: Alfred Knopf, 2001); Michael Phayer, *The Catholic Church and the Holocaust, 1930–1965* (Bloomington: University of Indiana Press, 2000); Susan Zuccotti, *Under His Very Windows* (New Haven, CT: Yale University Press, 2000); Robert Katz, *The Battle for Rome* (New York: Simon Schuster, 2003); Robert Katz, *Death in Rome* (New York: Macmillan, 1967); Gary Wills, *Papal Sin: Structures of Deceit* (New York: Doubleday, 2000); James Carroll, *Constantine's Sword: The Church and the Jews* (New York: Houghton Mifflin, 2001); Goldhagen, *A Moral Reckoning*, op. cit.

Chapter 1

1. Richard Evans, *Lying About Hitler* (New York: Basic Books, 2001), 3.

2. John Lewis Gaddis, *The Landscape of History* (New York: Oxford University Press, 2002), 136.

3. Michael Marrus, "The Nuremberg Trial: Fifty Years After," *American Scholar 66* (Winter 1997), 563. See also: Lukas, "Of Stereotypes and Heroes."

4. Conway in Delzell, 94–95.

5. Conway in Woolner & Kurial, 144. While Cornwell still accepts papal silence and by implication inaction to help Jews, he has recently admitted the lack of balance in his book, *Hitler's Pope*. He further stated, "I would now argue in the light of the debates and evidence following *Hitler's Pope*, that Pius XII had so little scope of action that it is impossible to judge the motives of silence during the war, while Rome was under the heel of Mussolini and later occupied by the Germans." Perhaps with a thorough reading of the published documents that were available to him at the time of the publication of his book, and now newly released documentation, Cornwell will come to see the serious flaws in his "research." *Economist*, "The Papacy: For God's Sake" (December 11, 2004), 82.

6. Yehuda Bauer, *Rethinking the Holocaust* (New Haven, CT: Yale University Press, 2001), 8–11; Samantha Power, *A Problem from Hell: America and the Age of Genocide* (New York: Basic Books, 2002), 15–19.

7. Eric Weiz, *A Century of Genocide* (Princeton, NJ: Princeton University Press, 2003),

7–8. How to apply and define genocide has recently come to light with the widespread atrocities in Darfur. Human rights organizations have criticized a UN report that found that the crimes against humanity in Darfur did not constitute genocide. Lydia Polgreen, "Both Sides of Conflict in Darfur Dispute Findings of U.N. Report," *New York Times*, February 2, 2005, A6.

8. Peter Novick, *The Holocaust in American Life* (New York: Houghton Mifflin, 1999), 133.

9. Bauer, *Rethinking the Holocaust*, 9, 12. Bauer defines genocide as "the planned attempt to destroy a national, ethnic, or racial group using measures outlined by Lemkin and the U.N. Convention, measures that accompany the selective mass murder of members of the targeted group." Stone's contention that the defense of the uniqueness of the Holocaust is ideological "stems from a historically explicable, but by now harmful belief that Jewish identity would be massively threatened if one of its mainstays (the fact that all Jews were potentially victims of Nazism) were to lose its 'sacred' aura, and also, unconsciously, a belief that the Holocaust's status as unique constitutes a bulwark against revivified anti–Semitism." Dan Stone, "The Historiography of Genocide; Beyond 'Uniqueness' and Ethnic Competition," *Rethinking History*, vol. 8 (March 2004), 129. For his critique of Bauer and those who hold to the Holocaust's uniqueness see 128–30.

10. Norman Finkelstein, *The Holocaust Industry* (New York: Verso, 2000), 48–49, 52.

11. Weitz, *A Century of Genocide*, 12. See also: Vahakn Dadrian, "Patterns of Twentieth Century Genocides: the Armenian, Jewish and Rwandan Cases," *Journal of Genocide Research*, vol. 6, no. 4 (December 2004), 494–95.

12. Weitz, *A Century of Genocide*, 8. Norman Finkelstein maintains that "The Holocaust dogma of eternal Gentile hatred also validates the complementary Holocaust dogma of uniqueness.... The persecution of non–Jews in the Holocaust merely becomes accidental and the persecution of non–Jews in history merely episodic." Finkelstein, *The Holocaust Industry*, 54. See also: Stone, *The Historiography of Genocide*, 127–42.

13. Weitz, 104.

14. Mark Mazower, "Evil Rising," *New York Times Book Review*, March 14, 2004, 3. See also: Stone, "Historiography of Genocide," 1; Lukas, *The Forgotten Genocide*, 37–39; Emmanuel Dongala, "The Genocide Next Door," *New York Times*, April 6, 2004, A23.

15. Yehuda Bauer, *A History of the Holocaust*, 308.

16. Mazower, 13. Christopher Browning, *The Origins of the Final Solution* (Lincoln: University of Nebraska Press, 2004), 12–35. Omer Bartov states that: "while there is no consensus on the nature of the tie between the decision on mass murder and the course of the Blizkreig in Russia, there is almost common unanimity on the connection ... between the Blitzkrieg and the implementation of genocide." Omer Bartov, *Germany's War and the Holocaust: Disputed Histories* (Ithaca: Cornell University Press, 2003), 51.

17. Novick, 21.

18. *Ibid.*, 22.

19. *Ibid.*, 23. Novick states: "If the mainstream press contained little about the Holocaust while it was going on, the same was true of much of the Jewish press," 37. Richard Breitman states that Rabbi Wise did not keep the Riegner report to himself. He shared it with other Jewish groups, but this information was not released to the press. Richard Breitman & Alan Kraut, *American Refugee Policy and European Jewry, 1933–1945* (Bloomington: University of Indiana Press, 1987), 152–53.

20. Novick, 26.

21. *Ibid.*, 25.

22. Bauer, *A History of the Holocaust*, 330. The issue of information is a complicated one and Professor Ruth Linn takes Bauer and a number of Israeli historians to task for misnaming, misreporting, misrepresenting, and the suppression of the Vrba-Wetzler report. Vrba and Wetzler escaped Auschwitz and provided information to the Hungarian Jewish Council regarding the forthcomng deportation. The council worked a deal with Eichmann that saved the Council and over 1,000 prominent Jews and withheld the information that it received from the masses who were to be deported. That information could have saved thousands of Hungarian Jews. Ruth Linn, *Escaping Auschwitz: A Culture of Forgetting* (Ithaca, NY: Cornell University Press, 2004).

23. Zuccotti quoted in Lawler, n. 6, 50.

24. Bauer, *Rethinking the Holocaust*, 224. The issue of information and its evaluation becomes complicated when one considers the suppression of the Vrba-Wetzler report. On April 7, 1944, two Slovakian Jews, Alfred Wetzler and Rudolf Vrba, escaped from Auschwitz. They succeeded in crossing the border into Slovakia and contacted the Slovakian Jewish Council and were debriefed by them. Wetzler and Vrba urged that their information be given to the Jews of Hungary, who were murdered, and to forestall additional planned deportations. This report, also known as the Auschwitz Protocols, never reached its in-

tended audience, and a half million Jews were deported and killed. The two men were certain that their report was suppressed. Ruth Linn argues Israeli historians have suppressed this report. According to Vrba the report was suppressed so that leading members of the Slovakian and Hungarian Jewish Councils could make a deal with Eichmann and exchanged their silence for their own survival. Many of them would occupy prominent positions in the newly established state of Israel. Official Israeli historians had no place for alternative interpretations of what happened in Hungary, or for any analysis of the role of the Judenrat and their collaboration with the Nazis. *Newsletter*, Association of Contemporary Church Historians, X, no. 11 (November 2004). Linn, *Escaping Auschwitz*.

25. Carl Amery, "The Harassed Pope," in Eric Bentley ed., *Storm Over the Deputy* (New York: Grove Press), 162.

26. David Alvarez, "U.S. Intelligence and the Vatican," in Woolner & Kurial, 264. See also: David Alvarez, "Vatican Intelligence Capabilities in the Second World War," *Intelligence and National Security*, 6 (July 1991), 593–607. Owen Chadwick, "The Pope and the Jews in 1942," W. J. Sheils, *Persecution and Tolerance* (London: Basil Blackwell, 1984), 436.

27. Cornwell, 240–41. José Sánchez, *Pius XII and the Holocaust*, 45.

28. Gallo, *Enemies*, 49, 60–78, 108–19.

29. *Casti connubii* (www.vatican.va/holy_father_pius_ xi/ encylicals/index.htm). Hereinafter cited Pius XI encyclicals. *Mystici corporis* www.vatican.va/holy_father/pius_xii/encyclicals/index.htm) hereinafter cited Pius XII encyclicals.

30. Conway in Woolner & Kurial, 145. See Tittman, 12, 21.

31. Peter Kent, *The Lonely War of Pius XII: The Roman Catholic Church and the Division of Europe, 1943–1953* (Montreal: McGill Queens University Press, 2002), 75.

32. *New York Times*, June 7, 1942, 1–4, 12. For the Vatican's opposition to the Nazi eugenics and euthanasia programs see: Henry Friedlander, *The Origins of Nazi Genocide: From Euthanasia to the Final Solution* (Chapel Hill: University of North Carolina Press, 1995), 112–16.

33. *New York Times*, June 10, 1943, 5, 20; *New York Times*, June 9, 1942, 6, 12.

34. OSS, "A Report from Switzerland on the German Churches," October 31, 1944, *NA*, RG226 Entry Frames 662.

35. OSS *RB* 226/16/11, October 10, 1944.

36. *New York Times*, May 26, 1943, 1.

37. *New York Times*, October 2, 1943, 3, 6.

38. *New York Times*, May 28, 1943, 4, 5.

39. *New York Times*, January 21, 1943, 2, 37.
40. William Z. Foster, *The Twilight of Capitalism* (New York: International Publishers, 1949), 158.
41. Max Bedacht, *The Menace of Capitalism*, cited in Irving Howe & Lewis Coser, *The American Communist Party* (Boston: Beacon Press, 1947).
42. *The Communist* (March 1930), 197.
43. *New York Times*, February 2, 1944, 1, 5–6, 11.
44. *New York Times*, February 4, 1944, 2, 14.
45. *New York Times*, February 6, 1944, 1, 7; *New York Times*, March 19, 1944, 3; *New York Times*, July 6, 1944, 1.
46. Kent, 73; *New York Times*, February 10, 1945, 3, 5.
47. *New York Times*, February 10, 1945, 6, 22. Kent, 73.
48. *New York Times*, April 17, 1945, 1, 5.
49. Kent, 73.
50. *New York Times*, February 19, 1945, 5, 22.
51. *New York Times*, April 17, 1945, 1, 5.
52. Adam Ulam, *Stalin* (New York: Viking, 1973), 325. See also: Simon Sebag Montefiore, *Stalin: The Court of the Red Tsar* (New York: Alfred A. Knopf, 2004).
53. Edvard Radzinsky, *Stalin* (New York: Doubleday, 1996), 249.
54. Ulam, 419.
55. Radzinsky, 413.
56. Anne Appelbaum, *Gulag: A History* (New York: Doubleday, 2003), 578–79.
57. Ulam, 487.
58. Appelbaum, 578–79.
59. Theodore Freedman, ed., *Anti-Semitism in the Soviet Union, Its Roots and Consequences* (New York, 1984). See also: Zvi Gitelman, *Jewish Nationality and Soviet Politics* (Princeton, NJ: Princeton University Press, 1972); "New Soviet anti–Semitism sees Jews as "little people," *Jerusalem Post*, April 13, 1980.
60. Mazower, 13.
61. Louis Rapoport, *Stalin's War Against the Jews* (New York: The Free Press, 1990), 58.
62. Rapoport, 58.
63. Ulam, 678. Jonathan Brent &Vladimir Naumov, *Stalin's Last Crime, The Plot Against the Jewish Doctors* (New York: HarperCollins, 2003).
64. Appelbaum, 454.
65. John Neuhaus, "Daniel Goldhagen's Holocaust," *First Things* (August-September 1996), 36. Willaim Allen Sheridan has concluded many people "were drawn to anti–Semitism because they were drawn to Nazism, not the other way around." *The Nazi Seizure of Power*, 84. See also: Browning, *Origins of the Final Solution*, 7–8.
66. Kent, "The Martyrdom of Archbishop Stepinac," in *The Lonely Cold War of Pius XII*, 155–76.
67. M. M. Scheinmann, *Der Vatikan in Sweiten Welreig* (E. Berling, 1945).
68. Scheinmann quoted in Conway, *Nazi Persecution of the Churches*, 81.
69. Alan Bullock, *Hitler and Stalin* (New York: Alfred Knopf, 1992), 956.
70. Poliakov, "The Vatican and the Jewish Question: The Hitler Period and After," *Commentary* (November 1950), 439–49. See also: Poliakov, "Pope Pius and Nazis," in Bentley, 222–23.
71. Cornwell, 112. See also: Kertzer, 40; Goldhagen, *A Moral Reckoning*, 43–44; Katz, *Battle for Rome*, 5.
72. Tittmann, *Inside the Vatican of Pius XII*, 95.
73. Cornwell, 288. The prevailing orthodoxy with reference to Pius XII's silence and inaction is perpetuated by Doris Bergen, *War and Genocide* (New York: Rowman & Littlefield, 2003), 109.
74. Phayer, xii.
75. John Conway, "How Not to Deal with History," in Joseph Bottum & David Dalin, *The Pius War* (Lanham, MD: Lexington Books, 2004), 70. Robert Lockwood review of Michael Phayer in *Newsletter of the Association of Contemporary Church Historians*, December 2000, 5. Hereinafter cited as *Newsletter*. See also: Sir Martin Gilbert interview with William Doino, *Inside the Vatican* (August 2003). For Cornwell's statement see: "For God's Sake," *Economist* (December 11, 2004) 82–83.
76. Bauer, *Rethinking the Holocaust*, 31.
77. Lawler, 105; Sánchez, 12.
78. Graham, 12–13. Saul Friedlander's principal theme is Pius XII's obsession with Communism. Friedlander, *Pius XII and the Third Reich* (New York: Knopf, 1966), 134, 236. Many revisionists repeat this same unproven assertion including Robert Katz, *The Battle for Rome*, 5. John Conway assessed Friedlander's claim: "He has chosen to overlook the most significant of the Papal protests, which despite his contention, are to be found in the sources he has used. This arbitrariness in selection is matched by a bias in interpretation which extends even to the translations in the various editions of his book." Conway, *The Nazi Persecution of the Churches*, 450. Conway's criticism is applicable to the many of the revisionists. To understand the Pope's view of Nazism and Communism see Robert Leiber, "Der Papst and die Verfolgung der Juden," in *Summa inuria oder Durfte der Papst schweigen?* Fritz J. Raddatz, ed. (Hamburg: Rowohlt, 1964), 104.
79. Novick, 65; Finkelstein, *The Holocaust Industry*, 12–38.

80. Eric Weitz review of Donald Bloxham, *Genocide On Trial* (New York: Oxford University Press) *American Historical Review*, vol. 109 (February 2004), 156–57.

81. Novick, 12.

82. Novick, 209. Novick observes that "more information about the Holocaust was imparted over those four nights than over all the preceding years."

83. Novick, 12. Richard Breitman takes issue with David Wyman's thesis in *Abandonment of the Jews*. He states that contrary to Wyman and Lipsstadt assertions, "Although anti-Semitism was present in the United States, it was not so virulent and corrosive that it dictated the outcome of refugee policy throughout the Roosevelt era." Breitman, *American Refugee Policy*, 4–6.

84. Erwin Piscator in Eric Bentley, ed. (New York: Grove Press, 1964), 11–15; Emanuela Barrasch-Rubenstein, *The Devil, the Saints, and the Church: Reading Hochhuth's* The Deputy (New York: Peter Lang, 2003).

85. John Weiss, *The Ideology of Death*, 1955. Hochhuth never altered his views despite the publication of new evidence at the time. See: Jenö Levai, *Hungarian Jewry and the Papacy* (London: Sands Publishing, 1968), 1–16. Ruth Linn has shed new light on the Hungarian deportations and the failure of Jewish leaders. Linn, *Escaping Auschwitz*.

86. Pius XI encyclicals. Pacelli as nuncio to Bavaria in a letter dated November 4, 1923, to the Gasppari, Cardinal Secretary of State, refers to Hitler's failed attempt to seize the government of Munich. The letter denounces the National Socialist movement as an anti–Catholic threat and notes that the cardinal of Munich had already condemned acts of persecution of Bavaria's Jews. See: Margherita Marchione, "New Archival Evidence Vindicates Pope Pius XII," *Catalyst* (November 2003).

87. *New York Times*, January 23, 1940, 1. See: Tornielli, *Pio XII*, 159–60, 167.

88. Pius XII encyclicals. For the positive coverage of Pius XII's actions by Jewish leaders, organizations, and the press see: Dimitri A. Cavalli, "The Good Samaritan: Jewish Praise for Pope Pius XII," *Inside the Vatican* (October 2000), 72–77; Cavalli, "Pope Pius XII and the Jewish Press," *Catholic New York*, April 15, 1999, 11.

89. *New York Times*, August 6, 1942, 1; *New York Times*, August 27, 1942, 1.

90. Rolf Hochhuth, *Sidelights on History*, 297–99. See: Tornielli, *Pio XII*, 38–40.

91. *Times* (London), May 20, 1963. Newly released documents reveal that Pius XII provided material and spiritual assistance to literally thousands of prisoners and victims of the war. Assistance was given to restore families separated by the conflict and to respond to numerous inquiries about refugees and missing military and civilians. The documents comprise two volumes and total 1,511 pages, and reveal that 20,000,000 messages were transmitted on the behalf of these victims. *Inter Arma Caritas* (2004). Monsignor Walter Brandmuller has documented the Holy See's intervention to prevent the persecution of Jews in Slovakia. See: *L'Olocausto nella Slovacchia e la Chiesa Cattolica* (Rome: Vatican Publishing House, 2004).

92. *American Jewish Monthly* (November-December 2002). Many scholars have criticized Goldhagen's works. Kristen Monroe in her review of Goldhagen's *Hitler's Willing Executioners* faults him for not putting forth "clearly established criteria of evidence," and says that his analyses have major flaws, that he ignores contrary evidence, and that he is polemical. She concludes, "Sadly, ironically, by condemning the German people en masse Goldhagen comes perilously close to the same kind of cultural and ethnic stereotyping that still leads to anti–Semitism, and which Goldhagen so passionately and rightly deplores." Kristen R. Monroe, "Review: Hitler's Willing Executioners," *Comparative Politics* (March 1977), 212–13. David Dalin excoriates Goldhagen's *A Moral Reckoning*. He states that the book, "is so flawed — its facts error-prone, its arguments tendentious, and its conclusion, equating Christianity in its essence with anti–Semitism, both bizarre and dangerous...," "History Bigotry," *Weekly Standard*, February 10, 2003. British historian Michael Burleigh has said Goldhagen's *A Moral Reckoning* is vile and a "strip cartoon view of European history."

93. Cornwell, 295–97; Goldhagen, 46–47, 56–57, 86, 141.

94. Goldhagen, 46.

95. Norman Finkelstein, who presents a devastating analysis of Goldhagen, writes, "Although bearing the apparatus of an academic study, *Hitler's Willing Executioners* amounts to little more than a compendium of sadistic violence." Finkelstein, *A Nation On Trial*, 64. Frederick Schweitzer says that similar faults that appeared in Goldhagen's earlier book reappears in *A Moral Reckoning*, "the book is ill organized, wordy and repetitious, endlessly and monotonously repetitious.... This is not so much a work of history — it does not rely on a chronological sequence (chronology is jumbled) or utilize a historical narrative — it is in turn a moralizing sermon and journalistic reportage." Schweitzer, "In Pursuit of guilt and accountability," 451–52. See also: Evans, *Coming of the Third Reich*, 204.

96. Ronald Rychlak, *Hitler, the War, and the Pope* (Columbus, MS: Genesis Press, 2000), 297–98. See: Andrea Tornielli, *Pio XII: Il Papa che salvo degli ebrei*, 50–76.

97. Cornwell, 71.

98. Michael Feldkamp, *Pius XII und Deutschland* (Gottingen: Vanderhoeck & Ruprecht, 2001), cited in *Newsletter*, vol. 7, no. 6 (June 2001), 5, 12.

99. Rychlak, 298–99. Professor Rychlak points out that Goldhagen accepts Cornwell's distorted mistranslation of the 1919 letter.

100. Goldhagen, 46. See: Schweitzer, "In Pursuit of guilt and accountability," 453–54.

101. Rychlak, 281–314.

102. Richard Evans, *Coming of the Third Reich* (New York: Penguin Press, 2004), 57.

103. Toland, *Adolf Hitler* (New York: Ballantine Books, 1976), 64.

104. Rychlak, 298–99. See also: Cornwell, 76–77.

105. Burleigh, *The Third Reich* (New York: Hill and Wang, 2000), 40. Letter of Pacelli to Gasparri, Zenit, March 5, 2003. See also: *Inside the Vatican* (March 2003).

106. Novick, 21–25.

107. Patrick Gallo letter to Abraham Foxman, October 29, 1999, regarding statement made Tuesday, October 21, 2003, on ABC-7 Eyewitness News. Chairman of the Yad Vashem Directorate Avner Shalev has criticized "The use of the Holocaust to manipulatively advance political stands is irresponsible. It deprecates the Holocaust and perverts the historical facts." *Jerusalem Post*, September 20, 2004, December 21, 2004, 1. Ruth Linn underscores the importance of a fully documented presentation of the Holocaust in order to assign responsibility. Linn criticizes the purposeful suppression of the Vrba-Wetzler Report that would have warned the intended victims. Ruth Linn, *Escaping Auschwitz, a Culture of Forgetting*.

108. Finkelstein & Birn, *A Nation on Trial*, 1–100.

109. Finkelstein, *The Holocaust Industry*, 55. For a complete refutation of Cornwell see Rychlak, 281–307. See: Peter Gumpel, "Cornwell's Pope: A Nasty Caricature of a Noble and Saintly Man," Zenit News Service, 16 (September 16, 1999).

110. *La Repubblica*, November 21, 2002, 2.

111. Vatican documents were published in 11 volumes as *Actes et Documents du Saint Siège relaifs à la Seconde Guerre Mondale* (hereinafter cited as *ADSS*). Vol. 1, *Le Saint Siège et la guerre en Europe, 1939–1940*; vol. 2, *Lettres de Pie XII aux Evêques allemands, 1939–1944*; vol. 3, *Le Saint Siège et la situation religiuse en Pologne et dans les Pays Baltes, 1939–1945*; vol.

4, *Le Saint Siège et la guerre en Europe, Juin 1940–Juin 1941*; vol. 5, *Le Saint Siège et la guerre mondale, Juillett 1941–Octobre 1942*; vol. 6, *Le Saint Siège et les victims de la guerre, Mars. 1939–December 1940*; vol. 7, *Le Saint Siège et la guerre mondiale, Novembre 1942–December 1943*; vol. 8, *Le Saint Siège et les victims de la guerre, Janvier 1941–Decembe 1942*; vol. 9, *Le Saint Siège de la guerre, Janvier 1943–Decembre 1943*; vol. 10, *Le Saint Siège et les victims de la guerre, Janvier 1944–Juillet 1945*; vol. 11, *Le Saint Siège et la guerre mondiale, Janvier 1944–Mai 1945*. Professor Marrus would be better served to consult *ADSS* vol. 2, 387–436, for the minutes of the meeting of the German cardinals with Pius XII. *La Repubblica* (November 21, 2002), 2. Vatican archives for the period 1922–1939 were opened in February 2003. Revisionist critics have not really read these volumes, perhaps in part because they can't read French or the other documents that are written in Italian.

112. *ADSS 9*, June 9, 1943 no. 224; June 23, 1943 no. 276. *ADSS 10*, March 32, 1944 no. 127: *ADSS 10*, May 16, 1944, no. 196; John Conway, "How Not to Deal with History," in Bottum and Dalin, *The Pius War*, 69.

113. Robert Trisco, "The Apostolic Delegation in Washington," in Woolner & Kurial, 239–43. For Pius XII's rescue efforts in Hungary see: Jenö Levai, *Hungarian Jewry and the Papacy*; *ADSS*, vol. 10, no. 273, 359; no. 396, 384; no. 418, 512–13; Breitman, *American Refugee Policy*, 213–14; *Summary Report-Hungary*, War Refugee Board Records, Box 34, 17–25, FDRL. For papal rescue in Slovakia see: Brandmuller, *L'Olocausto nella Slovacchia e la Chiesa Cattolica*, Linn, *Escaping Auschwitz*; Schweitzer, "In pursuit of guilt and accountability," 451–52.

114. Richard Breitman, Zenit News Service, July 7, 2000; *Corriere della Sera* (June 29, 2000); "Vatican Secret Archive Confirms Church's Opposition to Nazism," Zenit, November 15, 2002.

115. Bauer, *American Jewry and the Holocaust*, 18.

116. Adolf Hitler, *Mein Kampf* (New York: Houghton Mifflin, 1971), 60–75.

117. Fritz Stern, "The Worst Was Yet to Come," *New York Times*, February 23, 1997, 12. Some historians have argued that flushed with victory in the first phase of the war against Russia the Nazi elite were encouraged to begin the mass murder of European Jews. Others contend that the transition to genocide occurred after their failure to achieve their goals in Russia. Bartov, *Germany's War and the Holocaust: Disputed Histories*, 51.

118. Bauer, *Rethinking the Holocaust*, 28.

119. Klemperer, *I Shall Bear Witness*, vol. 2, 78.

120. Weitz, "The Primacy of Race," in *A Century of Genocide*, 102–43; Burleigh, *The Third Reich*, "Racial Wars Against the Jews," 574–629.

121. Gallo, *For Love and Country*, 40–41. See also: Gallo, *Enemies*, 115–16.

122. Kertzer, 282.

123. Martin Gilbert, *Righteous Gentile*, 356–80. See also: David Dalin, "Righteous Gentile: Pope Pius and the Jews," *Weekly Standard*, February 26, 2001.

124. Weitz, *A Century of Genocide*, 109.

125. Zuccotti, 63; Kertzer, 16; Goldhagen, "What Would Jesus Have Done," *New Republic*, January 12, 2002, 23; Robert Wistrich, *Hitler and the Holocaust* (New York: Modern Library, 2001), 129. See: Tittmann, *Inside the Vatican of Pius XII*, 111, 118–20, 124–25.

126. *New York Times*, October 28, 1939, 1.

127. The New York–based Jewish Telegraphic Agency was the equivalent of the Associated Press. See *Summi Pontificatus*, Pius XII encyclicals, paragraphs 32, 74, 96; Gallo, *For Love and Country, The Italian Resistance*, 31; Gallo, *Enemies*, 108; Mark Riebling, *The Eagle and the Cross: The Pope, the Jesuits, and the Plot to Kill Hitler* (New York: HarperCollins, 2005).

128. Rychlak, 177.

129. *New York Times*, December 25, 1942, 16. For the full text of Pius XII's Christmas message see *Acta Apostolicae Sedis* of 1943, vol. 35, 5–8; *Selected Encyclicals and Addresses* (London: Catholic Truth Society, 1949), 275–97; Lawler, 109–16; Gallo, *For Love and Country*, 40; Tornielli, *Pio XII*, 171–82.

130. *Report from the Reich Central Security Office*, January 22, 1943; Lawler, 115.

131. The other Nazi papers that the revisionists should consult include: *Der Andriff, Frankfuttr Zeitung, Volkisher Beobachter, Der Judenkener*, and *Der Weltkampf*. The SS journal *Das Schwarze Korps* should also be evaluated. See also: *Documents on German Foreign Policy 1918–1945, Series D (1937–1945)*, vol. 1, no. 633; Russel Lemmons, *Goebbels and Der Andriff* (Lexington: University of Kentucky Press, 1994).

132. Goldhagen, *A Moral Reckoning*, 40, 46–47, 56–57, 86, 158.

133. Gilbert, *Righteous Gentile*, 357–58.

134. Gallo, *For Love and Country*, 41. See: Martin Gilbert, *Inside the Vatican* (August 2003).

135. Pius XII encyclicals, paragraphs 32, 74, 96.

136. Tittmann, *Inside the Vatican of Pius XII*, 213; *New York Times*, May 28, 1943, 4. See also: *ADSS*, vol. 16, 12–13, 539 of appendix.

137. *ADSS*, vol. 6, 12–13, appendix 539; *ADSS*, vol. 18, 189; *ADSS*, vol. 8, document 165, 295–307, document 189, 334; Rychlak 362–63, no. 60; Tornielli, *Pio XII*, 237–50.

138. Lawler, 48. On September 9, 1941 the *Times of London* reported a Vichy order for the arrest of Roman Catholic priests who were sheltering Jews in the unoccupied zone. According to Martin Gilbert, "Cardinal Gerlier, the Archbishop of Lyons, had already issued a defiant refusal to surrender those Jewish children whose parents had already been deported, and who were being 'fed and sheltered' in Roman Catholic homes." On September 11 Maglione informed the French ambassador to the Vatican "that the conduct of the Vichy government towards Jews and foreign refugees was a gross infraction of the Vichy Government's own principles...." Gilbert, *Auschwitz and the Allies* (New York: Holt, Rinehart & Winston, 1981), 69; Tornielli, *Pio XII*, 250–70; *ADSS*, vol. 8, 295–307.

139. Zuccotti, *Under His Very Windows*, 301. For a thorough refutation of Zuccotti see: Ronald Rychlak's "Comments on Susan Zuccotti's, Under His Very Windows," The *Journal of Modern Italian Studies*, vol. 7 (Summer 2002), 218–33. Papal critics have seized on a purported Vatican document unearthed by Italian historian Alberto Melloni without critical assessment. The letter, dated October 23, 1946, apparently offers instructions to the apostolic nuncio in France, Angelo Roncalli. Papal revisionists such as Daniel Goldhagen and the *New York Times* and other publications seized upon the document, in which authorities were instructed that they should not return hidden Jewish children to their families after the war if they had been baptized. Ronald Rychlak has stated that Canon 750 of the 1917 Canon Law that was supplemented during World War II by orders of the Vatican and the French bishops made it clear that hidden Jewish children were not to be baptized without parental consent. Only a small number of such children were baptized. The letter was unsigned, not written on Vatican letterhead, with words not typical for directives from the Vatican. Moreover, it was addressed to the apostolic nunciature in Paris. Such a letter would have been written in Italian, not in French, since the Holy Office was staffed mainly by an Italian cleric who would have written to a counterpart in his own language. Furthermore there is no evidence that Archbishop Roncalli read it. He never referred to it in his diaries. The document was found in the French archives, not among the papers of the apostolic nunciature in France. The instructions were the exact opposite from those reported

and do not say that Jewish children should be kept from their families. The instructions referred to institutions, not families, and said that each individual instance had to be evaluated on a case-by-case basis. There are serious questions about the authenticity of the document. Finally, there is no evidence the instructions were approved by Pius XII. Ronald Rychlak, *Postwar Catholics, Jewish Children, and a Rush to Judgment*" (www.bliefnet.com). See also: Rychlak, "Jewish Children After World Word II: A Case Study" (www.bliefnet.com). See: Matteo Luigi Napolitano, "Pio XII, parliamo I documenti," *Avvenire*, January 18, 2005.

140. Lawler, 49–50. Martin Gilbert writes, "Throughout 1942, the problem confronting the Allies, and the Jews in Allied lands, had been the lack of information. This arose from the deliberated Nazi policy of deception, whereby the destination of the deportees, and their fate, was cloaked and concealed." Martin Gilbert, *Auschwitz and the Allies*, 339. Peter Novick notes that Gerhard Riegner forwarded his report "with due reserve" concerning the truth. This statement plus his informant's claim regarding "corpses turned into soap," furthered a will to disbelieve common among gentiles and Jews. By the fall of 1943 the U.S. State Department concluded that Riegner's report was "essentially correct." Novick, *The Holocaust in American Life*, 23.

141. Bauer, *Rethinking the Holocaust*, 23.

142. Rychlak, 402; Cavalli, "The Good Samaritan: The Jewish Praise for Pope Pius XII"; Margherita Marchione, *Pope Pius XII: Architect for Peace* (NJ: Paulist Press, 2000), 76–84, 123–31; *ADSS*, vol. 6, 211–14; Robert Graham, "Relations of Pius XII and the Catholic Community with Jewish Organizations," in Ivo Herzer, *The Italian Refuge: Rescue of Jews During the Holocaust* (Washington, DC: Catholic University Press of America, 1989), 231–53; Nicola Caracciolo, *Uncertain Refuge: Italy and the Jews During the Holocaust* (Urbana: University of Illinois Press, 1995) 37–39, 43–49; Tornielli, *Pio XII*, 184–86, 190–91.

143. Conway, *How Not to Deal with History*, 69. Zuccotti would be better served to read Harold Tittmann's memoirs on this matter. Harold Tittmann III, *Inside the Vatican of Pius XII*, 45, 143, 186–87. Cassulo and Safran statements in: *ADSS*, vol. 2, 950–51; *ADSS*, vol. 10, 428–29; *Civiltà Cattolica*, vol. 3 (1961), 462. For more on Tittmann see: William Doino & Joseph Bottum, *Books in Review*, "Inside the Vatican of Pius XII," *First Things* (November 2004), 39–42; Richard C. Lukas, *Of Stereotypes and Heroes*, 1; Gilbert, *Inside the Vatican* (August 2003). Peter Novick writes that generally

speaking "rescue was not a high priority for major American Jewish organizations or their leaders during the war." Novick, 40. See also: Feingold, *The Politics of Rescue*, 10–14; Rafael Medoff, "Conflict between American Jewish leaders and dissidents over responding to the news of the Holocaust: three episodes from 1942–1943," *Journal of Genocide Research*, vol. 5, no. 3 (September 2003), 439–45; Breitman, *American Refugee Policy*, 4–5.

144. Albert Einstein, *Time*, December 23, 1940, 38–40. Letter dated October 27, 1945. Giovanni Montini to Raffaele Cantoni, president of the Italian Jewish Communities, describing Kubwitsky's audience with Pius XII (Zenit, July 30, 1999). See also: Conway, "How Not to Deal with History," 69; David Dalin, "A Righteous Gentile: Pope Pius and the Jews," *Weekly Standard*, February 26, 2001; Tornielli, *Pio XII*, 167.

145. Antonio Gaspari, *Gli ebrei salvati da Pio XII* (Logos); *Testimonies on beatification of Pius XII*. For a summary of coverage of the Vatican and Pius XII by the *New York Times* see: Msgr. Stephen M. Di Giovanni, "Pius XII and the Jews: The War Years as reported by the *New York Times*" (New York: Catholic League), Pierre Blet, *Pius XII and the Second World War: According to the Archives of the Vatican* (NJ: Paulist Press).

146. *Newsletter*, February 2002, vol. 7, no. 2, 6. See also: *American Jewish Congress Monthly* (November–December 2002); Georg Denzler, *Wildersand ist nicht das richtge Wort: Katholische Prister, Brischoefe und Theologen im Dritten Reich* (Zurich: Pendo Verlag, 2003).

147. Georg Densler in *Newsletter* (February 2002) vol. 2, nos. 2, 6–7.

148. Feldkamp, *Newsletter*, 7.

149. Rubenstein, *Myth of Rescue* (New York: Routledge, 1997), 206.

150. Richard Breitman, *American Refugee Policy*, 6.

151. Saul Friedlander, *Nazi Germany and the Jews* (New York: HarperCollins, 1997), 3.

152. Saul Friedlander, 5.

153. Rubenstein, 216. For the central role of Hitler in decision-making see: Christopher Browning, *The Origins of the Final Solution* (Lincoln: University of Nebraska Press, 2004), 424–28.

Chapter 2

1. Goldhagen, 43.

2. Goldhagen, 43; Cornwell, 149–56.

3. Cornwell, 149–56.

4. Phayer, 18.

5. Heinrich Brüning, "Ein Bief," im *Eeutche Rundshau* (July 1947). Cornwell relies on

Klaus Scholder, who has been discredited by other historians.

6. Evans, *Coming of the Third Reich*, 250.
7. *Ibid.*, 251.
8. Toland, 211.
9. Evans, *Coming of the Third Reich*, 150–51.
10. Bullock, *Hitler: A Study in Tyranny*, 253.
11. Joachim Fest, *Hitler*, 367; Evans, *Coming of the Third Reich*, 283–84; Burleigh, *The Third Reich*, 140.
12. Goebbels, *My Fight in Germany* (London, 1935), 16–17.
13. Burleigh, 69.
14. Evans, *Coming of the Third Reich*, 152.
15. Bullock, *Hitler: A Study in Tyranny*, 253. Newly released Vatican documents reveal that Cardinal Secretary of State Pacelli reviewed Nuncio Cesare Orsenigo's New Year's speech. The draft of the speech, which was to be delivered before Paul von Hindenburg, president of the Reich, and Hitler, the new chancellor, was sent on November 25, 1933, and Pacelli replied on December 1 by secret code and told Orsenigo to remove the words that referred to Hitler as "leader of the German people." He also told him to remove an entire paragraph that praised Hitler. The cardinal deleted an entire paragraph on Hitler noting "that the praises contained in the address" should "undoubtedly be moderate, in consideration of the grave difficulties to which the Church is now exposed in Germany." (Entry 604, p.o. fascicle 113) In 1936 Cardinal Pacelli again edited Orsenigo's speech and deleted all the portions that praised the Führer's activity. Again in 1936 Pacelli instructed Orsenigo not to attend the Nazi Congress in Nuremberg with the foreign diplomatic corps. Orsenigo's New Year's address was to refer to the Olympics held in Berlin in 1936. Pacelli told him to delete this reference since the encyclical *Mit Brennender Sorge* had been issued assailing the Nazi regime. Later in April of 1937 Pacelli instructed Orsenigo not to attend a reception for Hitler's birthday. See: Marchione, "New Archival Evidence." See also: Zenit, May 1, 2003; Matteo Luigi Napolitano, *Il Giornale* (May 2003).
16. Bullock, *Hitler and Stalin*, 255.
17. *Mein Kampf*, 17.
18. Evans, *Coming of the Third Reich*, 329–32, 334–36.
19. ND 1390-PS, 262.
20. Bullock, *Hitler*, 269. For the full text of the Enabling Act see Baynes, vol. 1, 430–31.
21. Fest, *Hitler*, 407.
22. *Ibid.*
23. Bullock, *Hitler: A Study in Tyranny*, 270.
24. Evans, *Coming of the Third Reich*, 364.
25. *Ibid.*

26. Fest, *Hitler*, 410; Evans, *Coming of the Third Reich*, 349–55, 369–70.
27. Patrick Gallo, "Dachau's Priests," *Seattle Catholic*, March 28, 2003, 1. See also: Robert Krieg, *Catholic Theologians in Nazi Germany* (New York: Continuum, 2004).
28. Evans, *Coming of the Third Reich*, 346.
29. Cornwell distorts the entire issue regarding the origins of the concordat and its consequences. Cornwell, 141–48.
30. For Pius XII's assessment of Hitler see: Ivone Kirkpatrick, *Mussolini: A Study in Power* (New York: Hawthorn Books, 1964) Sr. M. Pascalina Lehnert, *Ich dufte ihm dienen: Erinbrugen an Papst Pius XII*, 4th ed. (Wurzburg: Verlag Johnann Wilhelm Naumann, 1983), 42–43; Conroy in Delzell, *The Silence of Pope Pius XII.*
31. Bauer, *A History of the Holocaust* (New York: Franklin Watts, 2001), 144.
32. Ivone Kirkpatrick to Sir Robert Vansittart, August 19, 1933. *Documents on British Foreign Policy, 1919–1939*, 2nd series (London: Her Majesty's Stationery Office, 1956), 5: 524–55. See: Robert Kreig, "The Vatican Concordat with Hitler's Reich," *America*, September 1, 2003, 5.
33. For the full text of the concordat see: *Documents on German Foreign Policy, 1918–1945, Series C (1933–1937)*, 80; Tornielli, *Pio XII*, 77–98.
34. Gallo, *Enemies*, 70–71; Burleigh, 722; Cornwell, 90–98; Phayer 133–38.
35. Cornwell; Phayer, 18; Goldhagen, 43. In 1933 Pacelli wrote to Orsengio to concern himself with the plight of the Jews. See: ASV, AES, *Germania 1932–36*, Pos. 631, fasc. 33; Godman, 89–90.
36. Rychlak, 296; Ludwig Volk, *Kirchliche Aketen über die Reichskonkordatsverhandlugen 1933* (Mainz: Matthias Grunewald Verlag, 1969); Konrad Repgen, "German Catholicism and the Jews: 1933–1945," in *Judaism and Christianity Under the Impact of National Socialism*, Otto Dov Kulka and Paul Mendes-Flohr, eds. (Jerusalem: The Historical Society of Israel and the Zalman Shazar Center for Jewish History, 1967).
37. Conroy, *Silence*, 87, 370–74, 378–83. Cornwell relies on Klaus Scholder, a Protestant, who is vigorously refuted by Ludwig Volk and Konrad Repgen.
38. Evans, *Coming of the Third Reich*, 377.
39. *Ibid.*, 377–78. Both Kertzer and Goldhagen treat this as an aside and do not pursue the reaction of the Nazis.
40. Breitman, *The Architect of Genocide*, 89. See also: Pacelli to Orsenigo, August 10, 1933. ACV, AES, *Germania 1932–36*, Pos. 632, fasc. 150. 3–5, 56r.

41. Evans, *Coming of the Third Reich*, 145; Goldhagen, 60–61, 178–79; Friedlander, *The Origins of Nazi Genocide*, 113–16.

42. Edwin Black, *War Against the Weak* (New York: Four Walls, Eight Windows, 2003), 233.

43. Black, 70, 232–33.

44. Friedlander, *The Origins of Nazi Genocide*, 21–23.

45. Alan Steinweiss (H-Net Catholic 1996), 1; Friedlander, 22.

46. Breitman, *Architect of Genocide*, 90.

47. Many historians of the Holocaust such as Henry Friedlander contextualize the persecution and murder of the Jews as part of a broader Nazi program of racial purification and territorial aggrandizement.

48. Black, 383–404; Friedlander, 23–28.

49. Nuremberg Doc. PS-846, PS-617, PS-615, PS-616. See: Nowak, "Euthanasie und Sterilisierung," 160; Hauptstaatsarchiv, Düsseldorf, RW, 18–26I, 173–75; Burleigh, *The Third Reich*, 383–404; Browning, *Origins of the Final Solution*, 184–93; Kevin Spicer, *Resisting the Third Reich: The Catholic Clergy in Hitler's Berlin* (DeKalb: Northern Illinois University Press, 2004), 63, 65, 121, 137.

50. Burleigh, 400.

51. Browning, 224, 264. See: Friedlander, 151–262.

52. Bullock, *Hitler and Stalin*, 751.

53. Goldhagen, 56–57. See: Pius XII encyclical; Robert Weisbord & W. P. Sillanpoa, *The Chief Rabbi, the Pope and the Holocaust* (NJ: Transaction Books, 1991), 40–41.

54. Pius XII Encyclical.

55. Evans, *Coming of the Third Reich*, 146–47; Spicer, *Resisting the Third Reich*, 47, 66, 73, 79–80, 110–17, 124–26, 156–57, 178–82.

56. Heike Kreutzer, *Ad Recichskirchenministerium im Gefuge der natinalisozialistchen Herschaft* (Duseldorf: Droste Verlag, 2000).

57. Zuccotti, *Under His Very Windows*, 21.

58. Gallo, *Enemies*, 73–74, 115; Gallo, *For Love and Country*, 40–41; Rhodes, *The Vatican in the Age of Dictators* (New York; Holt, Rinehart & Winston, 1973).

59. Zuccotti, *Under His Very Windows*, 21–23.

60. Kertzer, 277.

61. Gallo, *Enemies*, 74.

62. Victor Klemperer, vol. 1 (New York: Modern Library, 1999), 249.

63. *Acta Apostolicae Sedis*, 1943, vol. 3m, 508; H. E. Cardinal Hlond, *Reports of Primate of Poland to Pope Pius XII* (New York: Longmans Green, 1941).

64. Conway, *Nazi Persecution of the Churches*, 329. See: Godman, 112.

65. Kemperer, vol. 2 (New York: Random

House, 1999), 77. See also: Godman, "The Jesuits and the Racists," in *Hitler and the Vatican*, 58–70.

66. *New York Times*, January 14, 1939, 3, 5.

67. Gallo, *For Love and Country*, 40–41. See also: Gallo, *Enemies*, 115; Alvarez & Graham, *Nothing Sacred*, 49.

68. Gallo, "Dachau's Priests," 2. See: ASV, AES, *Germania 1935–38*, Pos. 692, fasc. 264, 10, 37, 44; Burleigh 441; Browning, 17–18, 32; Lukas, *The Forgotten Genocide*; Tittmann, 111–15; Richard Lukas, *Forgotten Survivors: Christians Remember the Nazi Occupation* (Lawrence: University of Kansas Press, 2004), 1, 6, 13; "Poland: The Church in Poland, 1939–1945," in *New Catholic Encyclopedia* (New York: McGraw Hill, 1967), XI, 481–83.

69. Gallo, "Dachau's Priests," 3; *New York Times* May 22, 1944, 2, 7. See also: *ADSS*, vol. 6, no. 196, 296–98.

70. *New York Times*, February 29, 1944, 1; *New York Times*, November 19, 1944, 6, 24. See: Gallo, "Dachau's Priests," 4, 5; Lukas, *Forgotten Survivors*, 6, 50–51.

71. Gallo, "Dachau's Priests," 3; Kevin Spicer, *Resisting the Third Reich*, 109–11, 115.

72. *New York Times*, April 26, 1943, 5, 6; *New York Times*, August 13, 1943, 3, 4; *New York Times*, October 6, 1943, 4, 6; *New York Times*, November 19, 1944, 5, 24; *New York Times*, June 24, 1945, 2–7.

73. Gallo, "Dachau's Priests," 3, 4; Burleigh, 200.

74. Gallo, "Dachau's Priests," 1.

75. Gallo, "Dachau's Priests," 4–5; Burleigh, 403.

76. *New York Times*, June 7, 1942, 1, 5, 12; June 9, 1942, 6, 12; June 10, 1042, 5, 20.

77. Pius XII encyclicals, paragraphs 43, 47.

78. *New York Times*, June 3, 1945, 1–22. The *New York Times* documented the arrest, deportation, and murder of priests and the religious. Tittmann records that Vatican Radio reported the atrocities committed against the Poles but suspended them because it provoked Nazi reprisals. See: Tittmann, *Inside the Vatican of Pius XII*, 111–12; Gallo, "Dachau's Priests," 4.

Chapter 3

1. This selection is reprinted with the permission of *Inside the Vatican*. It is an edited version of the article by Matteo Luigi Napolitano, "Pius XI, Pius XII and the Führer: Peter Godman Against Two Men of God," *Inside the Vatican* (August 2004), 46–51.

Chapter 4

1. This selection is reprinted with the permission of *Crisis* (Washington, DC) George Sim Johnson, "Papal Letter Never Sent," *Crisis*, December 28, 1997, 12–13.

Chapter 5

1. Cornwell, Katz, Zuccotti, Phayer, Wistrich, Friedlander, and Goldhagen do not touch this subject.

2. Conway in Woolner, 14.

3. *New York Times*, "Pius Appeals for Peace in First Public Act," March 4, 1939, 1. See: Tittmann, *Inside the Vatican of Pius XII*, 21, 23.

4. Gallo, *For Love and Country*, 28.

5. John Waller, *The Unseen War in Europe* (New York: Random House, 1996), 98–101. See: Max Gallo, *Mussolini's Enemies* (New York: Macmillan, 1973), 298–300; Harold Deutsch, *The Conspiracy Against Hitler in the Twilight War* (Minneapolis: University of Minnesota Press, 1968), 17–18; Terry Parssinen, *The Oster Conspiracy of 1938: The Unknown Story of the Military Plot to Kill Hitler and Avert War* (New York: HarperCollins, 2003).

6. Gallo, *For Love and Country*, 29. See also: Gilbert, *Inside the Vatican*, August 2003; Peter Gumpel, "Historian's Accusations Against Wartime Holy See Refuted," Zenit, November 21, 2002. Polish bishops were not favorable to public protests. Polish Cardinal Adam Sapieha, archbishop of Krakow, thanked Pius XII for his concern but felt a public protest would only increase the persecution of Poles. *ADDS*, vol. 3.

7. Gallo, *For Love and Country*, 29.

8. Deutsch, 53; See: Hans Gisevius, *To the Bitter End: An Insider's Account of the Plot to Kill Hitler* (New York: Da Capo Press, 1998).

9. Deutsch, 57. See: Hans Rothfels, *The German Opposition to Hitler: An Appraisal* (Chicago, 1962).

10. Joachim Fest, *Plotting the Death of Hitler* (New York: Henry Holt, 1996), 66, 68–69, 71–72.

11. Gallo, *For Love and Country*, 30. See: Alvarez & Graham, *Nothing Sacred: Nazi Espionage Against the Vatican 1939–1945* (London: Frank Cass, 1997), 24; Hans Mommsen, *Alternatives to Hitler: German Resistance Under the Third Reich* (Princeton, NJ: Princeton University Press, 2003), 26; Peter Ludow, "Pope Pius XII, the British Government and the German Opposition in the winter of 1939–1940," in *Vierteljahreshefte fur Zeitgesschichte* 22 (1974).

12. Deutsch, 107.

13. *Ibid.*, 110.

14. Diego von Bergen to Foreign Office, March 13, 1939, in *Documents on German Foreign Policy 1918–1945, IV, Series D (1937–1945)*.

15. Deutsch, 120. See: Gisevius, *To the Bitter End*. See also: Riebling, *The Eagle and the Cross*.

16. Jörgen Heidking and Christof Mauch, *American Intelligence and the Resistance to Hitler: A Documentary History* (Boulder, CO: Westview, 1996). The authors uncovered an OSS document that substantiates the Pope's role. See: Gallo, *For Love and Country*, 30–31.

17. Deutsch, 111. See: Tittmann, *Inside the Vatican of Pius XII*, 124–25.

18. Alvarez & Graham, *Nothing Sacred*, 27.

19. "Personal and Confidential Message from the British Legation to the Holy See," British Public Record Office, FO371/24405, January 12, 1940, February 7, 1940, February 19, 1940. See also: Waller, 98–101.

20. See Pius XII encyclicals.

21. Gallo, *For Love and Country*, 21–32.

22. Cornwell, 233–34.

23. Goldhagen's rant avoids any historical evidence that might challenge his preconceived agenda.

24. Alvarez & Graham, 25.

25. Deutsch, 127. See also: Roger Manvell & Heinrich Fraenkel, *The Canaris Conspiracy* (New York: David McKay, 1969), 75. For the memorandum see: Grosscurth papers. For the receptivity of the Vatican to the plan see: Hans Gisevius, *To the Bitter End* (Boston: Houghton Mifflin, 1947) 379–80, 385.

26. Fest, *Plotting Hitler's Death*, 132.

27. On the entire Müller mission see his reports in National Archives, microfilm T84, Roll 229, item EAP 21-x-15/2. See also: Josef Muller papers, IfZ, ED 92; Fest, *Plotting Hitler's Death*.

28. Tittman, *Inside the Vatican of Pius XII*, 111–12. See: Gallo, *For Love and Country*, 31.

29. Taylor Papers, FDR Library, Hyde Park, NY. Taylor to FDR, March 14, 1940. Hereinafter cited as Taylor Papers. *New York Times*, March 14, 1940, 1.

30. Burleigh, *The Third Reich*, 724. See also: Lukas, *The Forgotten Genocide*; Richard Lukas, *Forgotten Survivors, Polish Christians Remember the Nazi Occupation* (Lawrence: University Press of Kansas, 2004).

31. Alvarez & Graham, 26.

32. Telegram from Philips to the Secretary of State February 28, 1940, in U.S. Department of State, Foreign Relations of the U.S. Diplomatic Papers, 1940, vol. 1 (Washington DC: GPO, 1959) 126.

33. Memo from Undersecretary of State Sumner Wells, March 18, 1940, U.S. Depart-

ment of State, Foreign Relations of the U.S. Diplomatic Papers, 1940, vol. 1 (GPO, 1959), 108. For Britain's first response to Pius XII's peace proposal see: *ADSS*, vol. 1, no. 27, 127–28.

34. Deutsch, 143.

35. Deutsch, 339. See: Alvarez & Graham, 26; Richard Lamb, *Ghosts of Peace, 1935–1945* (London, 1987).

36. Alvarez and Graham, 33.

37. *Ibid.*, 59.

38. Owen Chadwick, *Britain and the Vatican During the Second World War* (Cambridge: Cambridge University Press, 1986), 168–70.

39. Alvarez, "U.S. Intelligence and the Vatican," in Woolner, 255; See: Alvarez and Graham, 145–48, 155–56.

40. Alvarez and Graham, 155.

41. Patrick Gallo interview with Frank Gilardi (August 1997; September 1998; November 3, 1998; April 5, 1999).

42. Gallo, *For Love and Country*, 94.

43. Alvarez in Woolner, 227 n. 27.

44. Fest, *Plotting Hitler's Death*, 309.

45. Deutsch, 127–28.

46. Fest, *Plotting Hitler's Death*, 202–36.

47. Fest, *Plotting Hitler's Death*, 255–91. See: Bullock, *Hitler*, 735–39, 743–52; Toland, 569–88.

48. Josef Muller Bis zur letgten Konsequenz (Munich, 1975) 225–50.

49. Zuccotti, 313.

50. *Ibid.*, 314.

51. Bullock, *Hitler*, 750–51.

52. Robert Katz and Susan Zuccotti have the same position with reference to Pius XII's opposition to unconditional surrender. They don't delve any deeper for an explanation that would challenge their preconceived judgments. See: *ADSS*, vol. 5, n. 473, 684–90; *ADSS*, vol. 6, n. 473, 684–90; *ADSS*, vol. 7, n. 303, 502–4; Tittmann, 133.

53. Pius XII, Christmas Message, December 25, 1948; Pius XII Message of October 3, 1953.

54. Deutsch, 352.

Chapter 6

1. This selection from *Popes and Politics* (New York: International Continuum Publishing Group, 2002) 109–16 is reprinted with the permission of the publishers.

Chapter 7

1. This article is reprinted with the permission of the *Political Science Reviewer*. Kenneth Whitehead, "The Pope Pius Controversy: A Review Article," *Political Science Reviewer*, vol. 31, 2002. This is an edited version of the original article.

2. Rolf Hochhuth, *The Deputy* (New York: Grove Press, 1964), 102.

3. Hochhuth, 204.

4. David Dalin, "Pope Pius and the Jews," *Weekly Standard*, February 25, 2001.

5. Daniel Jonah Goldhagen, *Hitler's Willing Executioners: Ordinary Germans and the Holocaust* (New York: Alfred A. Knopf, 1996).

6. Goldhagen, "Pius XII, the Catholic Church, and the Holocaust: What Would Jesus Have Done?" *New Republic*, January 21, 2002.

7. Dalin, Op. cit. note no. 23 supra.

8. José Sánchez, *Pope Pius XII and the Holocaust: Understanding the Controversy* (Washington, DC: Catholic University of America Press, 2002), 44; Zuccotti, *Under His Very Windows*, 90.

9. Cornwell, 236.

10. Rychalak, 140.

11. Cornwell, 313–15; Phayer, 100; Rychlak, 264–66; Zuccotti, 315–16.

12. Phayer, 132.

13. Zuccotti, 13.

14. Anthony Rhodes, *The Vatican in the Age of Dictators, 1922–1945* (New York: Holt, Rinehart, and Winston, 1973), 198.

15. Michael Burleigh, *The Third Reich: A New History* (New York: Hill and Wang, 2000), 402.

16. Phayer, xii.

17. Piere Blet, *S. J. Pius XII and the Second World War* (Mahwah, NJ: Paulist Press, 1999), 45.

18. Burleigh, note no. 33 supra, 316.

19. Blet, 64.

20. Rychlak, 261.

21. Margherita Marchione, *Pope Pius XII: Architect for Peace* (Mahwah, NJ: Paulist Press, 2000), 174–75.

22. Oscar Halecki and James F. Murray Jr. *The Crusade of Charity Pius XII: Eugenio Pacelli, Pope of Peace* (New York: Farrar, Straus, and Young, 1954), note 38 supra, 207–20.

23. Ralph McInerny, *The Defamation of Pius XII* (South Bend, IN: St. Augustine's Press, 2001), 59.

24. Blet, 286; Marchione, 2, 50; McInerny, 168–69; Rychlak, 240, 404.

25. Zuccotti, 303–04, 336 n. 11, 337 n. 20, 394 n. 7.

26. Robert Lockwood, "Pius XII and the Holocaust," at www.catholicleague.org.

27. Zuccotti, 192.

28. Kertzer, 16.

29. *Ibid.*, 213.

30. *Ibid.*, 216.

31. Pope Pius XI, "To the Directors of the Belgium Catholic Radio Agency," 1938. Quoted in the article "Anti-Semitism," in *New Cath-*

olic Encyclopedia, vol. 1, A–AZT (New York: McGraw Hill, 1967), 639.

32. Kertzer, 256–57.

33. William Teeling, *Pope Pius XI and World Affairs* (New York: Frederick A. Stokes, 1937), 67.

34. Phayer, xi.

35. *Ibid.*, 65.

36. Burleigh, note no. 33 supra, 418.

37. Wills, 29–45.

38. *Ibid.*, 48.

39. Waltraud Herbsrith, "Final Accounts," in the Edith Stein issue of *The Catholic Dossier* (November-December 2001), 12.

40. McInerny, 179.

Chapter 8

1. This selection is reprinted with the permission of Professor Arnold P. Krammer. Jenö Levai, *Hungarian Jewry and the Papacy* (London: Sands Publishing, 1968), 17–31, 43–47. This is an edited version of the pages cited.

2. Hochhuth, *The Representative*, 236. (Author's note: Hochhuth accuses Pope Pius of callously watching the Holocaust without extending any help. The play cites three exemplary individuals—Kurt Gerstein, a Nazi Waffen SS officer, and Alfred Wetzler and Rudolf Vrba, who escaped Auschwitz. They provided a detailed report to the Hungarian Jewish Council about the impending deportations. The council worked out its own deal with Eichmann, saved themselves and 1,684 prominent Jews. They kept the information to themselves that would have saved many of the 437,000 Jews who were subsequently deported. Meanwhile the publications of the Vrba-Wetzler report in the final days of June 1944 and by the Western Allies produced international denunciations. Vrba met with papal legate Monsignor Mario Matilotti who forwarded the ominous contents of the Vrba-Wetzler report to his superiors in the Vatican. The report was published in the Swiss press and by the Western Allies and by the BBC. This led to protests from the U.S. and Britain and the International Red Cross. On June 25, 1944, the pope issued an appeal in an open telegram to Horthy calling on him to "spare so many unfortunate people further sufferings." Horthy ordered a halt to the deportations from Hungary on June 7, 1944. Ruth Linn charges that Israeli historians have taken part in a cover-up of the Hungarian Jewish Council's actions. She calculates if only one percent of the 437,000 Hungarians had been told of the report, nearly 5,000 could have been saved. Ruth Linn, *Escaping Auschwitz*, 28–47. See: Breitman, *American Refugee Policy*, 213–14.)

3. G. Verolino, the secretary, told Levai this.

4. Nuremberg Documents NG 5523. (Author's note: Ruth Linn writes that in March of 1944 Eichmann "entered Hungary armed with detailed knowledge of Hungarian Jewry.... He knew that he would not encounter any opposition: The community was confused, divided, compliant, with a non-resisting leadership, and easily subjected to isolation, expropriation, ghettoization, concentration, entrainment, and deportation." Linn, *Escaping Auschwitz*, 35.)

Chapter 9

1. Katz, 84; Zuccotti, 103. British historian Martin Gilbert has characterized Zuccotti's book "not history but guesswork."

2. Katz, 54. David Kertzer, Daniel Goldhagen, Gary Wills, and James Carroll treat the deportation in a superficial manner and recycle the same interpretation.

3. Gallo, *For Love and Country: The Italian Resistance* (Maryland: University Press of America, 2003).

4. Christopher Duggan, review, *New York Times Review of Books, Under His Very Windows* (February 4, 2001), 34.

5. Katz, 4.

6. Dan Kurzman, *The Race for Rome* (Garden City, NY: Doubleday, 1975), 83.

7. Gallo, *For Love and Country*, 54.

8. *Ibid.*, 55–58.

9. Albert Garland and Howard McGaw Smith, *Sicily and the Surrender of Italy* (Washington: U.S. Department of the Army, 1965), 477–96, 498–504.

10. Gallo, *For Love and Country*, 58–64. See: B. H. Liddell Hart, *The Other Side of the Hill* (London: Cassell, 1951), 462–63. General Walter Bedell Smith believed the cancellation of Giant II to be a major mistake. Nigel Hamilton, *Monty: Master of the Battlefield, 1942–44* (New York: McGraw Hill, 1982), 401.

11. Katz, 29.

12. B. H. Liddel Hart, *A History of the Second World War* (New York: Putnam, 1987), 364–65, 462–63. See: Albert Kesselring, *A Soldier's Record* (Westport, CT: Greenwood Press, 1953), 221; Peter Tompkins, *Italy Betrayed* (New York: Simon & Schuster, 1966), 155–72; Samuel Elliot Morison, *History of United States Naval Operations, World War II* (Boston: Little, Brown, 1954), vol. 9, 241.

13. Gallo, *For Love and Country*, 73.

14. *Ibid.*, 121–22.

15. Taylor Papers, September 11, 1943.

16. Jane Scrivener, *Inside Rome with the Germans*, 65. Gerhard Schreiber, *I Militari Ital-*

iani Internati nei Campo diConcentramento Del Terzo Reich, 1943–1945 (Roma: Ufficio Storico SME, 1992).

17. Gallo, *For Love and Country*, 76–118.

18. *Ibid.*, 90.

19. Klemperer, *I Will Bear Witness*, vol. 2 (September 13, 1943), 257–58.

20. Tittmann, *Inside the Vatican of Pius XII*, 190; Katz, *The Battle for Rome*, 53.

21. Conway, *How Not to Deal with History*, 70. See: Katz, *The Battle for Rome*, 53. The O'Flaherty escape network is dealt with extensively in J. P. Gallagher, *Scarlet Pimpernel of the Vatican* (New York: Coward McCann, 1967. See: Raleigh Trevelyan, *Rome '44* (New York: Viking Press, 1981), 16–18, 59–60.

22. Galeazzo Ciano, *Mussolini segreto* (Bologna, 1958), 308. *ADSS*, vol. 1 (May 13, 1940), 422. See: *L'Osservatore della Domenica*, June 28, 1964, 68.

23. Gallo, *For Love and Country*, 89–90.

24. Goebbels in Lochner, *The Goebbels Diaries*, 505.

25. Telegram from Ribbentrop to Weizsäcker, October 4, 1943, in Saul Friendlander, *Pius XII and the Third Reich*, 182. Telegram to Ribbentrop, n. 372, Berlin 9, October 8, 1943, in Poliakow-Eulf, *Das Dritte Reich u die Juden*, Dokumente V Aufsaetze (Berlin, 1955), 52. Berlin's reply not to interfere in Poliakow: Dispaccio N 1645, 80.

26. Lenoard and Rennet Heston, *The Medical Casebook of Adolf Hitler* (New York: Stein &Day, 1980), 138.

27. Lochner, *The Goebbels Diaries*, 190, 195, 271, 279, 284, 300, 313, 328, 349. See: Conway, *The Nazi Persecution of the Churches*; Konrad Low, *The Guilt: Jews and Christians in the Opinion of Nazis and in Present Times*. Low provides massive documentation of the continuous and systematic persecution of Catholics.

28. Andrea Tornielli, *Pio XII: Il Papa degli ebrei.*

29. Albrect von Kessell, *L'Osservatore Romano della Domenica*, June 28, 1964, 68. See: Albrecht von Kessell, "The Pope and the Jews," in Bentley, 75.

30. Karl Wolff with Geoge Giese, "Wolff, I Want the Vatican," Niue Bildpost, May 5, 1974, 6–7. See also: *Testimonies of Karl Wolff before the Ecclesiastical Tribunal of Munich, Testimonies for the beautification of Pope Pius XII*, in keeping of the Society of Jesus at Borgo Spirito, Rome, 825, 832–37 (Hereinafter cited as Testimonies) See also: National Archives RG 982, reel 176; L'Osservatore Romano della Domenica, June 28, 1964, 68; Ernst von Weizsäcker, *The Memoirs of Ernst von Weizsäcker*, trans. John Andrews (Chicago: Henry Regn-

ery, 1951), 285–95; Lamb, *The War in Italy*, 44–46; Kurzman, *The Race for Rome*, 39–40; Meir Michaels, *Mussolini and the Jews*, 322–23. Michaels cites a written note by Lieutenant Heinz Rothke; Salvatore Massa, "Almeno due I piani nazisti per rapier Pio XII," *Avvenire* (January 18, 2005).

31. Goebbels in Lochner, *The Goebbels Diaries*, 460–75.

32. *Ibid.*, 468.

33. Giorgio Gariboldi, *Pio XII, Hitler e Mussolini: Il Vaticano fra le Dittature* (Milano: Mursia, 1995), 167–71. See: Corvin, *Canaris: Chief of Intelligence* (Maidstone, England: George Mann Publishers, 1973), 191; Waller, *The Unseen War*, 315.

34. Wolff quoted in Gariboldi, 202–06. See: Ian Kershaw, *Hitler: Nemesis*, 596. *ADSS*, 9. doc. 355; Alvarez &Graham, *Nothing Sacred*, 85–88. Tittmann, *Inside the Vatican of Pius XII*, 148, 186–87. Professor Anna Porta unearthed a letter in the archives of the archdiocese of Milan that revealed a plan — Rabat Fohn — to kill Pius XII and the cardinals. Further research is needed to fully authenticate this finding. *Il Giornale* (July 5, 1998); Margherita Marchione, *Pope Pius XII*, 72–73; Robert Graham, "Did Hitler Want to Remove Pius XII?" *Civiltà Cattolica*, I (1972), 319–27; Tornielli, *Pio XII*, 165–70.

35. Treveylan, 97. See: Zara Algardi, *Il Processo Caruso* (Rome, 1945; Piscitelli, *Storia della Resistenza Romana*, 279–80; Gallo, *For Love and Country*, 172–73; L'Osservatore Romano, February 9, 1944; *Il Messaggero*, February 7, 10, 11, 1944. Albrecht von Kessel approached Möllhausen and asked him to take part in an assassination plot to kill Hitler. Möllhausen refused.

36. J. P. Gallagher, *Scarlet Pimpernel of the Vatican* (New York: Coward McCann, 1968) 65–67, 77, 114–18. See: Gallo, 177–78. Treveylan, 63–64; Cesare De Simone, *Roma città prigioniera* (Milano: Mursia, 1949) 36–37.

37. Gallagher, *Scarlet Pimpernell of the Vatican*, 159–62. See: Gallo, *For Love and Country*, 241; Trevelyan, *Rome '44*, 227–28.

38. Gallo, *For Love and Country*, 95.

39. Israel (Eugenio) Zolli, *Before the Dawn* (New York: Sheed & Ward, 1954), 140–52. Zolli converted to Catholicism and took Pius XII's name, Eugenio, as his own. See: Michael Tagliacozzo, "La persecuzine degli ebrei a Roma," Liliana Picciotto Farigon, ed., *L'Occupazione tedesco e gli ebrei di Roma: documenti e fatti* (Roma: Carucci, 1979), 152; Robert F. Weisbord and W. P. Sillapoa, *The Chief Rabbi, the Pope and the Holocaust* (New Jersey: Transaction Books, 1991), 117–25.

40. Gallo, *For Love and Country*, 121.

41. *Ibid.*, 120. See: Miriam Zolli interview with Stefano Zurio, *Il Giornale* (March 21, 1999); S. Della Pergola dall'ebrasimo italiano (Roma, 1976), 54; Renzo De Felice, *Storia degli ebrei italiani sotto fascismo*, 13. Stille, *Benevolence and Betrayal* (New York: Summit Books, 1991), 170–73.

42. Gallo, *For Love and Country*, 122. See also: Taglicozzo, 152.

43. Tagliacozzo, *La Communita di Roma sotto l'incubo della svastica: La grande razzia del 16 Octobre 1943, Gli ebrei in Italia durante il fascismo 3* (Milano: Quaderni del Centro di Documentazione Ebracia Contemporanea, 1963), 9–10; Tagliacozzo, *AMT Archivio privato*; Michaelis, 353.

44. Zuccotti, *The Italians and the Holocaust* (Lincoln: University of Nebraska Press, 1996) 111; Robert Katz, *Black Sabbath* (New York: Macmillan, 1969), 54–61.

45. Gallo, *For Love and Country*, 123.

46. *Ibid.*, 123–24. See: Tagliacozzo, *L'occupazione tedesca* (1), 153–54.

47. Michaelis, 356. See: Stille, 193.

48. *ADSS*, vol. 9, n. 353, 494. See: Gallo, *For Love and Country*, 125. During the gold extortion, Father Benoît saved a large number of Jews by providing them with false identification papers. According to Martin Gilbert he was aided by the staffs of a number of embassies in Rome and "by a large number of Italians—among them the 'marshal of Rome,' Mario di Marco, a high official of the police, who was later tortured by the Gestapo but did not disclose what he knew." Gilbert, *The Holocaust*, 622; Friedman, *Roads to Extinction*, 418; Tornielli, *Pio XII*, 237–50.

49. Zuccotti, *Under His Very Windows*, 153–54.

50. Tagliacozzo in Zenit News Service, October 25, 2000.

51. Zuccotti, *Italians and the Holocaust*, 114. See: Zolli, 138–63; Renato Almansi, "Mio padre, Dane Almansi," *La Rassegna Mensile di Israel*, XLII (May-June 1976) 251–53; Michaelis, 358; *ADSS*, "Le Saint Siege il les victims de guerre" (Liberia Editrice Vataicano, 1975–Janvier-December 1943), 349; Stille, 199.

52. Katz, *Black Sabbath*, 197. See: Fausto Coen, *16 Ottobre 1943, La grande razzia degli ebrei di Roma* (Firenze: Giutina, 1993); Tornielli, *Pio XII*, 277–315.

53. Mölhausen's cable to Ribbentrop, October 6, 1943, GFM/132/123580. See: Gilbert, *The Holocaust: A History of the Jews of Europe During the Second World War* (New York: Henry Holt, 1986), 623; Michelis, 363–65; Tagliacozzo, *La Communita di Roma*, 20–37. Tagliacozzo on Mölhausen in Gaspari, 29–32.

54. *New York Times*, October 13, 1943, 1.

55. Gallo, *For Love and Country*, 95. See: *New York Times*, October 15, 1943, 1.

56. Martin Gilbert, *The Holocaust*, 623; See: *ADSS*, vol. 10, n. 227, 358–59; Gallo, *For Love and Country*, 142–43. Gaspari, 117–26. On Kunkel and Eichmann's testimony regarding the rescue by the Vatican see: Gaspari, 26–2; L'Intervista de Helmut S. Ruppert a Nichalau Kunkel, "La Maggior parte della ebrei a Rome se salvarono," *L' Osservatore Romano*, December 8, 2000; Robert Graham, "La Strana condotta di E. von Weizsäcker ambasciatore del Reich in Vaticano," *La Civiltà Cattolica*, anno 121, quad. 2879 (June 6, 1970), 455–71.

57. *ADSS*, vol. 9, n. 368, 505–06, 509–10. *ADSS* (December 1943) no. 373, 509–10. See: Gallo, *For Love and Country*, 142–43; Godman, 169. The revisionists might be better served if they consulted Antonio Gaspari, *Gli ebrei salvati da Pio XII* (Logos, 2001). Gaspari assembles numerous testimonies in support of Pius XII's efforts in saving Jews, including those from survivors of concentration camps, leaders of Jewish associations, and founders of the state of Israel. Gaspari, 127–31; A. Hudal, *Römische Tagebücher: Lebensbeichte eines alten Bishofs* (Graz, 1976), 215.

58. Hill, "The Vatican Embassy of Ernst von Weizsäcker," 148. For the text of Bishop's letter see Martin Wein, *Die Weizsäcker, Geshichte einer deutschen Famile* (Kanaur Sachbuch, 199), 574. The letter is also reproduced in Saul Friedlander, *Pius XII and the Third Reich* 205–06. See: *ADSS*, vol. 9, n. 368, 373 n. 14, 509–10; Gallo, *For Love and Country*, 177–78; Robert Graham, "La Strana Condotta di E. Von Weizsäcker ambascitore del Reich in Vaticana," *La Civiltá Cattolica*, June 6, 1970, 455–71. For Weizsäcker's communication with Stahel regarding Hudal's letter of protest see: Dispaccio Serie 2722. Inland iiG 56:2, Juden in Italian, 1943–44, E 42 1512; *The Jewish Chronicle* (London, October 29, 1943); Tornielli, *Pio XII*, 294–300.

59. Hill, *The Vatican Embassy of Ernst von Weizsäcker*. See: Diplomatic Telegram from Osborne to Foreign Office, British Public Record Office (October 31, 1943), FO 371/372555679. The letter of protest may be also found in Tagliacozzzo, *Gli ebrei in Italia durante il fascismo* (6), 30.

60. Martin Gilbert, *The Holocaust*, 623. See: Lamb, *The War in Italy*, 44; Zuccotti, *Under His Very Windows*, 189–214. Tagliacozzo, Zenit Dispatch, October 25, 2000; *The diaries of Adolf Eichmann* (Zenit, March 1, 2000); Tagliacozzo, *Gli ebrei in Italia durante il fascismo* (6) 30.

61. Zuccotti, *Under His Very Windows*, 156–57; Cornwell, 302–12; Phayer, 94–104; Gold-

hagen, 51–53. For how Himmler's deportation order became known to German military and diplomatic officials see Tagliacozzo, *Gli ebrei in Italia durante il fascismo* (6), 10–15.

62. Whitehead, 46. See: Zuccotti, *Under His Very Windows*, 71. There is no written document signed by Hitler that indicates he authorized the reprisals following the Via Rasella attack, nor is there a document ordering the Final Solution. Does Zuccotti contend that Hitler was not behind either of these two events?

63. The pope is also the bishop of Rome and as such St. John Lateran is his official church in Rome. An OSS intercept of a dispatch from Rome to Berlin dated October 26, 1943, 10 days after the Rome roundup, noted: "Vatican has apparently for a long time been assisting many Jews to escape. Tagliacozzo, Zenit, October 25, 2000. Cardinal Paolo Dezza, the rector of the Pontifical Gregorian University, published a signed article in 1964 stating in no uncertain terms that Pius XII told him to help the "persecuted Jews." Gaspari compiled documents and testimonies that provide evidence of the Pope's rescue efforts. See: Gaspari, *Gli Ebrei salvati da Pio XII*, 117–26, 127–36. Gaspari found new documents that provide evidence that Pius XII ordered churches and convents throughout Italy to shelter Jews. He found that as early as 1940 Pius XII explicitly ordered his secretary of state, Luigi Maglione, and his assistant, Giovanni Battista Montini (Paul VI) to send money to Jews who were protected by the bishop of Campagna; De Felice, *Storia degli ebrei italiani*, 628–32; John Patrick Caroll-Abbing, *But for the Grace of God* (New York: Delacorte Press, 1965), 48; Tornielli, *Pio XII*, 285–300; Gilbert, *The Holocaust*, 623; Tornielli, *Pio XII: Papa degli ebrei*; Alesandro Portelli, *The Order Has Been Carried Out* (New York: Palgrave Macmillan, 2003), 86.

64. Zuccotti, *Under His Very Windows*, 175. See: Martin Gilbert, Zenit News Service, February 20, 2003; Michaelis, 364–65.

65. Gallo, *For Love and Country*, 119–50.

66. Michaelis, 392. Except for his utility in this specific instance the Vatican kept Hudal at arm's length. Godman admits: "Hudal was only consulted in 1943 when the links he cultivated with the German high command in occupied Rome could be exploited." Hudal became embittered because of the Vatican's disassociation with him and provided "Rolf Hochhuth with material for *The Deputy*, so formative of Pius XII's negative image." Godman, 169–70. Goldhagen claims that Hudal was an important bishop and close friend of Pius XII and Paul VI. Hudal was never a

bishop and not an important prelate. Moreover, he was never a close friend of either pope.

67. Michaelis, 381–95. See: Zuccotti, *Italians and the Holocaust*, 170.

68. Jenö Levai, *Hungarian Jewry and the Papacy* (London: Sands, 1968), 112. See: Gallo, *For Love and Country*, 147; Lamb, 48; Gariboldi, 193–94; Blet, 216.

69. Levai, 112.

70. Michaelis, 377. See: Levai, 17–56; Gilbert, *The Holocaust*, 623.

71. James Carroll, *Constantine's Sword*, 534.

72. Rhodes, *The Vatican in the Age of Dictators*, 364. See: *ADDS*, ii, 324; Richard Leiber, "Pio XII e gli Ebrei di Roma," *Civilità Cattolica*, 1 (1961), 449; Blet, 64, 69–72.

73. José Sánchez, *Pius XII and the Holocaust* (Washington, DC: The Catholic University of America Press, 2002), 40. See: Lewy, *The Catholic Church and Nazi Germany*, 303.

74. Sanchez, 364.

75. Heathcote Smith to Myron Taylor, August 2, 1944, in Taylor Papers.

76. Harold Tittmann, *Inside the Vatican of Pius XII*, 122–23. See: Albrecht von Kessel, "Der Papst und die Verolgung der Juden," 103–04. See also: J. Fritz Raddatz, ed., *Summa injuria oder Durfe der Paps Schweigen* (Hamburg: Rowhalt, 1963), 169–70.

77. De Felice, *Gil ebrei in Italia durante il fascismo*, 538–39. See: Blet, 182–200; Steinberg, *All or Nothing* (London: Routledge, 1990), 80–81.

Chapter 10

1. It is unclear how many archives she reviewed. There are approximately 40 archdioceses and 182 dioceses in Italy. It does not seem that she reviewed the archives in all of them. See www.catholic-pages.com/dioceses/italy.htm.

2. Much of her argument, and even a great deal of "evidence" seems to have come from Sam Waagenaar's, *The Pope's Jews* (1974).

3. We now know that this is false.

4. Avvenire, June 27, 1996; CWN, "More Echoes on Pope Pius XII, Nazi Holocaust" June 27, 1996.

5. Ronald J. Rychlak, *Hitler, the War, and the Pope*, 128–32.

6. Curtis Bill Pepper, *An Artist and the Pope* (1968), 77.

7. Memorandum to General William Donovan from Fabian von Schlabrendorff, October 25, 1945 (Subject: Relationship of the German Churches to Hitler), posted on the Internet by Rutgers Law School and Cornell University at http://camlaw.rutgers.edu/publications/law-religion/nazimasterplan04.pdf.

8. John Patrick Caroll-Abbing, *But for the Grace of God — The Houses Are Blind* (New York: Delacorte Press, 1965), 48.

9. John Patrick Caroll-Abbing, *A Chance to Live: The Story of the Lost Children of War* (New York: Longman, Green & Co., 1952), 77.

10. Carroll-Abbing, *A Chance to Live*, 82, 141.

11. William Doino, "The Witness of the Late Monsignor John Carroll-Abbing," *Inside the Vatican* (July 12, 2001). Mr. Doino played portions of his tape recording of this interview. I note this because at a conference at Millersville University in 2002, Zuccotti raised the specter that Doino had fabricated the interview.

12. Susan Zuccotti, *The Italians and the Holocaust* (Lincoln,: University of Nebraska Press, 1987), 304.

13. Zuccotti, *The Italians and the Holocaust*, 230. See also: Robert Katz, *The Battle for Rome: The Germans, the Allies, the Partisans, and the Pope* (New York: Simon & Schuster, 2003), 174. Katz notes that no one was forced to leave.

14. Joseph L. Lichten, *A Question of Judgment: Pope Pius and the Jews*, originally released in pamphlet form by the National Catholic Welfare Conference and reprinted in *Pius XII and the Holocaust: A Reader*, Catholic League Publications (Milwaukee, 1988). See: Meir Michaelis, *Mussolini and the Jews: German-Italian Relations and the Jewish Questions in Italy 1922–25*. (Five thousand Italian Jews sought baptismal papers in hopes of surviving the Holocaust).

15. Peter Godman, *Hitler and the Vatican: The Secret Archives that Reveal the Complete Story of the Nazis and the Vatican* (New York: Free Press, 2004), 33.

16. Godman, *Hitler and the Vatican*.

17. Peter Novick, *The Holocaust in American Life* (New York: Houghton Mifflin, 1999), 316 n. 77.

18. Stephen M. Giovanni, *Pius XII and the Jews: the War Years* (2000), 30 (noting that the Communist charge of papal silence was false).

19. "Zuccotti and Michael Phayer have ignored (not the 'big picure,' but that too) clear evidence which refutes their basic contentions." Justus George Lawler, *Review Symposium: Proleptic Response*, 20 U.S. Catholic Historian (2000), 89, 93.

20. Eugenio Zolli, *The Nazarene: Studies in New Testament Exegesis* (Cyril Vollert, trans., 1999), 9.

21. Kenneth C. Davis, *Don't Know Much About the Bible: Everything You Need to Know About the Good Books but Never Learned* (2001).

22. Citing the rule see: Alana M. Fuierer, "The Anti-Chlorine Campaign in the Great Lakes: Should Chlorinated Compounds Be Guilty Until Proven Innocent?" 43 *Buffalo Law Review* (1995), 43.

23. Vad Vashem is Israel's Holocaust Marytrs' and Heroes Remembrance Authority.

24. "It is significant that the first initiative of the Holy See toward the government in Berlin concerned the Jews. As early as April 4, 1933, 10 days after the Enabling Act, the Apostolic Nuncio in Berlin (Orsenigo) was ordered to intervene with the government of the Reich on behalf of the Jews and point out the dangers involved in an anti–Semitic policy." Robert Leiber, "Mit brennender Sorge: März 1937," *Stimmen der Zeit*, vol. 169 (March 1962), 420. See: "New Proofs of Pius XII's Efforts to Assist Jews: Letter Targets 'Anti-Semitic Excesses' in Germany," Zenit News Service (February 17, 2003; "Pius XII's Directive Helped Save 800 Jews in 3 Cities, Papers Reveal," Zenit News Service, April 8, 2003 (further new evidence that undercuts Zuccotti's thesis). See: Adolf Eichmann's memoirs with reference to the events of October 16, 1943, in Gaspari, 26–29; Zenit Daily Dispatch, "Eichmann's Diary Reveals Church's Assistance to Jews" (March 1, 2000); Tornielli, *Pio XII, Papa deglli ebrei*.

25. As I understand it, these transcripts are now being maintained in a more private manner than they had been. This is due to the Vatican's conclusion that John Cornwell misrepresented them. I also have been told, however, that if Zuccotti had sought permission to view these transcripts when she conducted her original research, it would have been granted.

26. Pinchas Lapide, *The Last Three Popes and the Jews* (New York: Hawthorn Books, 1967), 137.

27. Lapide, 181. (Pope John XXIII personally told this to Lapide.)

28. *Inside the Vatican* (June 1997), 25. See: Pietro Palazzini, *Il clero e l'occupazione tedesca di Roma: Il rulolo del Seminario Romano Maggiore* (Rome: Apes, 1995) 16–17, 19, 29.

29. Interview with Zenit News Agency, October 26, 2000.

30. Personal correspondence with the author. See: Ronald Rychlak, "A Righteous Gentile Defends Pius XII," Zenit News Agency, October 5, 2002; "Holocaust Hero Defends Papacy," *The Wanderer*, September 30, 1983.

31. Interview with Don Aldo Brunacci: *The Secret Letter*, *Inside the Vatican*, January 2004, 74.

32. *Avvenire*, June 27, 1996 (direct order from Pius to admit Jews to hospital prior to police sweep). See: CWN, "More Echoes on

Pope Pius XII, Nazi Holocaust," June 27, 1996.

33. Antonoi Gaspari, *Gli ebrei salvati da Pio XII* (2001), 55; "New Revelations on Jews Saved by Pius XII," Zenit News Service, February 16, 2001; Testimony of Karl Otto Wolff, March 14, 1972, before the Ecclesiastical Tribunal of Munich, on the beatification of Pius XII (Eugenio Pacelli), 825.

34. Rychlak, *Hitler, the War, and the Pope*, 264–66. See: Ernst von Weizsäcker, *Memoirs of Ernst von Weizsäcker* (Chicago: H. Regnery, 1981), 155–56; Robert Payne, *The Life and Death of Adolf Hitler* (1995), 485.

35. Testimony of Karl Otto Wolff, March 14, 1972, before the Ecclesiastical Tribunal of Munich, 825; Rychlak, 420–21, n. 145.

36. Susan Zuccotti, "Pope Pius XII and the Holocaust: the Case in Italy," *The Italian Refuge* (Washington, DC: Catholic University of America Press, 1990), 254.

37. According to La Civilitá Cattolica the Pope was informed only after the roundup was completed. Giovanni Sale, La Civiltà Cattolica, December 5, 2003. See: John Thavis, "Jesuit Journal cites new evidence that Pius XII helped save Jews," Catholic News Service, December 4, 2003.

38. Owen Chadwick, *A History of Christianity* (New York: St. Martin's Press, 1995), 190; "The pope was obviously surprised. He said the Germans promised that they would not hurt the Jews, and knew of the 50 kilograms of gold." Owen Chadwick, Weizsäcker, "The Vatican and the Jews of Rome," 28, *Journal of Ecclesiastical History* (April 1977), 179.

39. L'Osservatore Romano, October 25–26, 1943; Zuccotti, "Pope Pius XII and the Holocaust: The Case in Italy" in *Italian Refuge* (Washington, DC: Catholic University Press, 1990), 255.

40. Actes et Documents, vol. 9, no. 369; *The Jewish Chronicle* (London: October 29, 1943).

41. Diplomatic (Secret) Telegram from Osborne to Foreign Office, October 31, 1943, British Public Record Office, FO 371/37255 56879.

42. "Dragnet: The Last Acceptable Bigotry," *This Rock* (April 2000), 7, 9. See: Zenit Daily Dispatch, "Eichmann's Diary Reveals Church's Assistance to Jews," March 1, 2000.

43. Andrea Tornielli, *Pio XII, Papa degli ebrei* (Piemme, 2001). See: Leonidas E. Hill III, "The Vatican Embassy of Ernst von Weizsäcker, 1939–1945," 29 *Journal of Modern History* (1967), 138–48.

44. Nikilasu Kunkel interview with German news agency KNA, March 1, 2001.

45. Actes et Documents, vol. 9, no. 373 n. 4.

46. Tagliacozzo interview, Zenit News Agency, October 26, 2000.

47. Sate of Ministry of Justice, *The Trial of Adolf Eichmann: Record of Proceedings in the District Court of Jerusalem*, vol. 1 (Jerusalem, 1992), 83. See: Antonio Gaspari, *Gli ebrei salvati da Pio XII* (2001); Zenit News Service, "New Revelations on Jews Saved by Pius XII," February 16, 2001.

48. *The Trial of Adolf Eichmann*, vol. 4, 1504–05.

49. Gaspari, *Gli ebrei salvati da Pio XII*, 112–17. See: Zenit News Service, "New Revelations on Jews Saved by Pius XII, February 16, 2001.

50. Professor Owen Chadwick dismissed Zuccotti's arguments as "not history but guesswork." See: "Pius XII's Terrifying Dilemma: Put Yourself In His Shoes," *The Tablet* (London: June 30, 2001), 950–51.

51. *Current Biography 1941*, Maxine Bock, ed. (H. W. Wilson, 1971).

52. Robert Speight, *Voice of the Vatican: The Vatican Radio in Wartime* (London: Sands, 1942).

53. La Civiltà Cattolica, January 17, 1976; *Pope Pius and Poland* (New York: The America Press, 1942) provides titles and dates of anti-Nazi broadcasts: January 13, 20, 27, April 25, December 20, 1940; March 28, April 4, 1941. See: Rychlak, 102, 119, 128, 135, 144, 149–51, 156–58; *Le Figaro*, January 4, 1964; Jenri de Lubac, *Christian Resistance to Anti-Semitism: Memories from 1940–1944* (San Francisco, CA: Ignatius Press, 1990), 118–22.

54. Lapide, *Three Popes and the Jews*, 254; Pierre Blet, *Pius XII and the Second World War* (Mahwah, NJ: Paulist Press, 1999), 214.

55. David Alvarez & Robert Graham, *Nothing Sacred: Nazi Espionage Against the Vatican 1939–1945* (London: Frank Cass, 1997), 143. See also: ADDS, vol. 4, 140.

56. "Catholic Historian's Report Details Perils of Marytrs of Vatican Radio," *National Catholic Register*, February 1, 1976.

57. Ibid. See also: H. E. Cardinal Hlond, *Reports of Primate of Poland, to Pope Pius XII, Vatican Broadcasts and Other Reliable Evidence*, "The Persecution of the Catholic Church in German Occupied Poland" (New York: Logmans Green, 1941), "Catholic Historian's Report Details Perils of Martyrs of Vatican Radio," *National Catholic Register*, February 1, 1976.

58. Catholic Historian's Report, citing directive January 19, 1940, from the Pope ordering German language broadcasts on the state of the church in Poland.

59. Gaspari, *Gli ebrei salvati da Pio XII*, 112–17.

60. Zenit News Service, February 16, 2001; Professor Israel Guttman, *Encyclopedia of the Holocaust* (New York: Macmillan, 1990). Guttman writes of the Jews hidden and saved in church institutions that "could only have taken place under the clear instructions of Pius XII."

61. Inter-office memorandum of World Jewish Congress, March 25, 1959, in a letter from Monty Jacobs to Edgar Alexander. The memo reports "The Catholic Church in Europe has been extraordinarily helpful to us in a multitude of ways. From Hinsley in London to Pacelli in Rome, to say nothing of the anonymous priests of Holland, France and elsewhere, they had [sic] done very noble things for us."

62. See photograph section in Margherita Marchione, *Yours Is A Precious Witness: Memoirs of Jews and Catholics in Wartime Italy* (Mahwah, NJ: Paulist Press, 1997).

63. Emilio Bonomelli, *I Papi in Campagna* (Roma: Cherado Casini Editore, 1953), 439.

64. Fernande Leboucher, *The Incredible Mission of Father Benoît* (London, 1970), 137.

65. Catholic World News, "Castel Gandolfo Celebrates 400 Years as Papal Residence," December 31, 1006. "During the pontificate of Pius XII in World War II, for example, 12,000 people took refuge in Castel Gandolfo, and the papal apartments were opened up to shelter pregnant women nearing the days of childbirth; some 40 infants were born there."

66. Neal H. Peterson, ed., *From Hitler's Doorstep: The Wartime Intelligence Reports of Allen Dulles, 1942–1945* (College Park: Pennsylvania State University Press, 1996). Document 3–43, Telegram 2341 (March 9, 1944).

67. *Ibid.* Document 3–112, Telegram 3282–91 (May 4, 1944).

68. Testimony of P. Guglielmo Hentrich, before the Ecclesiastical Tribunal of Rome on the beatification of Pius XII.

69. Zuccotti, *Under His Very Windows*, 180.

70. *Actes et Documents*, vol. 9, no. 356.

71. Zucotti, *Under His Very Windows*, 159. See: ADSS, vol. 9, no. 368.

72. *Actes et Documents*, vol. 7, no. 434. See: Blet, 234–36.

73. Tisserant interview, *Informations Catholiques* (April 15, 1974).

74. *New York Times*, February 26, 1964, 41.

75. Tisserant interview; Michael O'Carroll, *Pius XII: Greatness Dishonored* (Dublin: Laetare Press, 1980), 14, 69.

76. Zuccotti, *Under His Very Windows*, 144–47, 181. See: Ralph Stewart, *Pope Pius and the Jews* (New Hope, PA: St Martin de Porres, 1990); Robert Leiber, "Pio XII e Gli Ebrei di Roma, 1943–1944." *Civilitá Cattolica*, vol. 1 (February 1961), 449.

77. *Actes et Documents*, vol. 9, 412.

78. Zuccotti, *Under His Very Windows*, 184.

79. LeBoucher, *The Incredible Mission of Father Benoît*, 141.

80. LeBoucher, 141.

81. Ian Buruma, "Depravity Was Contagious," review of Kershaw's *Hitler 1936–45, Nemesis,* New York Times Books (December 10, 2000); Lapide, 187–88 cites Document no. CXLV a-60 in Archives of the Centre de Documentation Juive Paris.

82. José M. Sánchez, *Pius XII and the Holocaust: Understanding the Holocaust* (Washington, DC: The Catholic University of America Press, 2002), 99. Zuccotti is unable to find any document clearly linking Pius to the expulsion order. *Under His Very Windows*, 228–30.

83. Robert Katz, *Black Sabbath: A Journey Through a Crime Against Humanity* (New York: Macmillan, 1969), 134–39. See: Rychlak, 288.

84. Robert Graham, "La Strana Condotta di E. von Weizsäcker ambasciatore del Reich I Vaticana," *La Civiltá Cattolica*, June 6, 1970, 455–71. See: Owen Chadwick, *A History of Christianity* (New York: St. Martin's Press, 1995), 190.

85. Zuccotti, *The Italians and the Holocaust*, 127, 303.

86. Justus George Lawler, "Review Symposium: Postcriptum Response," 20 *U.S. Catholic Historian* (2002), 96, 113–17.

87. *New York Times*, January 10, 1949. The Vatican appointed Jewish scholars to the Vatican Academy of Science and another to the Vatican Library in March. *New York Times*, March 2, 1940.

88. Lapide, 269. See: Michael Burleigh, The Cardinal Basil Hume Memorial Lectures: "Political Religion and Social Evil," 3, *Totalitarian Movements and Political Religions* (Autumn 2002), 1, 38.

89. Her argument is that during the war editors at the *New York Times* wanted to court Catholics (and others) so they were less than honest in their reporting.

90. "A Vatican Visit." *London Times*, October 11, 1942; *Jewish Chronicle* (London), September 11, 1942; *Jerusalem Post*, January 22, 1946. See: Gaspari, *Gli ebrei salvati da Pio XII*, 117–225.

91. "The Rights of Man," broadcast, Christmas 1942. The original, in Italian, was published in the official *Acta Apostolicae Sedis 1943*, vol. 35, 5–8.

92. *Zanichelli's Italian and English Dictionary* (NTC Publishing Group, 1993), 304.

93. Kenneth D. Whitehead, "The Pope Pius XII Controversy," 31, *The Political Science Reviewer*.

94. Oscar Halecki, *Eugenio Pacelli: Pope of Peace* (New York: Creative Age Press, 1951), 340; Joseph Lichten, "A Question of Judgment: Pius XII and the Jews," in *Pius XII and the Holocaust: A Reader* (New York: Catholic League), 127.

95. Office of the U.S. Chief Counsel, vol. 1, 285–86; William L. Shirer, *The Rise and Fall of the Third Reich*, 324–25.

96. *La vostra presenza*, November 29, 1945. Extracts were published in *The Tablet*, December 8, 1945.

97. James W. Demers, *The Last Roman Catholic* (1991), citing Francis X. Murphy, *The Papacy Today* (1981), 15.

98. *The Tablet* (of London), August 24, 1946, 97. The full text entitled, "Nous sommes heureux," appears (in its original French) in the Vatican's official *Acta Apostolicae Sedis*, vol. 38, 1946, 322–23; *L'Osservatore Romano*, August 15, 1946; *New York Times*, August 15, 1946, C-3.

99. Zuccotti, *Under His Very Windows*, 308.

100. The doctrine of susidiarity can be found in *Pius XI*, 'Quadragesimo Anno, 1931).

101. Anne O'Hare McCormick, "Position of the Pope in Italy has been Enhanced by War," *New York Times*, August 21, 1944; Rychlak, *Hitler, the War, and the Pope* 220, 273–79; *Daily Telegraph* (London), October 28, 1939; Owen Chadwick, *Britain and the Vatican During the Second World War* (Cambridge: Cambridge University Press, 1986), 83–85; *Summi Pontificatus*, paragraph 84.

102. *New York Times*, October 28, 1939, December 25, 1941, December 25, 1942. *Time*, August 16, 1943; Herbert L. Mathews, "Happier Days for Pope Pius: Shadows of war are lifting for a Pontiff whose greatest interest is world peace," *New York Times*, October 15, 1944, 8.

Chapter 11

1. For a thorough analysis of the Italian resistance movement see: Gallo, *For Love and Country: The Italian Resistance* (Maryland: University Press of America, 2003).

2. Tompkins, *A Spy in Rome* (New York: Simon & Schuster, 1962), 72. See: Carlo D'Este, *Fatal Decision: The Battle for Rome* (New York: HarperCollins, 1991), 119, 132.

3. Kesselring, *A Soldier's Record*, 233. See: Sheehan, *Anzio* (Norman: University of Oklahoma Press, 1964), 31; Sigfried Wesphal, *The German Army in the West* (London: Cassell, 1951), 242; Graham & Bidwell, *Tug of War*, 140–41. For the role the resistance played in saving the Anzio beachhead see: Peter Tompkins, "The OSS Partisans' Contributions to the

Saving of the Anzio Beachhead," in *Gli Americani e La Guerra di Liberazione in Italia*, 317–24; Gallo, *For Love and Country*, 180.

4. Gallo, *For Love and Country*, 169.

5. Tompkins, *Spy in Rome*, 159–60.

6. Trial Transcript of Albert Kesselring, RG338 Box 816, National Archives II. Bentivegna interview with the author; Capponi interview with the author, July 13, 1994.

7. Jane Scrivener, *Inside Rome with the Germans* (New York: Macmillan, 1945), 133.

8. Gallo, *For Love and Country*, 186–87.

9. Fiorentini interview with the author, July 20, 1998; Bentivegna interview with the author, July 22, 1998.

10. Gallo, *For Love and Country*, 192.

11. *Ibid.*, 190–92.

12. Fiorentini interview with the author. For the Via Rasella plan see: Gallo, *For Love and Country*, 191–97; Bentivegna, *Achtung Banditen* (Milano: Mursia, 1983), 152–72.

13. Gallo, *For Love and Country*, 193–96. See: DeSimone & Bentivegna, *Operazione Via Rasella* (Roma: Editori Riuniti, 1996), 56, 92–93; Piscitelli, *Storia della Resistenza*, 281; Katz, *Death in Rome*, 2–55.

14. Bentivegna, *Achtung Banditen*, 161–64; Bentivegna interview with the author; Katz, *Death in Rome*, 65.

15. For a thorough discussion of the Via Rasella attack and its aftermath See: Gallo, *For Love and Country*, 20–205.

16. Gallo, *For Love and Country*, 205–07. See: Portelli, *The Order Has Been Carried Out*, 131–71.

17. Gallo, *For Love and Country*, 207. See: Transcript of Herbert Kappler's testimony in *Corriere della Sera* (June 5, 1948), 1–3; Piscitelli, 296–97.

18. Letter from Bruno Cassinelli to the Direttore del Panaorama a Milano, November 14, 1973, quoted by Dr. Peter van Mejl, SDS, "Da Via Rasella a Via della Conciliazione," *La Figura di Padre Panacrazio Peiffer, SDS durante I nove mesi di occupazione tedesca a Roma* (Rome: November 30, 1996), 10–11. See: Gariboldi, *Pio XII, Hitler e Mussolini*, 238–47; *Tribunale Militare di Roma, Processo Kappler* (Rome: June 5, 1948), 3.

19. Gariboldi, 236.

20. Katz, *Death in Rome*, 101–04. See: Katz, *Battle for Rome*, 232. Gallo, *For Love and Country*, 209; Gariboldi, 236–37. Katz's version of the fabricated Dollman-Pfeiffer meeting has been recycled even by those who are not revisionists such as Kuzman, *The Race for Rome*, 188; Treveylan, *Rome '44*, 215; Lamb, *War in Italy*, 57–58.

21. Katz, *Death in Rome*, 173; Katz, *The Battle for Rome*, 256.

22. Katz, 383 n. 19. Dollman subsequently recanted his original version that he called Pfeiffer on the evening of the 24th, however, Katz persists in weaving this tale. Dollman's version is also critically reviewed in Gariboldi, 243.

23. Naslli Rocca Testimony of May 6, 1976, in the trial of Robert Katz, *Transcript of the Supreme Court of Cassation*, 174; Rocca in Gariboldi, *Pio XII, Hitler e Mussolini* 246.

24. Gallo, *For Love and Country*, 210.

25. Richard Raiber, "Generalfeldmarschall Albert Kesselring, Via Rasella, and the 'Ginny Mission,' *Militargeschtliche Mittelungen*, 56 Heft I (January 1998), 71–82. Katz inaccurately states that Westphal was in a conference and that Hitler was at Wolfschanze. Katz, *Death in Rome*, 85.

26. Gallo, *For Love and Country*, 210.

27. Letter from Bruno Cassinelli quoted by Peter van Mejl in letter to author.

28. Katz, *Death in Rome*, 101–04.

29. Letter of Eitel Möllhausen to Gariboldi, June 8, 1981, reprinted in *Pio XII, Hitler e Mussolini*, 236, 242.

30. Gallo, *For Love and Country*, 284. See: Christopher Simpson, *The Splendid Blond Beast* (New York: Grove Press, 1993), 242–43.

31. Raiber, 72–106. Dr. Raiber has found telegrams, phone logs and documents as evidence. Raiber, "General Feldmarschall," 94. Katz has Möllhausen leaving at dawn on the 25th to go to Monte Soartte to meet Kesselring. Katz doesn't pursue this, if he did he may have questioned the whereabouts of Kesselring. Katz, *Death in Rome*, 182.

32. Fiorentini interview with the author, July 20 and July 23, 1998.

33. Bentivegna interview with the author. See: Portelli, *The Order Has Been Carried Out*, 150–51.

34. Gallo, *For Love and Country*, 220–23.

35. *Ibid.*, 224. See: Portelli, *The Order Has Been Carried Out*, 173–99.

36. *Ibid.*, 227. See: Robert Graham, "La rappresaglia Nazista alle Fosse Ardeatine: P. Pfeiffer, messagero della carita di Pio XII," *Civilitá Cattolica*, 124 (1973), 469–74; Erich Priebke, *La Stampa* (June 4, 1996), 12.

37. *Ibid.*, 227.

38. *Ibid.*, 227–28.

39. Fiorentini interview in *L'Unita*, August 7, 1997, 2. See: Fiorentini interview in *Il Manifeso*, January 14, 1998, 20–21.

40. Fiorentini interview with the author. See: Gallo, *For Love and Country*, 228.

41. Fiorentini interview with the author; Bentivegna and Capponi interview with the author.

42. Gallo, *For Love and Country*, 241–48.

Chapter 12

1. This article is reprinted with the permission of the Catholic League for Religious and Civil Rights. This version of Robert Lockwood's review article has been edited. For the complete article go to: www.CatholicLeague.org.

2. James Carroll, *Constantine's Sword, The Church and the Jews* (NewYork: Houghton Mifflin, 2001), 22. All further references to Carroll will be by page number alone.

3. Carroll, 70.

4. *We Remember: A Reflection on the Shoah* (1998).

5. Carroll, 425.

6. *Ibid.*, 250.

7. *Ibid.*, 476.

8. *Ibid.*, 510.

9. *Ibid.*, 539.

Chapter 13

1. Daniel J. Goldhagen, "What Would Jesus Have Done?" *New Republic*, January 21, 2002, reportedly the longest article ever published by that magazine. For a thorough critique of the *New Republic* article see Ronald Rychlak, "Goldhagen vs. Pope Pius XII," *First Things* (June–July 2002), 37–54.

2. Daniel J. Goldhagen, *Hitler's Willing Executioners: Ordinary Germans and the Holocaust* (New York: Knopf, 1996).

3. Imre Karacs, "Germans show democratic spirit to accuser supreme," *The Independent* (London: March 11, 1997); "U.S. Holocaust Scholar Admits to Germans His Book Has Flaws," *Reuters-Buffalo News*, September 6, 1996.

4. Similarly, James Carroll's resolution to the problems he identifies in *Constantine's Sword*, includes the convening of Vatican III.

5. Goldhagen takes many of his larger themes from Carroll.

6. In *The Battle for Rome*, Katz discounts the lawsuit, noting that because amnesty was granted in 1970, the litigation was ruled moot in 1983. The two findings on the merits, however, went against him. The original letter (April 18, 1919) appears (in Italian) in *Emma Fattorini, Germania e Santa Sede. Le nunziature di Pacelli fra la Grande Guerra e la Repubblica di Weimar* (Bologna: Società editrice il Mulino, 1992), 322–25. For a description of violent attacks on Pacelli while nuncio see: Oscar Halecki & James F. Murray, Jr., *Pius XII: Eugenio Pacelli, Pope of Peace* (1954), 46; Ian Kershaw, *Hitler, 1889–1935*, 108–16.

7. David G. Dalin, "History As Bigotry: Daniel Goldhagen Slanders the Catholic

Church," *Weekly Standard*, February 19, 2003. Transcripts of depositions taken as part of Pius XII's cause for sainthood date back to 1957. See: Ronald J. Rychlak, *Hitler, the War, and the Pope*, 341 n. 40. Because Goldhagen limited his research to a single and incomplete source, it is not surprising to find his comments only magnify the errors about the hidden encyclical. A much better book on the subject, edited by Anton Rauscher, recently appeared in Germany.

8. The anti–Nazi Catholic Resistance in Belgium was led by Cardinal van Roey, whose principled opposition to Hitlerism and anti–Semitism is revealed in *Le Cardinal Roey et L'Occupation en Belgique* (Brussels, 1945). See: Henri de Lubac, *Christian Resistance to Anti-Semitism: Memoirs from 1940–1944* (San Francisco, CA: Ignatius Press, 1990). On March 26, 1939, the Associated Press reported, "A pastoral letter condemning National Socialism and racial theories was read today in all Catholic Churches in Eastern Belgium...." In January 1939, the *National Jewish Monthly* reported "the only bright spot in Italy has been the Vatican, where fine humanitarian statements by the Pope have been issuing regularly." For Pius XI's 1938 statement regarding anti–Semtism see J. Derek Holmes, *The Papacy in the Modern World 1914–1978* (New York: Crossroad, 1981), 115. For the original text as it was delivered in French, see the Belgian publication: *La Libre Belgique* (September 14, 1938); the original text was also reproduced in the French documentary news service: *La Documentation Catholique*, vol. 39, no. 885 (December 5, 1938, columns 1459–60). Pius XII repeated his predecessor's words. *New York Times* (December 12, 1938, 1.

9. This was not true of Jewish leadership during the Nazi era. They recognized a serious difference between Christian and Nazi beliefs. See: Marvin Lowenthal, *The Jews of Germany: A Story of 16 Centuries* (Jewish Publication Society, 1939), 416.

10. It is perhaps not surprising that Goldhagen would want to show that the church has changed its doctrinal teaching over time.

11. Eugene Fisher, *Faith Without Prejudice: Rebuilding Christian Attitudes Toward Judaism* (American Interfaith Institute, 1993); Michael Shermis and Arthur Zannoni, eds. *Introduction to Jewish-Christian Relations* (1991); *The Jewish People and Their Sacred Scriptures in the Christian Bible*, by the Holy See's Pontifical Biblical Commission (available through the Vatican's Web page).

12. Hitler's Secret Conversations (New York: Signet Edition, 1961), 159, 624.

13. Konrad Low, *Die Schuld; Christen und*

Juden im Urteil der Nationalsozialisten und der Gegenwart (2003).

14. "The Rights of Man" broadcast of Pius XII, Christmas, 1942. The original was published in the official *Acta Apostolicae Sedis* of 1943, vol. 35, 5–8. *Pius XII Selected Encyclicals and Addresses* (London: Catholic Truth Society, 1949). For a discussion of the proper translation of the phrase "solely because of their nation or race."

15. British Public Record Office, FO 371/ 34363 59337 (January 5, 1943).

16. Pinchas Lapide, *The Last Three Popes and the Jews* (New York: Hawthorn Books, 1967), 201. For further details about anti–Nazi Catholic resistance in the Netherlands, see L. Bleys, "Resistance in the Netherlands," *Tablet of London*, October 14, 1944, 186 (an eyewitness account by a Dutch resistance priest, in which he provides details of how Pius XII communicated his support to Dutch bishops fighting Nazism).

17. *New York Times*, December 25, 1942.

18. "A Vatican Visit," *London Times*, October 11, 1942. See: Anthony Rhodes, *The Vatican in the Age of the Dictators, 1922–1945* (New York: Holt, Rinehart, &Winston, 1973); citing German Archives: A. A. Abteilung Inland, pak. 17, vol. 1 (January 22, 1943); J. Derek Holmes, *The Papacy in the Modern World, 1914–1978* (New York: Crossroad, 1981), 140.

19. Telegram from the German Ambassador (Bergen) to the Reich Minister, January 26, 1943, *NARA*, T-120, roll 361, 277668–70. See also: Telegram from the Minister in Switzerland (Harrison) to the Secretary State, January 5, 1943, in *Foreign Relations of the U.S., Diplomatic Papers*, 1943m vol. 2 (Europe), U.S. Government Printing Office (Washington, 1964), 91.

20. Goldhagen, "What Would Jesus Have Done?" *New Republic*, January 21, 2002.

21. Pierre Blet, *Pius XII and the Second World War* (Mahwah, NJ: Paulist Press, 1999). The entire text of broadcasts of January 21–22, 1940, can be found in *The Persecution of the Catholic Church in German Occupied Poland: Reports by H. E. Cardinal Hlond, Primate of Poland, to Pope Pius XII, Vatican Broadcasts and Other Reliable Evidence* (New York: Longmans Green, 1941), 115–17; See: "Vatican Radio Denounces Nazi Acts in Poland," *Jewish Advocate* (Boston: January 29, 1940), 1; Blet, 99; Phayer, *The Catholic Church and the Holocaust*.

22. See transcript of a Vatican Radio broadcast, in *The Tablet* (London: April 4, 1941), 264.

23. *The Tablet* (July 3, 1943. See: *La Voix du Vatican* no. 28 (September 14, 1942), no. 26

(June 30, 1942); no. 28; "Catholic Historian's Report Details Perils of Martyrs of Vatican Radio," *The National Catholic Register* (February 1, 1976).

24. Henri de Lubac, *Christian Resistance to Anti-Semitism.*

25. Figaro, January 4, 1964. See also: "Letters to the Editor: Pope Pius XII: An Eyewitness," *Inside the Vatican* (January 2000), 10. A former seminarian tells of papal orders to shelter Jewish victims and of reports given on Vatican Radio.

26. Richard John Neuhaus puts it that Carroll "committed" *Constantine's Sword*, as one might a crime. *First Things* (November 2002), 86. See: Ronald Rychlak, "At Cross Purposes: Review of Constantine's Sword," *Washington Post*, February 12, 2001, C3. Rychlak, "Spins of Deceit: Review of the Popes Against the Jews," *Crisis* (March-April 2002); Lapide, 251.

27. Kaus Gotto, *Die Katholiken und das Draitte Reich* (1990); *New York Times*, June 27, 1943, 16. See: *The American Jewish Yearbook, 1943–1944* (Philadelphia: Jewish Publication Society).

28. Frank J. Coppa, ed., *Controversial Concordats; The Vatican's Relations with Napoleon, Mussolini, and Hitler* (Washington, DC: Catholic University of America, 1999), 2; Cornwell, *Hitler's Pope*, 263; Nicholas Cheetham, *The Keeper of the Keys: A History of the Popes from St. Peter to John Paul II* (1982), 284–86.

29. L'Osservatore Romano, June 28, 1940, 68–69.

30. Minutes dated September 10, 1941, British Public Record Office, FO 371/30175 57750. See: Robert A. Graham, *The Vatican and Communism During World War II: What Really Happened?* (1996), 156–57; Pius XII to Kallay, April 3, 1943, National Archives (Washington Hungarian Selection/T973/1/1–120/1153ff; Nicholas de Kallay, *Hungarian Premier: A Personal Account of the Second World War* (1954), 169.

31. Michael Ready, auxiliary bishop of Cleveland, was assigned to head a campaign to clarify *Divini Redemptoris* in the United States. William Langer & S. Everett Gleason, *The World in Crisis and American Foreign Policy: The Undeclared War 1940–1941* (1953), 796–97.

32. Barrett McGurn, *A Reporter Looks at the Vatican* (1962), 16. McGurn notes that a significant Communist population was tolerated in Castel Candolfo. See: "At the time of Pus XII's death, the Communist Daily Worker commented, Progressives throughout the world will remember Pius XII with gratitude for his reiterated appeals on behalf of Ethel and Julius Rosenberg, an intervention unprecedented in Vatican history." See: *The Tablet* (London: October 25, 1958).

33. Guenter Lewy, *The Catholic Church and Nazi Germany* (New York: DaCapo, 2000), 9–20.

34. The Polish Catholic clergy also strongly resisted the Nazis.

35. Richard Lukas, *The Forgotten Genocide* (New York: Hippocrene Books, 2001), 13–15; Memorandum to General Donovan from Fabian von Schlabrendorff, Relationship of the German Churches to Hitler (October 25, 1945) posted on the Internet by Rutgers Law School and Cornell University at www.camlaw.rutgers.edu/publications/law-religion/nazimasterplan04.pdf. The memorandum may also be found in Leo Stein, *Hitler Came for Niemoeller* (New York: Penguin, 2003), 253–57.

36. Official Report by William Donovan, *The Nazi Master Plan: Annex 4: The Persecution of the Christian Churches* (July 6, 1945) reprinted in Stein, 272–73. See: Rychlak, *Hitler, the War, and the Pope*, 35–41.

37. Richard Seigmann-Gall, *The Holy Reich: Nazi Conceptions of Christianity, 1919–1945* (New York: Cambridge University Press, 2002) 67.

38. *Hitler's Secret Conversations*, 83, 112, 296, 330, 389, 397–98, 482, 583, 624.

39. *Ibid.*, 98–99.

40. Peter Matheson, *The Third Reich and the Christian Churches* (Edinburgh: T&T Clark, 1994).

41. OSS Research and Analysis Branch, *The Nazi Master Plan* (July 6, 1945). See: Michael Burleigh, "The Cardinal Basil Hume Memorial Lectures: Political Religion and Social Evil," 3, *Totalitarian Movements and Political Religions* (Autumn 2002), 1, 29.

42. For the official papers of Cardinal Faulhaber see: Ludwig Volk, ed., *Akten Kardinal Micahel von Faulhaber, 1917–1945*, vol. 1 (Mainz: Mattias Grunewald-Verlag, 1975–78), 705; Theodore Hamerrow, *On the Road to the Wolf's Lair: German Resistance to Hitler* (Cambridge, MA: Harvard University Press, 1997), 75; Jurgen Heideking & Christof Mauch eds., *American Intelligence and the German Resistance to Hitler* (1996).

43. OSS, *The Nazi Master Plan*.

44. *Ibid.*

45. This encyclical is central to Pius XII's approach to the war. Rychlak, *Hitler, the War, and the Pope*, 273–77. Goldhagen has only one passing quote from this encyclical in his text (page 158), without mentioning its name. He refers to *Summi Pontificatus* in an obscure footnote (321 n. 95).

46. *The Tablet* (London: April 27, 1940), 398; See: "La figure e l'opera di PioXII," *L'Osservatore Romano*, April 14, 1940, 1; "German Court

bars sale of book on Roman Catholic during Nazi era after complaint about photo," Associated Press, October 8, 2002; Rychlak, *Goldhagen vs. Pius XII* (June-July 2002) 37–54; Stephen Wise, *Servant of the People* (1969); *Selected Letters* (Jewish Publication Society, 1959); "Christendom and the Jews," *The Jewish Chronicle* (London: September 11, 1942); Stephen Wise, *As I See It* (New York: Marstin Press, 1944).

47. Piet Oudendikik, *Pope Pius XII and the Nazi War Against the Catholic Church* (1944), 179; See: Burns and Oates, *The Persecution of the Catholic Church in the Third Reich* (London: W. Mariaux, 1940), 421. The authors quote Julius Streicher on von Galen in *Der Sturmer; Heinrich Portmann, Cardina von Galen* (London: Jarrolds, 1957).

48. For Pius XII's February 24, 1943, letter to von Galen see *Actes et Documents*, vol. 2, 306. Even earlier, he congratulated Faulhaber on February 2, 1942, for two bold sermons in the face of Nazism. *Actes et Documents*, vol. 2, 2360237. Pius XII's April 30, 1943, letter to Bishop Konrad von Preysing (Berlin) and March 3, 1944, letter to Archbishop Joseph Frings (Cologne) on the difficulty of speaking out without risking reprisals. *Actes et Documents*, vol. 2, 318–27, 365 respectively. Pius XII's wartime letters to the German bishops have been published, Burkhart Schneider, ed., *Die Briefe. An die Deutschen Bishöfe 1939–1944* (Grünewald: Mainz, 1966).

49. Ronald J. Rychlak, "The Church and the Holocaust," Wall Street Journal (Europe), March 28, 2002.

50. Michael Burleigh writes of the Nazi leaderships efforts to compel the church to tolerate euthanasia: "Negotiations collapsed when on 2 December 1940 Poe Pius XII unequivocally condemned the killing of 'life unworthy of life.'" Michael Burleigh, *The Third Reich: A New History* (New York: Hill & Wang, 2001), 400. See: Robert A. Graham, "The 'Right to Kill' in the Third Reich: Prelude to Genocide," LXII, *The Catholic Historical Review* (January 1976), 56, 68.

51. Robert Kemper, U.S. deputy prosecutor at Nuremberg commented on the mistaken notion that von Galen's protests caused the Nazis to halt the mercy killing program. "This is not in accord with the facts, for even after the protests this programme of murder was strictly enforced in secret right up to the end of the war." See: Jenö Levai, *Hungarian Jewry and the Papacy*; Michael Burleigh, *The Third Reich*, 723; Michael Burleigh, *Death and Deliverance; Euthanasia in Nazi Germany, 1900–1945*, 994; Michael Burleigh, The Cardinal Basil Hume Memorial Lectures: Political Re-

ligion and Social Evil, 3, *Totalitarian Movements and Political Religions*, 1 (Autumn 2002), 32–33.

52. José Sánchez, *Pope Pius XII and the Holocaust: Understanding the Holocaust* (Washington, DC; Catholic University Press, 2002). See: Robert Graham, *The Pope and Poland* (London: Veritas, 1968); *ADSS*, vol. 3, 633–36; 713–17; 736–39.

53. Casmir Papée, *Pius XII e Polska* (Rome, 1954).

54. Holmes, *The Papacy in the Modern World*, 164–65.

55. Lubac, *Christian Resistance to Anti-Semitism*, 161–62. See: Joseph Lichten, "A Question of Judgement: Pius XII and the Jews," in *Pius XII and the Holocaust: A Reader* (Milwaukee, Catholic League Publications, 1988), 114–15.

56. On Vatican Radio broadcast of Pius's protest see Joseph L. Lichten, "A Question of Judgment: Pius XII and the Jews," in *Pius XII and the Holocaust: A Reader*. On Gerlier see *Australian Jewish News*, April 16, 1943). Pius's protest to Petain see: *New York Times*, August 6, 1942; Nuncio Valeri's ciphered message on August 7, 1942, to Maglione regarding the protest. British Public Record Office, No. 320/81. D'Arcy Osborne cable to British Foreign Office confirmed the "Nuncio at Vichy had protested against the persecution of Jews in France." British Record Office, Reference Number 371 32680; Henri de Lubac, *Christian Resistance to Anti-Semitism: Memories from 1940–1944*. On Stephen Wise's praise of Pius regarding the French deportations see: "Christendom and the Jews," *Jewish Chronicle* (London), September 11, 1942; Stephen Wise, *As I See It* (New York: Marstin Press, 1944).

57. Memo by Tardini, October 18, 1944, *Actes et Documents*, vol. 10, 446 n. 4 (no. 357. See: Lapide, 151; Pius personally drafted the telegrams to Horthy. Domenico Cardinal Tardini, *Memories of Pius XII* (Newman Press, 1961), 123; Levai, *Hungarian Jewry*, 17–54; Graham, *Pope Pius and the Jews of Hungary*, 5–6; Blet, chap. 5. For his telegram to Seredi see: Holmes, *The Papacy in the Modern World*, 163. For Horthy's arrest see: Robert A. Graham, *The Vatican and Communism During World War II: What Really Happened?* (1996), 163; Robert A. Graham, *Pope Pius and the Jews of Hungary in 1944*, 19–22; Lapide, 161. For the World Jewish Congress's telegram see: Lapide, 161. For the American Jewish Congress telegram see Blet, chap. 9.

58. Lapide, 138; Tardini recorded in his notes of October 21 and 23, 1942, that if the pro-Nazi statements attributed to Tiso were actually made by him, the Holy Father wanted his name to be removed from a list of prelates

designated for special praise. *Actes et Documents*, vol. 5, no. 123; *Actes et Documents*, vol. 8, 598, no. 426.

59. Lapide, 138. See also: *Actes et Documents*, vol. 8, no. 305 (Vatican Secretary of State's concern expulsion of Jews from the Slovak Republic). *Actes et Documents*, vol. 9, no. 87.

60. *Official Report for the Prosecution and Trial of Major War Criminals Office of the U.S. Chief Counsel*, 283.

61. Michael O'Carroll, *Pius XII; Greatness Dishonored* (1980), 105–106; Lapide, 141.

62. Holmes, 159–60. See also: *Actes et Documents*, vol. 7, no. 346; *Actes et Documents*, vol. 9, 141.

63. Many similar situations that would have influenced Pius XII's thinking along these lines are set forth in *Hitler, the War, and the Pope*. The simple fact is that no one spoke out more explicitly than the Dutch bishops, and no other country had a higher percentage of Jews killed. Eva Fogelman, *Conscience and Courage*, 172; in Holmes, 165.

64. Camile Cianfarra, *The Vatican and the War* (New York: Literary Classics, 1944) Pius XII considered having L'Osservatore Romano publish a protest when the events from Holland were reported back to him. Testimony of Senior Pacalina Lehnert (October 29, 1968– January 24, 1969) Tribunal of the Vicariate of Rome on the beatification of Pius XII, Part I, 77, 85; Testimony of Maria Conrada Gramair (May 9, 1969–May 29, 1969), Tribunal of the Vicariate of Rome, Part I, 173–74.

65. Religious News Service, "Holocaust Hero Defends Papacy," *The Wanderer* (September 30, 1983). See: Gaspari, *The Jews Saved by Pius XII*; Zenit News Service, "New Reve-lations on Jews Saved by Pius XII," February 16, 2001.

66. *Opere et caritate [By Work and by Charity]*. Fernande Leboucher in *The Incredible Mission of Father Benoit* (1969) wrote that Pius XII's 1942 "command to all Christians and particularly the clergy, to the effect that every means available must be employed to save as many lives as possible. Vatican Radio defense of Jews (January 1940). See also: Lapide, 118.

67. The bishops replied with a letter pledging "anew to the Holy Father our best efforts in the fulfillment of his mission of apostolic charity to war victims." "Holy Father Extends Thanks to American Catholics for Aid," *Catholic News*, November 21, 1942.

68. "CBS Television Report Seeks to Discredit Church," Zenit News Service, March 19, 2000.

69. *The Nazi Master Plan: The Persecution of the Christian Churches*.

70. Alice von Hildebrand, *The Soul of a Lion: The Life of Dietrich von Hildebrand* (Ignatius Press, 2000).

71. *L'Osservatore Romano della Domenica*, June 28, 1964, 49. Lapide, 266, 366 n. 221.

72. Kempner in prologue, Levai, *Hungarian Jewry*, xi.

Epilogue

1. Joseph Bottum's essay is an edited version of the original and it is reprinted with the permission of the Association of Contemporary Church Historians, and published in the association's *Newsletter* (July-August 2004), 1–5. The essay was first published in *First Things* (April 2004), 18–25.

About the Contributors

Editor

Patrick Gallo received his PhD from New York University, where he is an adjunct professor of political science. He has taught at American University, SUNY–Purchase, William Paterson University and Queens College–CUNY. Professor Gallo is the author of 10 books: *For Love and Country: The Italian Resistance*; *Enemies: Mussolini and the Antifascists*; *The American Paradox: Politics and Justice*; *Old Bread, New Wine: A Portrait of the Italian Americans*; *Ethnic Alienation: The Italian Americans*; *The Urban Experience of Italian Americans*; *Swords and Plowshares: The United States and Disarmament*; *India's Image of the International System*; and *Patterns of American Foreign Policy*. He has been a scholar-in residence at the American Academy-in-Rome, a Fulbright Scholar, and an NEH Fellow. Dr. Gallo has received an Excellence in Teaching Award from the University of Chicago.

Contributors

Joseph Bottum is Books and Arts editor of the *Weekly Standard*, and poetry editor of *First Things*. He is the coauthor of *The Pius War: Responses to the Critics of Pius XII*.

George Sim Johnson is a graduate of Harvard University. He is a three-time winner of the Journalism Award given by the Catholic Press Association. Mr. Johnson is a freelance writer who has contributed articles on church history and religious issues. He has written for the *Wall Street Journal*, *Harper's*, *Commentary* and numerous publications.

Justus George Lawler has been the editor of five publishing imprints and of two quarterly and two monthly journals. He has taught at St. John's University and St. Mary's University. Mr. Lawler is the author, editor, and translator of a score of books on religious and cultural issues.

Dr. Jenö Levai was recognized as one of the leading authorities on Hungarian Jewry and was hailed for his groundbreaking book, *Hungarian Jewry and the Papacy*. He died in 1983.

Robert Lockwood, a graduate of Fairfield University, served as the research director for the Catholic League for Religious and Civil Rights. He was the publisher and editor of *Our Sunday Visitor* and currently writes a column for that publication. He is the author of numerous articles and books including *Anti-Catholicism in American Culture* and *A Faith for Grown Ups*. At present he is the communications director for the Pittsburgh Diocese.

Matteo Luigi Napolitano teaches history of treaties, international politics, and history of state-church relations at the Faculty of Political Science of the University of Urbino, Italy. He is the author of *Pius XII Between War and Peace*.

Ronald Rychlak is professor of law and associate dean of academic affairs in the University of Mississippi School of Law. Professor Rychlak is one of the leading authorities in the United States on Pope Pius XII and is the author of the widely acclaimed *Hitler, the War, and the Pope*. Professor Rychlak has contributed articles to numerous journals, newspapers, and magazines. He has also lectured widely and has made extensive television and radio appearances.

Kenneth Whitehead was educated at the University of Utah and the University of Paris. He is a former U.S. assistant secretary of education. Prior to that he was for 10 years a career Foreign Service officer who served in Rome, the Middle East, and the State Department's Office of German Affairs. He is the author of dozens of articles and of eight books.

Index